# THE COMPLETE ENCYCLOPEDIA OF

# WILD ANIMALS

THE COMPLETE ENCYCLOPEDIA OF

# WILD ANIMALS

ESTHER VERHOEF-VERHALLEN

REBO
PUBLISHERS

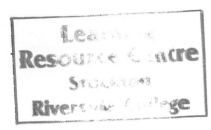
© 2001 Rebo International b.v., Lisse, The Netherlands

This 3rd edition reprinted in 2006.

Text: Esther Verhoef-Verhallen
Photographs: Esther Verhoef-Verhallen/Furry Tails
Illustrations: Angelique Kok
Editors: Willy Temmerman, Blanka Rambousková
Layout and design: Signia, Winschoten, The Netherlands
Cover design: Minkowsky Graphics, Enkhuizen, The Netherlands
Coordination and production: TextCase, Groningen, The Netherlands
Typesetting: Artedit, Prague, The Czech Republic

ISBN-13: 978-90-366-1595-2
ISBN-10: 90-366-1595-X

# Contents

# 1. Amphibians (Class *Amphibia*)

Amphibians are found in most regions of the world, except in the North and South Poles. Although several species have penetrated colder regions, such as Northern Scandinavia, these are exceptions and most species can be found in (sub)tropical and warm regions. Amphibians have a soft skin which generally offers insufficient protection against dehydration. This is one of the reasons that most of these animals are found in damp habitats, particularly near or in fresh water. Amphibians are never found in salt water. Just like reptiles, amphibians depend on the surrounding temperature for their own body temperature. They are particularly sensitive to overheating and will, therefore, seek out cooler locations.

A typical characteristic, of amphibians is that they do not drink water but absorb it

The European common toad (*Bufo bufo*)

The European common frog (*Rana temporaria*)

The edible frog

through their skin. To prevent them from absorbing too much water when they are in water, amphibians have glands in their skin which they can use to secrete a slime which acts as a protective layer. Many species can hibernate or aestivate. This is a natural adaptation which protects the animal from unfavorable or even fatal conditions, such as a drop or increase in temperature or a shortage of food. Amphibians are so dependent on high humidity or the presence of water that they go into a type of hibernation during a period of drought. They withdraw to a safe area, often into an underground hole, or bury themselves underground and only return to the surface when the rainy season starts or when conditions are more favorable. Most amphibians spend a part of their lives in water and some of them bury themselves in the riverbed. The best chance of seeing an amphibian while out walking is during rainy, very humid and warm weather, particularly in the evening. Many, but not all, amphibians remain underground or in a sheltered location during the day and are only active at dusk or during the night. An amphibian has a slow metabolism and, consequently, does not require much oxygen. Remaining temporarily underground does not, therefore, present a problem. It is striking that many amphibians use gills to breathe during their larval stage and develop lungs only later. Although they have

Edible frog tadpoles in shallow water

Mating European common frogs

Mating European common frogs

European fire salamander with larvae

European fire salamander with larvae

lungs, they can absorb oxygen through their skin and the mucous membrane of their mouth.

Amphibians have many enemies, including reptiles, birds and many kinds of small and large predatory mammals. In some countries, humans also eat certain amphibians, but their largest threat comes from the reduction of their natural habitat due to the construction of houses and roads. To protect themselves from their natural enemies, almost all amphibians can secrete poison (bufotoxin) which does not usually affect humans. However, some species, such as the poisonous frogs, also secrete a strong toxin which can kill humans. The place from where the toxin is secreted varies from species to species, but it is always secreted through glands in the skin. Many amphibians are territorial and usually remain within their own territory, moving only during the mating season. A well-known phenomenon is the migration of the common toad, where a large number of toads congregate in the same area with the intention of finding a partner and laying eggs. Many animals die during this migration because they

European tree frog

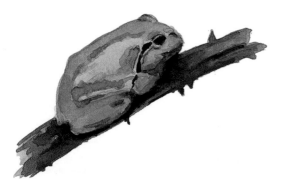
European tree frog

Embryo in its capsule (Alpine newt)

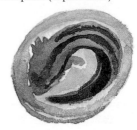
Embryo in its capsule (Alpine newt)

8

Various stages of development of frogs, frogspawn

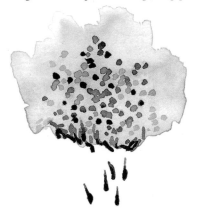

Various stages of development of frogs

Various stages of development of frogs

Various stages of development of frogs, tadpoles

must leave their familiar and protected area. Motorways which intersect the route to the final location are often fatal for many toads; this is why animal protectionists build special tunnels under recognised crossings, so that the animals can cross the road unharmed. Toads are not the only animals which display this behavior, but their migration is the best known.

Most amphibians lay eggs, usually in water or sometimes on land, but some amphibians give birth to live young. Some amphibians show brood care in the sense that they watch over the eggs and some species which lay their eggs on land help their hatched larvae to reach the water. The midwife toad goes one step further and the male carries strings of eggs, which he wraps around his hind legs. Most amphibians, however, lay their eggs in a sheltered area and leave them there; brood care is not a normal occurrence for amphibians.

When the eggs hatch, most amphibians do not look like their parents. Most species first undergo a larval stage before they assume their permanent, adult form. While in the larval stage, they often eat food different from the adults of the species. Adult amphibians are almost entirely carnivorous, while their larvae will often eat vegetable matter.

Many species of amphibians do not live for much longer than a year, but some species have lived for more than 20 years (in terrariums), considerably longer than most people believe possible.

Amphibians (Class *Amphibia*) are divided into three orders:

• Salamanders (Order *Urodela*)
• Caecilians (Order *Gymnophiona*)
• Toads and frogs (Order *Anura*)

# Salamanders (Order *Caudata*)

Families: *Rhyacotritonidae, Dicamptodontidae, Hynobiidae, Cryptobranchidae, Sirenidae, Proteidae, Salamandridae, Amphiumidae, Ambystomatidae* and *Plethodontidae*.

## European fire salamander (*Salamandra salamandra*)

The European fire salamander is the largest and best-known species of salamander in Europe. The length of the body can vary according to the subspecies, but is generally between 8 and 12 inches in length. The female is usually larger than the male. Different subspecies of the European fire salamander can be found in certain regions of Europe (particularly in southern and Central Europe), North Africa and the bordering areas of Asia. Since the markings can vary for each animal, diversity is very large, even in the same area. The female European fire salamander gives birth to live larvae, which are already reasonably developed and have sometimes already undergone full metamorphosis. The European fire salamander is a member of the true salamander family (*Salamandridae*).

European fire salamander (*Salamandra salamandra*)

## Black salamander (*Aneides flavipunctatus*)

The black salamander can be found mostly near streams in the south-western United States, particularly in California. Little is known about the reproduction of this species. It is believed that the animal does not lay its eggs in water, but in an (existing) underground hole. The black salamander is approximately 6 inches long.

Axolotl (*Ambystoma mexicanum*)

Black salamander (*Aneides flavipunctatus*)

Tiger salamander (*Ambystoma tigrinum*)

## Axolotl
## (*Ambystoma mexicanum*)

The axolotl can be found in Mexico, particularly in the Chalco and Xochimilco lakes. A characteristic of this animal is that many of them are sexually mature while still in the larval stage and do not really develop any further (neoteny). This characteristic is also found in a small number of other salamander species, but only on a small scale. It has been discovered that the animal does finally undergo metamorphosis if given a thyroid hormone. The axolotl grows to about 12 inches in length. Although it is usually a dark, grey-green color, it is the occasional albino, bred for scientific purposes, which has

become much better known. There are also different colored axolotls, such as speckled and black axolotls, but these are less common. The animal eats a variety of living creatures, such as water insects and larvae. The female can be distinguished from the male by thickness; the female is somewhat thicker than the male. The male also has a longer tail and is usually larger. It normally produces only one clutch of eggs per year. This annual clutch contains hundreds of eggs. An axolotl can live to be fairly old–some animals have been known to live for 25 years. The axolotl is a member of the mole salamander family (*Ambystomatidae*).

## Tiger salamander
## (*Ambystoma tigrinum*)

The tiger salamander can grow to be 12 inches in length, which makes it the largest land salamander known to man. The animal is seldom found in water outside the mating season, but prefers to bc in damp places. This animal becomes active at dusk

Tiger salamander (*Ambystoma tigrinum*)

Olm (*Proteus anguinus*)

and at night and feeds on a variety of living creatures from snails and rain worms to small rodents. There are no major differences between the male and female. The eggs are laid on water plants. Various subspecies of tiger salamander can be found in almost all regions of the United States, parts of Canada and Mexico. Populations which live in northern regions hibernate during the winter months. This species can have many different colors and markings, even within the same population or subspecies.

## Olm (*Proteus anguinus*)

The olm, also called the cave olm, grows to a length of approximately 10 inches. It lives in subterranean rivers in caves, particularly in the Carpathian Mountains in the former Yugoslavia. Since it generally lives in the dark, it does not need its eyes and they

Alpine newt (*Triturus alpestris*)

are, therefore, not fully developed and entirely covered with skin. Although it always lives in or close to water, it can remain on land for some weeks without experiencing any visible discomfort. Despite its relatively small and thin limbs, it can move on land. Its diet consists mainly of crustaceans. It has a typical reproduction system. Some female olms lay eggs, while others bear live young. Mating and egg laying take place in water. It can take three months for the eggs to hatch, but the parents usually remain near the eggs during this time to offer protection.

## Alpine newt (*Triturus alpestris*)

The alpine newt is most often found in the mountainous regions of southern and Central Europe, but can also be found in other regions. The female usually grows to a length of 4.5 inches, while the male only grows to be 4 inches or less. The female is usually also much thicker. During the mating season, the male, with its white and black markings, can be distinguished easily from its female counterpart. The male deposits a *semen parcel* to which it leads the female. The female absorbs this semen parcel and fertilisation then takes place internally. The eggs are laid in water. The young do not leave the water until they have undergone full metamorphosis, during which time they feed on a variety of small water animals. It can take three or more years before the young reach sexual maturity.

## Alpine salamander (*Salamandra atra*)

The alpine salamander lives in the high mountains of Central and Eastern Europe, mainly in the Balkans. It can grow to a length of 6 inches. The largest part of its life is spent on land. Its diet consists of

Alpine salamander (*Salamandra atra*)

a variety of worms and insects. The female always gives birth to two young, which have already undergone full metamorphosis. Due to this far-reaching adaptation, it no longer needs water to reproduce.

## Eastern newt
### (*Notophthalmus viridescens*)

The eastern newt can be found in south-eastern Canada and the eastern portion of the United States. In addition, some newts have been spotted close to large expanses of water in the southern United States. The color and pattern of this species vary. It reaches sexual maturity between the ages of 2 and 3.5 years. During the breeding season, hundreds of eggs are laid in the water, usually between plants. The larvae hatch after an incubation period of between one and a couple of months and reach an intermediate stage a couple of months later, in which they are neither larvae nor adult newts. It lives on land during this period. This species of newt grows to a length of between 3 and 6 inches.

Eastern newt (*Notophthalmus viridescens*)

# Order Apoda (Caecilians)
# (*Gymnophonia*)

Families: *Rhinatrematidae, Ichthyopidae, Uraeotyphlidae, Scolecomorphidae, Caeciliaidae* and *Typhlonectida*

## Yellow-striped caecilian
### (*Ichtyophis kohtaoensis*)

The yellow-striped caecilian is a primitive caecilian. Very little is known about this species, since this animal leads a very withdrawn life. It usually lives underground or under a layer of humus during the daytime and rarely comes to the surface. It only comes to the surface at night to eat. Its diet consists of a variety of small animals, ranging from insects to worms. The eggs are laid in an underground hole and are looked after by the female. The larvae live in water until they have undergone full metamorphosis. The yellow-striped caecilian is found in South-East Asia.

## Island caecilian
### (*Schistometopum thomense*)

This species of caecilian is found in the forests on the African island of Soa Tomé,

Yellow-striped caecilian (*Ichtyophis kohtaoensis*)

Island caecilian (*Schistometopum thomense*)

which lies in the ocean to the west of Gabon. The animal grows to approximately 12 inches in length and has a diameter of almost 0.5 inch. Just like all other caecilians, this species does not have any limbs. It spends the largest part of its life underground. It has a sticky tongue with which it can easily catch its prey, which includes small insects and worms. The female is fertilised internally. It is ovoviviparous, which means that the eggs develop inside the female's body.

# Frogs and toads
# (Order *Anura*)

Families: *Ascaphidae, Leiopelmatidae, Pipidae, Discoglossidae, Pelobatidae, Pelodytidae, Rhinophrynidae, Centrolenidae, Heleophrynidae, Bufonidae, Brachycephalidae, Hylidae, Pseudidae, Rhinodermatidae, Leptodactylidae, Myobatrachidae, Sooglossidae, Dendrobatidae, Hyperoliidae, Microhylidae, Ranidae* and *Rhacophoridae*

## Edible frog
## (*Rana esculenta*)

The edible frog can be found in almost all regions of Europe, except for the Iberian peninsula and most parts of the British Isles and is found only in the southern-most areas of Scandinavia. It is strongly dependent on water, which it seldom leaves. It lives in ditches and in small pools which have sufficient overgrowth

Edible frog (*Rana esculenta*)

American bullfrog (*Rana catesbeiana*)

European common frog (*Rana temporaria*)

and shelter. The edible frog is quite gregarious. Particularly during the mating season, groups of edible frogs can be heard very easily. The eggs are laid between April and July. The larvae hatch from the eggs after approximately 2 to 4 weeks, and 16 weeks later, most have undergone full metamorphosis. Some larvae, however, only undergo metamorphosis during the spring of the following year.

The edible frog eats a variety of insects and insect larvae, worms and sometimes even small (nesting) mice. It grows to about 3 to 3.5 inches in length.

## American bullfrog
## (*Rana catesbeiana*)

The bullfrog can be found in the central and eastern parts of the United States, as well as in Central America. Man has also introduced this animal into other parts of the world, including Europe. It can breed very quickly and can lay up to 20,000 eggs in a single clutch. It has a great ability to adapt and is aggressive. It is possible for bullfrogs to oust indigenous species, which is why they are not very welcome in regions where they do not originate. It takes a long time, up to several years, before the larvae develop into adult frogs. The name "bullfrog" originated in the United States, because the call of the male

during the mating season sounds like a bull. It is very low, extremely loud and carries far. The female bullfrog is approximately 8 inches in length, while the male is usually 2 to 3 inches smaller and more colorful. Just like other species of frog, the bullfrog eats insects and larvae but its size allows it to eat larger animals as well, such as small reptiles and mammals. It is mainly active at dusk and at night. The bullfrog hibernates during the winter.

## European common frog
## (*Rana temporaria*)

The common frog is native to almost all regions of Europe and the bordering areas of Asia. It can withstand lower temperatures and can, therefore, also be found in northern regions. The animal is territorial and does not like to move to new loca-

European common frog (*Rana temporaria*)

Brazilian horned frog (*Ceratophrys varia*)

## Green-and-black poison dart frog (*Dendrobatus auratus*)

This small species of terrestrial, territorial frog can be found in the rain forests of Central America. It belongs to the poisonous frog family (*Dendrobatidae*) and its skin toxin can be very harmful. Just as with most poisonous frogs, its color and markings can vary greatly. The green-and-black poison dart frog is approximately 1 inch long. The male of this species can be distinguished from the female by his smaller size. This species displays brood care. The eggs are fertilised by the male after they have been laid. The male then remains close by and keeps the eggs moist so that they do not dry out. The larvae hatch from the eggs after about 2 weeks. They then crawl onto the back of the male, who takes them to the water. From then on, the young larvae have to fend for themselves and develop into frogs, a process which takes approximately 1.5 months. The green-and-black poison dart frog eats a variety of small animals.

tions, so it can often be found in the same area. It spends the largest part of its life on land. They seek out water only for mating purposes. It is striking that this frog always returns to the same water to mate where it grew as a larva. It usually reaches sexual maturity only in its third year. In contrast to the edible frog, the common frog does not make a great deal of noise, not even during its mating season, which is considerably shorter than that of the edible frog.

Its diet includes insects. It is approximately 3 to 4 inches in length. Just as with many other frogs, its color and markings vary.

Green-and-black poison dart frog (*Dendrobatus auratus*)

## Brazilian horned frog (*Ceratophrys varia*)

The Brazilian horned frog is also called the colored horned frog. This species is found in tropical South America and can grow to a length of 8 inches. Since this animal has bony protrusions on its jaw which function like teeth, it can eat offensive prey, such as large insects, small rodents and worms. It reproduces similarly to other species of large frogs, in that it lays its eggs in water and the larvae remain in the water until they have undergone full metamorphosis.

## Yellow-and-blue poison dart frog (*Dendrobates tinctorius*)

This poisonous frog can be found in parts of Suriname, Guyana and Brazil. This species has many different colours and markings. Just as with most species of frogs, the female is larger. She grows to about 2.5 inches in length, while the male is generally a 0.5-inch shorter. The yellow-and-blue poison dart frog is diurnal and lives in the damp, boggy soil of rain forests. The eggs are laid on land instead of in water before being fertilised by the male. The male watches over the eggs and takes care of them. The larvae which hatch from the eggs are collected and taken to shallow water where they develop into frogs. The adult eats a variety of small insects, such as ants, termites, flies and larvae.

## Phantasmal poison dart frog (*Epipedobates tricolor*)

This small, poisonous South American frog is a member of the poisonous frog family (*Dendrobatidae*). It eats a variety of small insects and their larvae. The female lays an average of 20 eggs on land. The eggs hatch two weeks later and the male takes the larvae to the water, where the young develop further. After 8 weeks, they have undergone full metamorphosis

Yellow-and-blue poison dart frog (*Dendrobates tinctorius*)

Phantasmal poison dart frog (*Epipedobates tricolor*)

into frogs. The reproduction of this species is not related to a certain season and the female usually lays eggs at very regular intervals.

Golden poison dart frog (*Phyllobates terribilis*)

Antsouhy tomato frog (*Dyscophus insularis*)

European tree frog (*Hyla arborea*)

## Golden poison dart frog (*Phyllobates terribilis*)

This South American species of frog is a member of the poisonous frog family (*Dendrobatidae*) and is one of the most feared species of frog. The skin contains a very strong toxin that can be fatal to humans. It is also called the *poison-arrow frog* because this is one of the species used by the indigenous tribes of the Amazon for making poisonous arrowheads. This species eats small insects and insect larvae and displays brood care.

## Antsouhy tomato frog (*Dyscophus insularis*)

The antsouhy tomato frog can be found in Madagascar and is predominantly active at dusk and at night. The male of the species is approximately 2 inches in length, while the female can grow to a length of 3.5 to 4 inches. When it feels threatened, it can make its body swell up. The skin of this animal is not poisonous but it does give off an irritating substance. It eats a variety of insects and insect larvae, but the larger female can also eat small vertebrates.

## European tree frog (*Hyla arborea*)

The European tree frog can be found in most regions of Europe. Although it is always green, many different shades are possible. For example, a tree frog may turn blue (temporarily) due to stress or weather. The European tree frog gets its common name from the fact that it spends a large part of its life in trees and bushes. For this purpose, it has developed adhesive disks on its feet, which allow it to

European tree frog (*Hyla arborea*)

obtain a better grip and make it possible for the animal to climb up the most slippery of surfaces. It eats insects and their larvae. Although the tree frog is not often found in water, it always mates in water. Hundreds of eggs are laid, which hatch fairly quickly. The metamorphosis begins after approximately 16 weeks and the larvae change into small frogs. The adult European tree frog grows to approximately 1.5 to 2 inches in length. As with most amphibians, the European tree frog hibernates during the winter. It hibernates in mud or other sheltered areas.

## European common toad (*Bufo bufo*)

This toad is a member of the family of true toads (*Bufonidae*). It is the most common and best known toad in Europe but it can also be found in large areas of Asia and North Africa. It hides during the day and only goes searching for food at dusk and at night. The toad eats small, live animals. Animals in northern regions hibernate. Once awoken from hibernation, they form large groups and return to the water where they were born to mate (*toad migration*). The eggs are laid in water and are connected to each other to form

European common toad (*Bufo bufo*)

Midwife toad (*Alytes obstetricans*)

a string which can be several feet long. The development of the eggs and the larvae is, as with several animal species, dependent on the temperature and the food supply. The eggs usually hatch after approximately 10 days. The toad can grow to 6 inches in length, but remains smaller in certain regions. In a single population, the female is usually larger than the male.

## Midwife toad (*Alytes obstetricans*)

The midwife toad can be found in different regions of Europe and is generally not much larger than 2 inches in length. The midwife toad displays a special kind of brood care. The female lays the eggs, which are connected in long gelatinous tubes, on land. The male then winds these tubes of eggs around his hind legs and carries them around for 3 to 7 weeks, during which time he regularly moistens them. After this time, he takes the eggs into the water and the larvae hatch a short time afterward.

European green toad (*Bufo viridis*)

European spadefoot toad (*Pelobates fuscus*)

## European green toad
## (*Bufo viridis*)

The European green toad can be found mainly in southern and Eastern Europe, but also in North Africa and in the bordering areas of Asia. Although it lives mostly near water, it prefers to live on dry land. The European green toad is mostly active at night and at dusk. It generally eats a variety of insects and worms. The female green toad grows to 4 inches in length and is larger than the male. The green toad is a member of the family of true toads (*Bufonidae*).

## Colorado River toad
## (*Bufo alvarius*)

The Colorado River toad may look harm-

Colorado River toad (*Bufo alvarius*)

less but its skin toxin is extremely poisonous and can be fatal in some cases. Its size can vary greatly. An adult male is between 3 and 6 inches in length, while the female is at least 3.5 inches; the female can often be 1 inch larger than the male. Despite its fairly large appearance, it usually does not produce a loud noise. Even during the mating season, the animal is relatively quiet. The Colorado River toad can be found in the desert regions of the southern United States where there is very little water. Nevertheless, the animal always mates in water. The Colorado River toad is a member of the family of true toads (*Bufonidae*).

## European spadefoot toad
## (*Pelobates fuscus*)

Various subspecies of the spadefoot toad can be found in certain regions of Europe, from the Netherlands to Spain. The spadefoot toad can also be found in a few regions of North Africa, the Middle East and western Asia. This species of toad prefers sandy soil, since it likes to bury itself. It is nocturnal and is rarely seen during the daytime. The male is approximately 2 inches in length and the female measures approximately 3 inches. The larvae, however, are sometimes two to three times as large.

# 2 Reptiles (Class *Reptilia*)

Reptiles are cold-blooded animals. This does not mean that their blood is cold, but rather that they depend on the surrounding temperature to regulate their body temperature. It is for this reason that most species are found in tropical and subtropical regions. Some species do, however, live in more temperate regions, such as Central Europe, although no reptiles are found in extremely cold regions, such as the North Pole.

An unusual characteristic of cold-blooded animals is that their body functions adapt to the surrounding temperature. The warmer it is, the more they move and the faster they can digest their food. When the temperature drops, their body functions adapt and the animal requires little or no food and very little oxygen. The animal hardly moves, if at all, during a cold period. Various reptiles, in particular tortoises, hibernate during the winter. However, a long-lasting cold period, a fast drop in temperature or freezing temperatures are fatal for a reptile.

Reptiles are predominantly terrestrial animals, although many of them live partly on land and partly in the water. Only a few species live exclusively in water, such as the sea snake and the sea turtle. The keratinised skin of reptiles consists of shells or scales and provides protection against dehydration. Unlike amphibians, reptiles cannot breathe through their skin.

West African dwarf crocodile

Dabb spiny-tailed lizard (*Uromastyx acanthinurus*)

The monitor is considered to be the most intelligent reptile.

African spurred turtle

They absorb oxygen through their lungs, although these are not as well developed as those of mammals. The heart and circulatory system are also not as well developed as those of mammals.

Reptiles exhibit internal fertilisation. The male has one or two penises, but only one is used during copulation. Most reptiles are oviparous, meaning that they lay eggs. The eggs can have a limy shell and are softer for some species than for others. The shell always has a structure which protects the embryo from drying out. Most reptiles bury their eggs on land to protect them from large temperature fluctuations and to make it more difficult for predators to steal them. The yolk is relatively large and rich in nutrients. Young reptiles hatch from the eggs using a strong egg tooth and look like small versions of their parents. Theoretically, they are able to fend for themselves as soon as they hatch, although they are often clumsy and vulnerable. They need to be able to fend for themselves because, except for the crocodile, reptiles do not display brood care.

There are also ovoviviparous reptiles and these tend to be found among the snakes and lizards. With these animals, the young develop in the egg inside the female's oviduct and the young are fed by the nutrients in the yoke. The young are born when they are large enough and sufficiently developed. There is no brood care whatsoever after the animals are born; the young animals usually disappear quickly from the mother after birth.

Feeding time for American alligators on an alligator farm

Helmeted turtle (*pelomedusa subrufa*)

Helmeted turtle

African slender-snouted crocodile

Eyesight is the best developed sense for almost all reptiles. One of the exceptions to this is the New Guinea blind lizard (*Dibamus novaeguinae*), which is completely blind. The sense of hearing is only slightly developed in most reptiles; it is believed that they are able to hear only low frequencies. Another unusual characteristic is that most reptiles make little or no noise, except for crocodiles and geckos. Almost all reptiles have a well-developed sense of smell. Tortoises and crocodiles have nostrils which they use to smell, but other reptiles, such as snakes, pick up smells with their tongues, using an olfactory organ in the mouth called the Jacobson organ. Almost all reptiles have teeth, except for tortoises, which have extremely sharp, hard, ossified jaw edges. Most reptiles are carnivorous (meat eaters) but some reptiles are herbivorous (plant eaters) or omnivorous (meat and plant eaters). Another characteristic of reptiles is that they continue to grow throughout their entire lives, although the growth stagnates somewhat as the animals get older. The largest reptile in the world is a snake, the green anaconda (*Eunectes murinus*), which can grow to a length of more than 30 feet.

The following orders are reptiles (class *Reptilia*):

- Tortoises and turtles (Order *Testudines*)
- Crocodiles, alligators and gavials (Order *Crocodylia*)
- Lizards and snakes (Order *Squamata*)
- Tuatara (Order *Rhynchocephalia*)

Gould's monitor

# Turtles and tortoises
# (Order *Testunides*)

Suborder cryptodires (Cryptodira)
Families: Dermatemydidae, Chelydridae, Kinosternidae,
Platysternidae, Emydidae, Testudinidae, Cheloniidae,
Dermochelyidae, Carettochelyidae and Trionychidae

## Leatherback turtle
## (*Dermochelys coriacea*)

The leatherback turtle is the heaviest turtle known to man. The animal has an average weight of approximately 750 pounds and a length of approximately 5 feet but specimens weighing almost 1,300 pounds and measuring almost 7 feet have also been found. The leatherback turtle is a marine turtle and gets its common name from its unusual shell, which has a leathery covering. The species is found in all the tropical and subtropical oceans and has even been observed along the Canadian coast, as far north as Nova Scotia. Its diet consists mainly of molluscs and fish, but it also eats a small amount of plant material. This turtle leads a solitary life. As with all marine turtles, its lungs have an extra function; they also serve as a float for swimming. The leatherback turtle lays its eggs in a hole on land and then covers them over with soil to protect them from predators and strong fluctuations in temperature. The eggs have a limy shell to protect them from drying out. The

Leatherback turtle (*Dermochelys coriacea*)

Common green turtle (*Chelonia mydas*)

leatherback turtle does not display brood care. When the young animals hatch, they must dig themselves out of the nest and make their own way to the water–many turtles perish during this perilous undertaking. The leatherback turtle is a member of the family *Dermochelyidae*.

## Common green turtle
## (*Chelonia mydas*)

The common green turtle is a marine turtle and is found in almost all the tropical and subtropical oceans. It is herbivorous. The common green turtle lays a relatively large number of eggs, a clutch usually containing approximately 100 eggs. The eggs are laid on a beach, which the animal sometimes travels hundreds of miles to reach. Some beaches are favorite laying beaches and attract large numbers of animals during a certain period. The eggs hatch after approximately 8 to 12 weeks. The common green turtle is a member of the sea turtle family (*Chelonidae*).

## Red-eared turtle
## (*Chrysemys scripta elegans*)

This well-known aquatic turtle is found mainly in the marshy regions of Florida, but is also found in other areas of the

Red-eared turtle or slider (*Chrysemys scripta elegans*)

United States and in northern Mexico. The red-eared turtle forms, together with the yellow-eared turtle (*C. scripta troosti*), a subspecies of the slider (*P. scripta*), which is much more widely distributed.

The species is a member of the cryptodires suborder and the terrapin family (*Emydidae*). The red-eared turtle is gregarious. It is predominantly carnivorous and eats fish, crustaceans, insects and their larvae and snails. It always eats its food in the water, never on land. The sex of adult animals can be distinguished easily, for example, by the extended nails on the front feet. It lays an average of 10 eggs, which, depending upon the temperature, hatch after about 70 days. The shell of a red-eared turtle can grow to a length of approximately 12 inches. Unfortunately, this animal is quite popular as a pet. To meet the large demand for red-eared turtles, it is bred in large commercial nurseries. The animals are sold to the consumers when they are still babies and only

Red-eared turtle or slider (*Chrysemys scripta elegans*)

an inch or so long. Only 1% of the animals reach adulthood due to ignorance of the animals' needs. This unacceptably high death rate has led some western countries to introduce a stricter policy regarding the trade and keeping of this animal by private individuals.

Helmeted turtle (*Pelomedusa subrufa*)

Helmeted turtle (*Pelomedusa subrufa*)

## Helmeted turtle
## (*Pelomedusa subrufa*)

This species of turtle can grow to a length of approximately 10 inches. Its diet consists mainly of mosquito larvae, although it also eats other small animals and plant matter. It prefers to live in marshy regions and comes onto land only to bask. During persistent dry weather, the helmeted turtle buries itself for protection to stave off dehydration. It sometimes falls into a kind of aestivation, from which it awakes when the rains break. The helmeted turtle is a member of the family *Pelomedusidae.*

## Alligator snapping turtle
## (*Macroclemys temincki*)

With a maximum length of 30 inches and a weight of up to 200 pounds, the alligator snapping turtle is one of the heaviest species of turtle. It is a river turtle and is found mainly in the Mississippi River basin. The alligator snapping turtle has

a special way of catching its fish. It lies on the riverbed with its mouth wide open and moves the bright red appendage on its tongue from side to side. An unsuspecting fish sees this as a worm and voluntarily swims into the turtle's mouth. The alligator snapping turtle is a member of the snapping turtle family (*Chelidridae*).

## Snapping turtle
## (*Chelydra serpentina*)

The snapping turtle is a member of the cryptodires and is closely related to the alligator snapping turtle. This hardy animal is widely distributed. This species is found in large parts of the central and southeast United States, Central America, the northeast of South America and has also been observed in Canada. It can grow to a length of approximately 18 inches, but most animals remain somewhat smaller. The sex can be distinguished by the tail, which is longer on the male. The snapping turtle lives up to its common name. It is an aggressive animal and, if necessary, actively hunts to catch its prey. Its diet consists of a variety of animals, including fish, snakes, frogs and even birds, which it catches both in the water and on land. It also eats carrion, which it can easily locate using its excellent sense of smell. This turtle is not completely harmless for humans and can react quickly and give a nasty bite if disturbed.

Alligator snapping turtle (*Macroclemys temincki*)

Snapping turtle (*Chelydra serpentina*)

New Guinea plateless turtle (*Carettochelys insculpta*)

## Bog turtle
## (*Clemmys muhlenbergii*)

The bog turtle is considered to be the smallest species of turtle in the world. An adult measures 3 to 3.5 inches, although turtles an inch longer have also been found. When the young animals hatch, they are 1 inch long. It grows very slowly and reaches its adult size only when it is 8 years old. Just like all reptiles, the bog turtle continues to grow after that age, although this growth is minimal. The male of this species can be recognised by its longer tail and the head is often larger as well. The species is found in the marshy regions of the United States.

Bog turtle (*Clemmys muhlenbergii*)

## New Guinea plateless turtle
## (*Carettochelys insculpta*)

The New Guinea plateless turtle is a freshwater turtle which is found mainly in the rivers of New Guinea and northern Australia. This species lives predominantly in water and rarely comes onto land, usually only to lay eggs. It eats aquatic plants and soft, sweet fruit which has fallen into the water, as well as crustaceans and worms. It uses its characteristic trunk, for which it is also sometimes called the pignosed turtle, as an antenna which it sticks above the surface of the water to breathe. An adult can grow to a length of 19 to 23 inches and weigh more than 45 pounds. The sex can be distinguished easily by the length of the tail; a male New Guinea plateless turtle has a significantly longer tail. The New Guinea plateless turtle is a member of the family *Carettochelyidae*.

## Ornate box turtle
## (*Terrapene ornata*)

The ornate box turtle is found in several of the southern American states. The sex of this species can be distinguished easily. An adult male is more colorful and has a longer tail than the female. The shell of an adult ornate box turtle does not measure much more than 6 inches. It is omnivorous and eats worms, insects and soft fruit. The ornate box turtle is a member of the family *Emydidae*.

Ornate box turtle (*Terrapene ornata*)

## African spurred turtle (*Geochelone sulcata*)

The African spurred turtle is one of the larger terrestrial turtles. Its shell can reach a length of approximately 30 inches. It inhabits the dry regions of Central Africa and is herbivorous. If the conditions are bad, for example a long-lasting heat wave or drought, this turtle can aestivate and will then not require any food. It is a member of the family *Testudinidae*.

## South American red-footed tortoise (*Geochelone/Chelonoidis carbonaria*)

The South American red-footed tortoise gets its common name from its red feet which, according to legend, it got from burning them on a charcoal fire. The South American red-footed tortoise is found in the northern part of South America. It is predominantly herbivorous but sometimes also eats worms. The sex can be distinguished by the tail–the tail on the female is shorter. The eggs are laid in a nesting hole and hatch after approxi-

South American red-footed tortoise
(*Geochelone/Chelonoidis carbonaria*)

African spurred turtle (*Geochelone sulcata*)

Galapagos tortoise (*Geochelone nigra*)

mately 5 months, but this can vary greatly according to the circumstances. The South American red-footed tortoise grows slowly and does not reach sexual maturity until the age of 6 years. The length of an adult shell can vary from approximately 12 inches to 24 inches.

## Galapagos tortoise
## (*Geochelone nigra*)

This well-known terrestrial tortoise can grow to a length of 43 inches and can weigh in excess of 440 pounds. The Galapagos tortoise and various subspecies are found only on several of the Galapagos Islands. The Galapagos tortoise is gregarious and herbivorous. As with all other tortoises, this species has no teeth and does not chew its food. Its strong jaw has very hard, ossified edges which allow it to chop its food into manageable pieces. The male is larger than the female. The Galapagos tortoise is a member of the family *Testundinidae*.

## Spur-thighed tortoise
## (*Testudo graeca*)

The shell of this terrestrial tortoise can grow to a length of approximately 12 inches. The spur-thighed tortoise and various subspecies are found in several North African countries, the Middle East and southeast and southwest Europe. The spur-thighed tortoise is predominantly herbivorous, but also eats insects, snails and worms. It lays an average of 10 to 13 relatively large eggs, which hatch after 3 to 4 months. The species was popular as a pet for some time. It is a member of the family *Testundinidae*.

Spur-thighed tortoise (*Testudo graeca*)

## Marginated tortoise
## (*Testudo marginata*)

The marginated tortoise originates from the south of Greece but has also been introduced into Sardinia. It has sections on its shell, which is predominantly black on an adult animal. The marginated tortoise is predominantly herbivorous. The sexes can be distinguished by their size; the male is usually smaller than the female, although the tail of the male is longer. It lays its eggs in a hole in the ground and covers them with soil. The eggs hatch after approximately 60 days. The marginated tortoise can grow to a length of approximately 14 inches.

Marginated tortoise (*Testudo marginata*)

# Turtles and tortoises (Order *Testunides*)

*Suborder pleurodires (Pleurodira)*
*Families: Pelomedusidae and Chelyidae*

## Yellow-spotted Amazon River turtle (*Podocnemis unifilis*)

The yellow-spotted Amazon River turtle can grow to a length of approximately 18 inches. It is found in the northern part of South America, where it lives in and close to fresh water. It is predominantly herbivorous and is a member of the family *Pelomedusidae*.

## Matamata (*Chelus fimbriatus*)

The matamata is undoubtedly one of the most unusual turtles known to man. The matamata is found in the northern part of South America. It is aquatic and rarely leaves the rivers in which it lives. Although it spends most its time in the water, the matamata is not a good swimmer. When it moves, it usually walks on the riverbed and when it wishes to breathe, it only sticks its nostrils above the surface of the water. It prefers to live in reasonably still water and is often found in shallow water along the riverbank. Its diet consists mainly of fish and amphibians. The matamata rests during the day and becomes active only at dusk and during the night. The number of eggs laid by the female varies greatly but a clutch contains an average of 20 eggs. The matamata can

Matamata (*Chelus fimbriatus*)

Yellow-spotted Amazon River turtle (*Podocnemis unifilis*)

Macquarie turtle (*Emydura macquarii*)

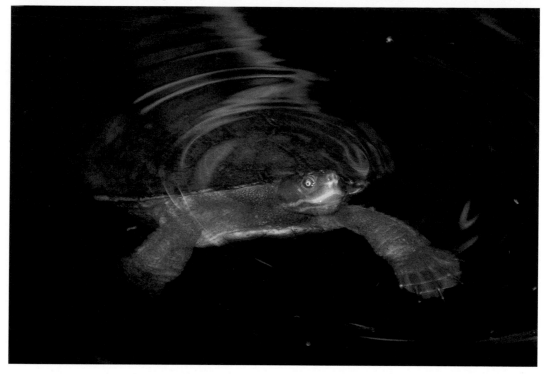

grow to a length of more than 15.5 inches. It is a member of the snake-necked turtle and matamata family (*Chelidae*).

## Australian snake-necked turtle (*Chelodina longicollis*)

The Australian snake-necked turtle is carnivorous and its diet includes fish and frogs. It is a quick turtle which actively hunts its prey and is quickly irritated. It is very agile, both on land and in the water. Its shell can grow to a length of approximately 11 inches and its neck can be just as long. The Australian snake-necked turtle lives in the marshy regions of southeast Australia.

## Macquarie turtle (*Emydura macquarii*)

The Macquarie turtle is found in the rivers of southeast Australia. It eats small animals, amphibians and, to a lesser extent, plant matter. It can grow to a length of approximately 11 inches. It usually lays 12 to 16 eggs, which the female buries in the soil near the water. The eggs hatch after approximately 2.5 months. The species is a member of the snake-necked turtle and matamata family (*Chelyidae*) and the genus of short-necked turtles (*Emydura*).

Australian snake-necked turtle (*Chelodina longicollis*)

# Crocodiles, alligators and gavials (*Crocodylia*)

Families: *Crocodylidae, Alligatoridae and Gavialidae*

## American alligator (*Alligator mississippiensis*)

The American alligator is by far the best-known member of the alligator and caiman family (*Alligatoridae*). It is found mainly in the southeastern United States. The American alligator is approximately 8 to 10 inches long at birth. At the beginning of the 20th century, some animals found were 20 feet long but such long animals are seldom seen today. An adult male measures approximately 15 feet and the female 10 feet. Although the young alligators grow quickly, it can take some time before they reach sexual maturity, often not until they are approximately 7 years old. The female lays an average of 40 eggs, which hatch after 65 to 80 days. As with all crocodiles, the American alligator displays brood care. The female guards the

An alligator farm in Orlando (*American alligators in the foreground*)

nest and carries the young to the water in her mouth after they hatch. The young animals remain with their mother for several years. The American alligator can live for 50 to 60 years in the wild but animals kept in captivity can live for a further 10 years. The American alligator is one of the most well-liked crocodilians because it usually shows little or no aggression toward humans. The American alligator was threatened by extinction in the middle of the 20th century. It is now bred in large numbers on special crocodile farms and is no longer endangered.

## Chinese alligator (*Alligator chinensis*)

The Chinese alligator is the only species of alligator which is not found in America. This species is found in China, mainly in a reserve in the province of Anhui. An adult is approximately 6.5 feet long. It is predominantly nocturnal and eats mainly fish and crustaceans, although it will also eat birds and similar animals if given the opportunity. Like all crocodilians and related animals, the Chinese alligator has no sweat glands and cools itself by opening its mouth.

American alligator (*Alligator mississippiensis*)

## Nile crocodile
## (*Crocodylus niloticus*)

The Nile crocodile is a member of the family of true crocodiles and has a notorious reputation for eating humans. Most species of crocodile do not often disturb humans as long as they are not extremely hungry and are not disturbed or seriously threatened by them. The Nile crocodile is an exception to this rule and, for this reason, is often feared. The Nile crocodile spends the night in the water and usually spends the day basking on land. The animal reaches sexual maturity when it is approximately 10 years old. It lays an average of 50 eggs, which have a limy shell. The mother digs a hole as a nest, which she covers with a thick layer of plant material and mud to form a mound. The warm sun acts on the plant material to create a hot climate within the mound, which in turn incubates the eggs. The

Nile crocodile (*Crocodylus niloticus*)

mother fanatically protects the mound from predators. Once the young hatch, they alert their mother by making a loud quacking noise. The mother reacts instinctively to this and digs the young out. The young animals remain under their mother's protection for up to 2 years, although this does not guarantee a prosperous life. Young crocodiles are a favorite food of many animals, such as some birds of prey and large carnivorous turtles. An adult measures, on average, between 14 and 16 feet and can weigh 2000 pounds, although animals of more than 23 feet have also been recorded. The species is found throughout Africa, except in the northern and northwestern regions. The species is also native to Madagascar.

## Salt water crocodile
## (*Crocodylus porosus*)

Another much feared species of crocodile is the salt water crocodile, or the *Saltie*. The largest salt water crocodile ever recorded was more than 30 feet long, although the animals are seldom longer than 16 feet long, with the female being 8 feet shorter. This animal is very widely distributed, partly because it can swim long distances. It is found from India to China and from Indonesia to Australia, where it lives mainly in salt or brackish water. The young animals, however, are

33

Salt water crocodile (*Crocodylus porosus*)

African slender-snouted crocodile

make blowing or hissing sounds. The salt water crocodile can live for as long as 50 to 60 years.

## African slender-snouted crocodile (*Crocodylus cataphractus*)

This species is found in central and West Africa. An adult animal is usually 8 feet long, but can grow to be more than 13 feet long, although this is exceptional. The African slender-snouted crocodile eats mainly fish and other aquatic animals. The female digs a hole in the riverbank, in which she lays an average of 20 relatively large eggs. The hole is then covered and the eggs are left to be incubated by the sun. The eggs hatch after approximately 100 days. The mother then digs the young out of the nest, so that they can reach the water without too much difficulty.

## Spectacled caiman (*Caiman crocodilus*)

The spectacled caiman is the most common species of caiman. It is found in the tropical regions in northern South America, as well as in Central America. An adult can grow to a length of approximately 9 feet, but most animals are considerably shorter, usually between 5 and 6.5 feet. The spectacled caiman was once popular not only because of its expensive skin, but also as a stuffed animal for

usually reared in fresh water. In Australia, the salt water crocodile is often kept on special crocodile farms, where it is bred for its meat and skin. As with almost all crocodiles, the salt water crocodile can sometimes be very noisy. The male makes a heavy and penetrating howl during the mating season and during confrontations with other males. The mother generally communicates with her children through sound. The sound that the young crocodiles emit is similar to the croak of a frog or the call of a crow, but they can also

Gavial (*Gavialis gangeticus*)

Spectacled caiman (*Caiman crocodilus*)

tourists. The spectacled caiman lives between 30 and 40 years.

## Gavial
## (*Gavialis gangeticus*)

The gavial is the only species of the gavial family (*Gavialidae*) which is not extinct. It distinguishes itself from the true crocodiles, alligators and caimans by its much narrower and longer snout. It lives in rivers and almost never comes out of the water. In contrast to most species, the gavial is not very agile on land. As a result of its way of living, its diet consists mainly of fish and amphibians. An adult male can be easily recognised by the unusual lump at the end of its top jaw. The gavial is one of the largest crocodilians and the male can grow to a length of between 20 and 23 feet. It lays an average of 35 eggs, which hatch after approximately 85 days.

The gavial is found in India and surrounding countries, such as Pakistan and Nepal, although it is quite rare. There are currently several on-going projects which should preserve the species from extinction.

## West African dwarf crocodile
## (*Osteolaemus tetraspis*)

One of the smaller crocodiles is the dwarf crocodile, sometimes also called the broad-snouted crocodile. It is a member of the true crocodile family (*Crocodylidae*) and an adult can grow to a length of between 5 and 6.5 feet. There is a considerable difference between the color of the young and adult animal. The adult is almost completely black, while the young animal has bright markings. The natural habitat of this species is the tropical rain forests of West Africa and the western part of central Africa. Its diet consists mainly of fish and it leads a somewhat withdrawn, solitary life.

West African dwarf crocodile or broad-snouted crocodile (*Osteolaemus tetraspis*)

# Lizards (Order *Squamata,* suborder *Sauria*)

Families: *Gekkonidae, Pygopodidae, Dibamidae, Iguanidae, Agamidae, Chamaeleonidae, Scincidae, Feyliniidae, Anelytropsis, Cordylidae, Xantusiidae, Teiidae, Lacertidae, Anguidae, Anniellidae, Xenosauridae, Helodermatidae, Varanidae, Lanthanotidae, Bipedidae, Amphisbaenidae and Trogonophidae*

Moorish gecko (*Tarentola mauritanica*)

## Leopard gecko (*Eublepharius macularius*)

The leopard gecko is one of the few species of gecko with moveable eyelids. It is a member of the large family of geckos (*Gekkonidae*). An adult gecko can grow to a length of 10 inches. The leopard gecko sheds its skin, just like all the other geckos, and eats it.

Leopard gecko (*Eublepharius macularius*)

Leopard gecko (*Eublepharius macularius*)

The leopard gecko is found in western India, Afghanistan and Pakistan in both urban areas and inhospitable deserts. It lays approximately 2 eggs, which initially have a very sticky and soft shell, but which becomes harder with time. Since the fresh eggs are sticky, a gecko can stick them against almost any object, usually somewhere sheltered and difficult for possible predators to reach. This animal does not display brood care. The leopard gecko is one of the most popular terrarium pets. Animals kept in a terrarium usually live for 10 to 15 years.

## Moorish gecko (*Tarentola mauritanica*)

The Moorish gecko is one of the best-known species of geckos. It grows to a length of approximately 6 inches. It is predominantly nocturnal and eats a variety of insects. The species is found in North Africa, the Canary Islands and southern Europe, where it usually lives close to humans. The Moorish gecko has a large number of *hooks* under its toes which allow it to climb very slippery, even vertical, surfaces.

Madagascar giant day gecko

## Madagascar giant day gecko (*Phelsuma madagascariensis*)

The Madagascar giant day gecko and various subspecies are found in Madagascar. It is diurnal and eats small insects and soft fruit. The male of this species can grow to a length of approximately 12 inches, 2 inches longer than the female. It reaches sexual maturity when it is approximately 1.5 years old. The female always lays 2 eggs, which she sticks in a protected location. The incubation period varies according to the conditions. The young animals are approximately 1.5 inches long when they hatch. The Madagascar giant day gecko lays more than one clutch of eggs per year.

Green tree gecko (*Naulitinus elegans*)

## Green tree gecko (*Naulitinus elegans*)

The green tree gecko is a striking green color. It varies from most other geckos in two ways: it is diurnal and it does not lay eggs. In fact, it is ovoviviparous, but since the green tree gecko gives birth to live young, it appears to be viviparous. Ovoviviparous animals must, however, not be confused with viviparous animals, such as mammals, because viviparous animals feed and supply oxygen to the unborn animal via the female's ingenious system of blood vessels. With ovoviviparous animals, the young are fed by the nutrients in the yoke of the egg. The eggs are, in fact, incubated in the mother's body, where they are relatively safe. The green tree gecko is found in New Zealand and grows to a length of approximately 8 inches.

Tokay gecko (*Gekko gecko*)

## Tokay gecko
## (*Gekko gecko*)

The tokay gecko is a member of the gecko family (*Gekkonidae*) and is found throughout Asia, particularly in Indonesia. The species can grow to a length of approximately 14 inches. The tokay gecko is considered to be rather noisy; the male can make considerable noise during the mating season. The species is a popular terrarium pet throughout the world. The tokay gecko is nocturnal and eats mainly insects, although it may also eat young mice and nestlings. The tokay gecko is not a particularly friendly animal and when disturbed, it can be fairly aggressive and give its enemy a nasty bite. It can sometimes also be particularly unfriendly to its own species. As with most other geckos, the tokay gecko does not seem to have eyelids. Its eyelids are transparent and have grown together to cover the whole eye so that they cannot move. The tokay gecko uses its long tongue to keep its eyes moist and clean.

## Gliding gecko
## (*Ptychozoon kuhli*)

The gliding gecko is a member of the gecko family (*Gekkonidae*). The species gets its common name from the folds of skin which enable it to glide from tree to tree and from branch to branch. The gliding gecko lives in wooded areas and only comes out at dusk and during the night. Its diet consists of a variety of insects. It is found in southeast Asia and can grow to a length of approximately 6 inches.

## Burton's legless lizard
## (*Lialis burtonis*)

The Burton's legless lizard, which looks very much like a snake, is a member of the flap-footed lizard family (*Pygopodidae*). It is found in the forests and semi-arid regions of certain parts of Australia and New Guinea. It is active both during the

Gliding gecko (*Ptychozoon kuhli*)

Burton's legless lizard (*Lialis burtonis*)

Spotted rock lizard (*Platysaurus guttatus*)

Giant zonure (*Cordylus giganteus*)

day and at night. The Burton's legless lizard is an active hunter and eats insects and other species of lizard. Its flexible jaw allows it to eat relatively large prey. It grows to a length of approximately 24 inches.

## Spotted rock lizard (*Platysaurus guttatus*)

The spotted rock lizard is a member of the girdle-tailed lizard family (*Cordylidae*). It is found in South Africa and can grow to a length of 12.5 inches. The sexes can be distinguished easily by their color and size; the male has a much more striking color and is also larger than the female. It eats a variety of large insects, such as grasshoppers. The female lays 2 eggs in a sheltered alcove in some rocks. The heat of the sun then incubates the eggs.

## Giant zonure (*Cordylus giganteus*)

This species is a member of the girdle-tailed lizard family (*Cordylidae*) and grows to a length of approximately 15 inches. It lives on the ground and eats mainly insects, although it also eats other prey, such as young mice and nestlings

which have fallen out of their nest. It is diurnal and spends its life in an underground network of tunnels. The giant zonure is ovoviviparous. Its young are relatively large at birth and are usually longer than 4.5 inches. The female usually gives birth to only 2 young per year. The giant zonure is found in South Africa.

## New Guinea blind lizard (*Dibamus novaeguineae*)

The New Guinea blind lizard is one of three species which belong to the blind lizard family (*Dibamidae*). The species is found in New Guinea and on the Asiatic islands to the Northwest. The animal can grow to a length of approximately 12 inches. The New Guinea blind lizard is completely blind, but does not appear to experience any difficulty with this, since it spends a large part of its life in the dark underground. It is carnivorous.

New Guinea blind lizard (*Dibamus novaeguineae*)

## Marine iguana
### (*Amblyrhynchus cristatus*)

The marine iguana is found mostly on the island of Santa Cruz and the Galapagos Islands, where it lives on the inhospitable rocks along the coast. Its diet consists mainly of sea algae, but it also eats animals, such as grasshoppers. The marine iguana often enters the water to catch its food. It is an excellent swimmer and diver; a marine iguana can remain under water for almost 1 hour. The marine iguana does not reproduce very quickly. The female usually lays 2 eggs, which hatch after approximately 3.5 months. The male can grow to a length of 5 feet, while the female is considerably smaller.

## Fiji Island banded iguana
### (*Brachylophus fasciatus*)

The Fiji Island banded iguana is a spectacularly colored iguana. It is omnivorous and eats mainly leaves, flowers and insects. It is found in the forests on the islands of Fiji and Tonga. The female usually lays 4 eggs in a hole, which she then covers over with soil. The eggs hatch after 4 to 7 months. An adult measures approximately 35 inches, but the tail accounts for three quarters of this.

Marine iguana (*Amblyrhynchus cristatus*)

Fiji Island banded iguana (*Brachylophus fasciatus*)

Green iguana (*Iguana iguana*)

## Green iguana
### (*Iguana iguana*)

The green iguana is one of the largest species of iguanas. It can grow to a length of 6.5 feet, although the body is only 16 to 20 inches long. The male is bigger than the female. Adults are predominantly herbivorous and eat leaves, flowers and fruit, while young animals also sometimes eat insects. The species gets its common name from the bright green color of the young animal. As it gets older, the darker bands become wider and the bright color becomes weaker. The green iguana lives in the wooded regions which are abundant with water in the northern part of South America, in Central America and on several neighboring islands. It prefers to remain on the strong branches along the riverbank. The green iguana is an excellent swimmer. It is also a good climber and is often found many feet above ground level. It has an interesting mating ritual and the female lays her eggs approximately 2 months after mating. A clutch normally consists of approximately 30 eggs, although it is possible for it to contain twice as many. She usually buries the eggs in the sand and they hatch after about 3 months. The green iguana is very popular as a terrarium pet and is one of the few reptiles which can be tamed in a general sense.

## Malayan sail-finned water dragon (*Hydrosaurus amboinensis*)

The Malayan sail-finned water dragon can grow to a length of more than 3 feet. It is found mainly in the rain forests of New Guinea and is agile both on land and in the water. On land, it sometimes only walks on its powerful rear legs but it is significantly faster and more at home in the water. An adult eats an equal proportion of plant material and insects. The sexes can be distinguished easily; the male has a crest on the top of

Malayan sail-finned water dragon (*Hydrosaurus amboinensis*)

Philippine sail-finned water dragon

its tail. The female lays an average of 9 eggs, which hatch after approximately 65 days.

## Philippine sail-finned water dragon (*Hydrosaurus pustulatus*)

The Philippine sail-finned water dragon is a very closely related to the Malayan sail-finned water dragon. As its common name suggests, it is an excellent swimmer. This water dragon lives in the forests in the Philippines where there is abundant water. It is omnivorous, although the young animals are predominantly carnivorous. The sexes can be distinguished easily by the fin on their backs, which is larger and better developed on the male.

The Philippine sail-finned water dragon is somewhat smaller than the Malayan sail-finned water dragon and the female is often smaller than the male.

Texas horned lizard (*Phrynosoma cornutum*)

Dabb spiny-tailed lizard (*Uromastyx acanthinurus*)

## Texas horned lizard
## (*Phrynosoma cornutum*)

This horned lizard is one of the smallest species of iguana. An adult grows to a maximum length of almost 7 inches, but is usually much smaller. It is a very peculiar animal. It is found in the southern United States, including Texas, Oklahoma and Kansas and has also been observed in Mexico. Although the animal looks rather frightening, it has a friendly and peaceful character. When it feels threatened, it makes its body as flat as possible and remains still for some time. When it feels in extreme danger, it can spray blood out of its eyes, something not very common in the animal kingdom. It eats a variety of insects but is particularly fond of ants. The female digs a small tunnel in the ground where she lays 15 to 45 eggs, which hatch after 35 to 60 days.

## Dabb spiny-tailed lizard
## (*Uromastyx acanthinurus*)

This diurnal lizard is found in the (semi-) arid regions of North Africa. The dabb spiny-tailed lizard spends the day searching for food and buries itself in a hole under the ground at night. A male has his own territory, which it shares with several females. Its diet consists of a variety of plant material, which it sometimes supplements with insects and other small animals. The dabb spiny-tailed lizard cannot be recognised by its color because its markings and color can vary greatly. The animal is oviparous and the female lays 10 to 20 eggs, which she buries in the ground. Although it does not display brood care, the female initially protects the eggs from predators. An adult dabb spiny-tailed lizard can grow to a length of approximately 16 inches. It gets its com-

A young bearded dragon (*Pogona barbata*)

mon name from its prickly tail. It can store fat in its tail, which it can draw on when food is scarce.

## Bearded dragon
## (*Pogona barbata*)

For a long time, this species was known by the scientific name *Amphibolurus barbatus,* but is now a member of the genus *Pogona.* It gets its common name from the prickly scales that cover its throat sack, which it can inflate when threatened or when it wishes to impress an opponent. The species is found throughout Australia, but mainly along the east coast. It can grow to a length of approximately 9 inches, not including its tail. The bearded dragon is omnivorous. It can lay more than one clutch of eggs in a single season, usually 2 or 3. A clutch contains an aver-

A young green crested basilisk (*Basiliscus plumifrons*)

Green crested basilisk (*Basiliscus plumifrons*)

age of 25 eggs. The eggs are buried in the ground and the animal does not display any further brood care. The eggs hatch after approximately 8 to 10 weeks. When the eggs hatch, the young animals are approximately 4 inches long.

## Green crested basilisk
## (*Basiliscus plumifrons*)

Including its long tail, a green crested basilisk can grow to a length of 30 inches. It is found in the northern countries of South America and in Central America, where it inhabits dense forests. It eats mainly a variety of insects, although it also sometimes eats fruit. The sexes can be distinguished easily by the crest, which is not as large on the female. The female lays more than one clutch of eggs in a single season. The number of eggs varies greatly, but is not usually more than 26. The eggs hatch after approximately 70 to 85 days.

## Frilled lizard
## (*Chlamydosaurus kingii*)

The frilled lizard is a member of the agama family. It is found in New Guinea and in certain parts of Australia. A peculiar characteristic of this animal is the way it moves very quickly by running on its rear legs. This species gets its common name from its collar, which under normal cir-

Frilled lizard (*Chlamydosaurus kingii*)

cumstances, remains folded up and is carried as a cape. The male inflates this collar during the mating ritual or if he wants to impress another male. When the collar is inflated, it has a diameter of approximately 10 inches. The frilled lizard is diurnal and is found mainly in wooded regions. It is predominantly insectivorous. The frilled lizard can grow to a length of approximately 27.5 inches.

## Sand lizard
## (*Lacerta agilis*)

The sand lizard is a member of the true lizard family (*Lacertidae*). It can grow to a length of more than 4 inches, although the tail is usually (much) longer than the body. It is common throughout Europe, including Great Britain and western Russia. It lives up to its common name because it prefers to live in sandy regions. This diurnal animal hibernates during the winter. Its diet includes insects.

Sand lizard (*Lacerta agilis*)

During the mating season, the male's color changes to green. Outside the mating season, the male can be recognised by its striking markings and color. The sand lizard is oviparous.

## Ocellated lacerta
## (*Lacerta lepida*)

The ocellated lacerta is found in several southern European countries and North Africa. Including the tail, the male can grow to a length of 31.5 inches, which makes it one of the largest species of lizards found in Europe. The female is quite a bit smaller. Not only can the male be recognised by its size but also by its head, which is much larger and wider than that of the female. The ocellated lacerta lays as many as 20 eggs, which hatch after 2 to 3 months. When the young hatch, they are already 2

A male ocellated lacerta (*Lacerta lepida*)

A female ocellated lacerta (*Lacerta lepida*)

Sand skink (*Scincus scincus*)

Western blue-tongued skink (*Tiliqua occipitalis*)

inches long. The ocellated lacerta hibernates.

## Sand skink
## (*Scincus scincus*)

The sand skink is believed to have healing properties. It measures approximately 8 inches and is found in various deserts and similar habitats in North Africa and the Middle East. This diurnal animal has a great need for warmth and eats a variety of insects. The sand skink is also called *sandfish* and is ovoviviparous.

## Western blue-tongued skink
## (*Tiliqua occipitalis*)

The genus of blue-tongued skink (*Tiliqua*), which is a member of the skink family, contains 10 different species which are almost all found in Australia. The western blue-tongued skink is a member of this genus and is found in Australia, Tasmania and New Guinea. The blue-tongued skink gets its name from its bright blue tongue. The species is predominantly herbivorous, but also likes to eat insects. This skink, in turn, is a welcome addition to the diet of certain snakes and birds of prey and is also consumed by humans. The species is ovoviviparous. The young animals often remain close to their mother for a year or more and go their own way only when

they reach sexual maturity. The western blue-tongued skink can live for 20 to 30 years.

## Blue ameiva
## (*Ameiva ameiva*)

This small lizard is a member of the tegu family and is found in Central America. It can grow to a total length of 20 inches. The sexes can be distinguished easily by the color of the belly. The female has a white belly, while the male's belly is blue. The blue ameiva is oviparous. It is diurnal and predominantly insectivorous, although it also eats plant material, such as soft fruit. It is also called a jungle runner because of the speed with which it runs when it feels threatened.

Blue ameiva (*Ameiva ameiva*)

## Tegu lizard
(*Tupinambis teguixin*)

The tegu lizard is a member of the tegu family (*Teiidae*). It grows to a length of approximately 4.5 feet, almost half of which constitutes its tail. It is found in central South America where it lives in forested regions, as well as near human settlements. It eats a variety of animal food, such as eggs, birds, rodents, frogs and insects.

## Prehensile-tailed skink
(*Corucia zebrata*)

The prehensile-tailed skink is the largest member of the skink family. From its head to the tip of its tail, it measures more than 23.5 inches. In contrast to all other skinks, the prehensile-tailed skink is not terrestrial, but arboreal. It is herbivorous.

Prehensile-tailed skink (*Corucia zebrata*)

## Slow-worm
(*Anguis fragilis*)

The slow-worm is found throughout Europe, North Africa and western Russia. It can grow to a length of approximately 16 inches. The species is often mistaken for a snake. A layman cannot be blamed for this, because the two can easily be mixed up at first sight. One of the typical characteristics of this animal is the many different colors it may have. The color ranges from almost white (albino) to dark grey, but red animals have also been found. The slow-worm

Slow-worm (*Anguis fragilis*)

Tegu lizard (*Tupinambis teguixin*)

Gila monster (*Heloderma suspectum*)

feels at home in almost all habitats. Its diet consists mainly of rain worms, slugs and snails. The slow-worm is ovoviviparous and gives birth to approximately 10 young after a gestation period of about 3 months. The young slow-worms can be recognised by the clearly visible stripes along their length, which are not present on the adult animal. On average, a slow-worm lives for 30 years but some have also been known to live for twice as long.

## Gila monster
## (*Heloderma suspectum*)

The Gila monster is a member of the small family of Gila monsters and bearded lizards (*Helodermatidae*) and can grow to 12 inches in length, including its tail. It is found in several arid areas in the southern United States and in northern Mexico. It is nocturnal and eats mainly young rodents and birds, but also likes to eat eggs. Its dark pink to red markings make it one of the most colorful species of lizard. It is oviparous and lays its eggs in an underground hole, so that they are reasonably protected from large temperature fluctuations and predators. The bite from

a Gila monster is very poisonous and can be fatal for humans.

## Jackson's chameleon
## (*Chamaeleo jacksonii*)

The male Jackson's chameleon has three horns, while the female has a varying number of horns; she may have no horns, 1 horn or 3 horns and they are always smaller than the male's. The Jackson's chameleon is a relatively small animal. Including its tail, it can grow to a length of approximately 9.5 inches, although half of this length is made up of its tail. The animal originates from the rain forests of countries such as Uganda and Tanzania, but is nowadays also native to Hawaii, where some animals were accidentally released several years ago.

Jackson's chameleon (*Chamaeleo jacksonii*)

## Common chameleon (*Chamaeleo chamaeleon*)

This species of chameleon is found in North Africa, the southern parts of various Middle Eastern countries, India, the Canary Islands, southern Portugal and Spain. It is the only species of chameleon found in Europe. It usually lives alone and is fairly aggressive to other common chameleons. It has its own territory, in which it does not tolerate any other animals of the same species outside the mating season. The female lays approximately 25 eggs, which she buries in the ground. The common chameleon can grow to a length of approximately 11 inches. The chameleon is well known because it can change color. It does not, in fact, change its color to match its background, but rather to reflect its mood. All chameleons, and therefore also the common chameleon, can move their eyes independently from each other. It has a very long, sticky tongue which it uses to catch food, mainly insects, without having to move too much. This is a useful adaptation, because the animal is not very agile and does not actively hunt. The tail acts as a grip to move from branch to branch and is a very important means for moving through dense foliage. If the tail of the common chameleo breaks off, it does not grow back and its chances of

survival are considerably reduced.

## Nile monitor (*Varanus niloticus*)

The Nile monitor is diurnal and can grow to a length of more than 6.5 feet, although most animals remain smaller. The species is found in large parts of Africa, where it prefers to live near and in water. Its diet consists mainly of fish and amphibians, such as frogs and toads. It also eats crocodile eggs and ventures near the nesting place of crocodiles for this purpose. The Nile monitor can be very daring and aggressive. Part of its diet also consists of shellfish, for which it will sometimes dive to the bottom of the river to catch. It uses its excellent vision to hunt. The Nile monitor is oviparous. It lays eggs with a soft shell, which it buries under a layer of rotting plants. When the eggs hatch after 4.5 to 7 months, the young animals are approximately 10 inches long.

## Gould's monitor (*Varanus gouldii*)

The Gould's monitor is carnivorous and actively hunts for its food. It is one of the fastest monitors, if not the fastest. Its diet consists of small animals, such as rodents, birds and nestlings, but it also eats insects and small lizards. The Gould's monitor is found in the (semi-) arid regions of Aus-

Nile monitor (*Varanus niloticus*)

Gould's monitor (*Varanus gouldii*)

tralia and New Guinea. An adult measures approximately 4 feet.

## Rough-necked monitor (*Varanus rudicollis*)

The rough-necked monitor gets both its common and scientific name from its large, somewhat thick neck scales. It is a slim monitor, and is found in Indonesia where it prefers to live in trees. It eats a variety of small animals, which it finds in the branches and leaves. An adult

Rough-necked monitor (*Varanus rudicollis*)

rough-necked monitor can grow to a length of 4 feet.

## Komodo dragon (*Varanus komodoensis*)

Although there are only a small number of Komodo dragons and although it is found only on a small number of islands to the east of Java (including the Island of Komodo), it is the best-known species of monitor lizard. This is possibly due to its impressive appearance and its considerable size; it can grow to a length of 10 feet and weigh 300 pounds. The Komodo dragon is carnivorous and hunts mostly for hoofed animals, such as deer. It is diurnal and is considered one of the most intelligent species of lizard.

## Merten's water monitor
### (*Varanus mertensii*)

The Merten's water monitor is found in northern Australia, near water and in regions with high humidity. Its body is well adapted to its living environment; for example, its tail is flat for faster swimming. A Merten's water monitor can grow to a length of approximately 4 feet.

## Bornean earless monitor
### (*Lanthanotus borneensis*)

The Bornean earless monitor inhabits marshy regions and is the sole representative of its genus, the earless monitor. The species is found only on the island of Borneo, where it lives a withdrawn life close to shallow water. During the day, it hides in a hole or underwater and it appears only at dusk. Its diet consists mainly of fish. The Bornean earless monitor is rather clumsy on land. It does not use its legs and moves like a snake along the ground. The species can grow to a length of approximately 16 inches. It is believed to be oviparous.

Merten's water monitor (*Varanus mertensii*)

Bornean earless monitor (*Lanthanotus borneensis*)

Komodo dragon (*Varanus komodoensis*)

# Snakes (Order *Squamata,* suborder *Serpentes*)

Families: *Typhlopidae, Leptotyphlopidae, Aniliidae, Uropeltidae, Xenopeltidae, Acrochordidae, Boidae, Colubridae, Elapidae, Hydrophiidae, Viperidae and Crotalidae*

## False coral snake (*Anilius scytale*)

This brightly colored and marked snake is a member of the small family of burrowing snakes (*Aniliidae*), which is composed of three genera. The species is found in wooded areas throughout the northern half of South America, except in the area to the west of the Andes. The animal can grow to a length of approximately 31.5 inches. It eats lizards, amphibians and smaller species of snakes. It lives partly underground and, like all snakes of its type, is a good burrower. In contrast to what its coloring suggests, this snake is not venomous. The false coral snake is ovoviviparous.

False coral snake (*Anilius scytale*)

## Green tree python (*Chondropython/Morelia viridis*)

The green tree python is found mainly in the forests of New Guinea, northern Australia and the Solomon Islands, where it spends most of its time high up in trees. It can move quickly and often uses its tail to gain an excellent hold of branches. It is carnivorous and often eats birds and nestlings. Most animals are green with white markings, but some animals of a bluer color have been found. The green tree python can grow to a length of approximately 6 feet.

## Royal python (*Python regius*)

The royal python is found in the wooded regions of central and West Africa, where it lives partly on the ground and partly in

Green tree python (*Chondropython/Morelia viridis*)

Royal python (*Python regius*)

trees. It eats a variety of small animals, such as small birds, amphibians and small reptiles. Although it can grow to a length of 6.5 feet, the average royal python is no longer than 4.5 feet. It reaches sexual maturity between 3 and 5 years of age. The female lays 4 to 10 eggs, which hatch after 3 months. During this period, the mother winds herself around the eggs to protect them and keep them warm. Once the eggs hatch, the young snakes go their own way and receive no further care. The young snakes are approximately 12 inches long when they hatch. The royal python is very popular as a pet in terrariums and has been successfully bred in captivity. If it is handled from a young age, it is one of the few reptiles which can, in a general sense, be tamed. Animals kept in terrariums live an average of 20 to 30 years. The oldest known royal python lived in captivity for almost 50 years.

Reticulated python (*Python reticulatus*)

## Reticulated python (*Python reticulatus*)

The reticulated python is, together with the green anaconda, one of the largest snakes known to man, as well as the largest reptile. The reticulated python can grow to a length of more than 30 feet, although most snakes are several feet shorter. Like all other pythons, the reticulated python displays brood care. It is found in Asia, particularly in the Philippines. It eats its prey whole and has a very flexible jaw which allows it to eat large prey. It can unhinge the joint of its lower and top jaws, so that they are connected to each other only by elastic tendons. The flexibility of the stomach and skin is also well adapted to this way of eating. It can take quite some time for it to consume its prey, during which time the reticulated python gets oxygen via its stretched lungs. The lungs have air bags which enable the snake to store oxygen in the rear and absorb this oxygen into the body. This way of eating is characteristic of all snakes.

## Giant sand boa (*Eryx tataricus*)

The giant sand boa is a member of the genus *Eryx*. The members of this genus distinguish themselves from all other species of large snakes by their habitat. The giant sand boa is found in the desert

Giant sand boa (*Eryx tataricus*)

Emerald tree boa (*Boa caninus*)

## Boa constrictor
## (*Boa constrictor*)

The average boa constrictor is 10 feet long but animals measuring 15 feet have also been recorded. Despite its large size, the species is harmless to humans and does not normally attack them. It prefers to use its sharp fangs when it feels threatened. Various subspecies of boa constrictor are found in Central America and the northern part of South America. It is predominantly terrestrial, lives in dense wooded habitats and eats rodents, birds and various species of lizards. It overpowers its prey by biting it with its strong, backward-pointed fangs and then quickly wrapping its strong body around the prey until it suffocates. The species is ovoviviparous.

regions of certain parts of Asia. It eats small prey, such as rodents, which it overpowers by constriction. The giant sand boa grows to a length of approximately 3 feet and is ovoviviparous. As with all snakes, it has transparent eyelids which do not move. When it sheds its skin, it also sheds the transparent skin that covers its eyes. A relative of the giant sand boa is the (common) sand boa, which is found in Europe and is somewhat smaller.

## Emerald tree boa
## (*Boa caninus*)

This snake is arboreal and rarely ventures onto the ground. Its diet consists mainly of birds and nestlings. The emerald tree boa can grow to a length of approximately 6.5 feet but is often about a foot shorter. The species is found in the rain forests of central and northern South America and is ovoviviparous. The sexes can be distinguished by their size; the female is usually bigger than the male and the male often has a larger head. The emerald tree boa is a member of the family *Boidae*.

## Green anaconda
## (*Eunectes murinus*)

The green anaconda is one of the most feared species of snake. It is a member of the boa family (*Boidae*) and the genus anaconda (*Eunectes*). The green anaconda can grow to a length of more than 30 feet, but is usually approximately 23 feet long and weighs about 450 pounds.

Boa constrictor (*Boa constrictor*)

Green anaconda (*Eunectes murinus*)

This is one of the few species of large snakes that present a danger to humans because they regard humans as prey. This species spends most of its time in water, but seldom eats fish. Its diet consists mainly of mammals, but it sometimes also

Russian rat snake (*Elaphe schrencki*)

eats large reptiles and birds. It requires relatively little food, however, and can go without it for weeks or even months. The green anaconda is ovoviviparous. The number of young varies according to the size and age of the mother, but averages between 40 and 50. The young are already 27 inches long when born and can fend for themselves. Although an adult green anaconda does not have any natural enemies, its young have many predators. The green anaconda is found in the rain forests of South America.

## Russian rat snake (*Elaphe schrencki*)

The Russian rat snake is a member of the family *Colubridae*. It is found in the wooded regions of China, Korea and the neighboring regions of the former USSR. It can grow to a length of approximately 6 feet. Although it can give a nasty bite if it feels threatened, its venom is harmless to

Grass snake (*Natrix natrix natrix*)

Rat snake (*Elaphe obsoleta*)

humans. It eats small animals, such as birds, nestlings and rodents and may sometimes also eat eggs.

its name implies that it only eats rats, it also eats other rodents, as well as birds, amphibians and small lizards. What the rat snake shares with all the other colubrids is its short venomous fangs and a venom that is relatively harmless to humans. There are several subspecies which vary in length, with the largest measuring 8 feet. There is also a striking difference in the colors and markings of the various subspecies; they vary from a slightly dark color to being speckled or brightly striped. The rat snake is oviparous. The female usually lays 1 or 2 clutches of eggs per year containing 10 to 40 eggs, which hatch after 8 to 10 weeks.

## Rat snake
## (*Elaphe obsoleta*)

The rat snake is a member of the very large family of colubrids (*Colubridae*). Several subspecies are found in Canada, the United States and Mexico. Although

## Grass snake
## (*Natrix natrix natrix*)

The common grass snake is a striking member of the colubrid family. It is a member of the water snakes (genus *Natrix*). The species is venomous, but its

Green vine snake (*Oxybelis fulgidus*)

venomous fangs are not normally used in defence. When threatened, the grass snake emits a foul-smelling substance which usually results in the animal being left in peace. If it is in serious danger, a grass snake will sometimes play dead, something it can do for a considerable time. It is oviparous. It prefers to live near water, and its diet consists mainly of amphibians and fish. The common grass snake can grow to a length of approximately 5 feet. It is found in Central and Eastern Europe, as well as western Russia. If the subspecies of the common grass snake are included, the joint natural habitat is much larger and includes almost all of Europe, western areas of Asia and areas in North Africa. Certain subspecies, such as the spotted grass snake (*N. natrix Helvetica*) are about a foot longer than the average grass snake.

## Green vine snake (*Oxybelis fulgidus*)

The green vine snake is a member of the family *Colubridae*. It is found in Central America and in the northern part of South America. The green vine snake is arboreal and hunts for food in the trees both during the day and at night with breaks in between. Its diet consists mainly of nestlings and small lizards. An average adult green vine snake is approximately 5 feet long, but some have been recorded up to a foot longer.

## Indian cobra (*Naja naja*)

The Indian cobra can expand its neck to make itself look bigger to opponents. The neck usually has a spectacle-like marking. The Indian cobra and several subspecies are found in Asia and are members of the coral snake family (*Elapidae*). As with all coral snakes, the venom of the Indian

cobra is harmful to humans. Its venom acts on the nervous system by paralysing its prey or enemy. The average size of the Indian cobra is 5 feet, although some subspecies can be more than 6.5 feet in length. The Indian cobra is the best-known species of cobra. The snake is known for its ability to perform with snake charmers, where the snake appears to be "dancing" to the music of a flute. Snakes are actually deaf, so it is not reacting to the music, but rather to the movement of the snake charmer. The Indian cobra may have many different colors and markings, which means that it can be recognised only by its build. It is oviparous and the mother protects the eggs from predators.

Cape cobra (*Naja nivea*)

Indian cobra (*Naja naja*)

Eastern coral snake (*Micrurus fulvius*)

## Cape cobra
## (*Naja nivea*)

This species of cobra is found in the mountainous regions of South Africa. Its fast-acting venom is very harmful to humans and acts on the nervous system. When the Cape cobra feels threatened, it points the front part of its body vertically upward and expands its neck so that it appears larger and broader than it actually is. The Cape cobra can grow to a length of 5 to 6.5 feet.

## Eastern coral snake
## (*Micrurus fulvius*)

The eastern coral snake is one of the most colorful species of snakes known to man. The species is found in the southern United States and Mexico. Its diet consists mainly of small reptiles and snakes. The eastern coral snake is extremely venomous and harmful to humans. The chances of encountering an eastern coral snake are, however, not very great, since the animal usually lives a withdrawn life in rodent burrows and is active only in the early morning and at dusk. It is oviparous and usually lays between 4 and 12 eggs. It does not display any form of brood care. The eastern coral snake can

grow to a length of approximately 24 inches.

## King cobra
## (*Ophiophagus hannah*)

The king cobra is a member of the coral snake family (*Elapidae*). It can grow to a length of more than 16 feet, but is usually a couple of feet shorter. It is found in China, Malaysia, the Philippines, Indonesia and India. It prefers to live in wooded and sheltered locations and eats mainly smaller species of snakes and, to a lesser extent, lizards (monitors). Just like the python, the king cobra also displays brood care but the care that the king cobra gives to its offspring goes one step further. Usually, the male king cobra also remains with the nest and the parents leave only when the eggs hatch. A clutch of eggs usually consists of about 30 eggs. A young king cobra is usually approximately 1.5 feet long when it hatches. The venom of a king cobra is considered to be the most dangerous and fastest-acting venom in the world; it can kill a human within 15 minutes and a single bite is fatal for very large mammals, such as elephants. Nevertheless, a king cobra would prefer to

King cobra (*Ophiophagus hannah*)

Yellow-lipped sea snake (*Laticauda colubrina*)

avoid a threatening situation than attack an opponent. Like all species of cobra, when threatened, the king cobra raises its body vertically and expands the loose skin around its neck to make itself look more imposing.

## Yellow-lipped sea snake (*Laticauda colubrina*)

The yellow-lipped sea snake is found on several coral islands on and around New Caledonia to the east of Australia. The tail of the yellow-lipped sea snake has a characteristic shape that helps it to swim and turn in the water. Its diet consists mainly of fish, which it paralyses with a venomous bite that acts on the nervous system. A bite from a yellow-lipped sea snake can be fatal for humans, but this seldom happens since the animal is usually not aggressive. The yellow-lipped sea snake grows to a length of more than 3 feet.

## Eastern diamondback rattlesnake (*Crotalus adamanteus*)

The eastern diamondback rattlesnake is found in the desert regions in the souteastern United States. It can grow to a length of 8 feet and is the largest species of rattlesnake. There are almost 100 known species and subspecies of rattlesnakes. It is a member of the true rattlesnake genus (*Crotalus*) and the pit viper family (*Crotalidae*). All pit vipers have an organ that can measure temperature. The organ, which is called the *pit organ*, is located between the nostrils and the eyes and gives this animal its unusual appearance. A characteristic of all rattlesnakes is that they can make a rattling noise by moving the end of their tail very quickly back and forth. The end of the tail is made from various, clearly distinguishable, horny segments. All rattlesnakes are extremely venomous and their bite can be fatal to humans. They usually hibernate in large numbers, often in a hole in rocks. It is not uncommon for hundreds of rattlesnakes to be found in the same location. A rattlesnake usually eats small rodents, but may also eat small snakes and lizards. Like all other species of rattlesnake, the eastern diamondback rattlesnake is ovoviviparous.

Eastern diamondback rattlesnake (*Crotalus adamanteus*)

Long-nosed viper (*Vipera ammodytes*)

## Long-nosed viper
## (*Vipera ammodytes*)

The long-nosed viper can be easily recognised by the horny bulge on its nose. It is a member of the viper family (*Viperidae*), which has the longest venomous fangs of all the venomous snakes. The fangs are so long that they do not fit inside the mouth vertically and must be folded backwards along the top jaw. When a viper bites, it hinges its jaw forward and upward, in order to release its fangs. The viper's venom usually acts quickly and kills small prey, such as lizards and mice, in a short time. The species is found mostly in Central Europe and the Balkans. It prefers sandy soil, but is also found in rocky regions and urban areas. The long-nosed viper is ovoviviparous and gives birth to an average of 10 young each year. The long-nosed viper can grow to a length of approximately 35 inches.

## Tuatara
## (*Rhynchocephalia*)

This order is represented by 2 species, the *Sphenodon punctatus* and the less well-known *Sphenodon guntheri*. It is found only on North Brother Island near New Zealand, which covers an area of 10 acres. The tuatara occupies a special place among the class of reptiles. Fossils of this species have been found which must be between 130 and 200 million years old. It is remarkable that these fossils are almost identical to the current population of tuataras. This animal is, therefore, also called the *living fossil*. An adult male is approximately 26 inches long and the female is usually much smaller. The tuatara is predominantly carnivorous and eats small lizards, which it captures at dusk and during the night. It usually remains hidden in a sheltered location during the day. The tuatara can live to be quite old, but how old exactly is not known. In any case, it has been established that a 60-year-old female is still able to reproduce normally. The age of reaching sexual maturity gives an indication of the supposed age that an animal can reach and this species reaches sexual maturity only when approximately 20 years old. The frequency with which the female lays eggs is very low; on average she lays eggs only once every 2 to 4 years. A usual clutch contains 9 eggs. It can take a very long time before the eggs hatch, usually 1 to 1.5 years.

Tuatara (*Rhynchocephalia*)

# 3 Birds (Class *Aves*)

Common cuckoo (*Cuculus canorus*)

Just like mammals, birds are warm-blooded animals, which means they can regulate their own body temperature. Species that live in cold climates have a plumage which has been adapted to the cold to prevent them from losing too much heat. Most birds shed part of their feathers each year; a characteristic which is called moulting. This moulting requires so much energy that many birds lose a considerable amount of weight when moulting. Some species cannot fly during the moult-

Hummingbirds are members of the family *Apodiformes*

ing period and are, therefore, more vulnerable. Most, but not all, birds can fly. Penguins, for example, have to rely on their swimming ability, while flightless birds, such as the ostrich and rhea, can run very fast. One of the fastest species of bird is, without doubt, the peregrine falcon. When swooping down on its prey from a great height, it can reach a speed of 200 miles per hour.

The eating habits of birds vary greatly. There are birds which only eat seeds, there are carnivorous birds and every possibility in between. The shape of the beak can often indicate what type of food a bird will eat.

One characteristic that all birds share is that they are oviparous (i.e., they lay eggs).

Emperor goose (*Anser canagicus*)

Common rhea (*Rhea americana*)

Emu (*Dromaius novae hollandiae*)

Most bird species build a nest, but the size and shape can vary from a carefully woven spherical shape to an untidy construction of twigs. There are also birds which do not take the trouble to build a nest and lay their eggs in a hole in the ground. Nests can be built in all sorts of locations, including trees, bushes, rocks, holes, rooftops and even the ground.

There are also species of birds whose nests more or less float on water. Some species of birds brood in colonies, while other species have their own territory where no other bird of the same species, or sometimes even the same color, is permitted. Naturally, there is a correlation between the size of the eggs and the size of the species. Ostriches, for example, lay

Eagle owl (*Bubo bubo*)

Blue peacock (*Pavo cristatus*)

the largest eggs. Their eggs can weigh as much as 3.5 pounds, while the eggs of the hummingbird sometimes only weigh a tenth of an ounce. Birds usually display intensive brood care. Almost all parent animals, except for the cuckoo and several related breeds, incubate their eggs. In many cases, the female carries out this task alone, but there are many examples where the partners take turns. In several rare cases, it is exclusively, or mainly, the male that takes responsibility for incubating the eggs.

Young, newly hatched birds can be either precocial or altricial. Precocial birds can often leave the nest on the day they hatch and walk or swim with their parents. The task of the parents then consists of teaching the young what is edible, protecting them and keeping them warm. Altricial birds do not only require food from their parents (which is often pre-digested), but

Cormorant (*Phala crocorax carbo*)

also warmth, because they cannot maintain their body temperature, as they have not yet grown feathers and down. They are often naked, blind and completely helpless.

Birds rely heavily on their vision. Birds of prey, for example, pick out their prey thanks to their sharp vision. The paring and mating rituals of many species of birds are based on appearance. During the mating season, the males often have a differ-

Black stork (*Ciconia nigra*)

Grey heron (*Ardea cinerea*)

Yellow grosbeak (*Pheucticus chrysopeplus*)

to wing tip, measured with outstretched wings, can reach almost 12 feet.

Birds are often remarkably light in weight, more so when the weight is compared to the size and wingspan. This is because the skeleton of almost all birds is mostly hollow. Feathers weigh very little, but they account for a relatively large proportion of a bird's weight.

Common gallinule (*Gallinula chloropus*)

A coot in its nest.

ent, more colorful plumage or some other eye-catching characteristic with which to catch the interest of the broody females. The hearing of most birds is also reasonably well developed, as demonstrated by the songs of many species which are used to mark out the boundaries of their territory or to attract partners. For several species, particularly vultures, the sense of smell is the best developed sense.

Birds can be found throughout the world and have adapted to the most divergent climates and circumstances. Some species of birds remain in the same area all their lives; these birds are called sedentary birds. There is also a considerably large number of species whose breeding ground and the location where they spend the winter are hundreds of miles to tens of thousands of miles apart. These birds are called migratory birds. There are, however, also examples of species in which several populations are migratory, while animals belonging to the same species, but residing in a different area, are sedentary. The size of adult birds varies greatly. The smallest birds are hummingbirds. Some species of hummingbirds are smaller than 2.5 inches in length, including the tail. The bird with the largest wingspan is the albatross and the distance from wing tip

Common barn owl

In total, there are between 9,000 and 10,000 different species of bird divided into 28 different orders.

## The following orders are birds (Class *Aves*):

- Ostriches (*Struthioniformes*)
- Rheas (*Rheiformes*)
- Emus and cassowaries (*Casuariiformes*)
- Kiwis (*Apterygiformes*)
- Tinamous (*Tinamiformes*)
- Penguins (*Sphenisciformes*)
- Loons (*Gaviiformes*)
- Grebes (*Podicipediformes*)
- Albatrosses, shearwaters and petrels (*Procellariiformes*)
- Pelicans, boobies, tropic birds, cormorants and frigate birds (*Pelecaniformes*)
- Herons, storks, ibis and flamingos (*Ciconiiformes*)
- Screamers and wildfowl (*Anseriformes*)
- Birds of prey (*Falconiformes*)
- Grouse, pheasants, quail and turkeys (*Galliformes*)
- Cranes, rails, coots, seriemas and bustards (*Gruiformes*)
- Plovers, sandpipers, gulls, terns and auks (*Charadriiformes*)
- Sandgrouse (*Pteroclidiformes*)
- Pigeons and doves (*Columbiformes*)
- Parrots (*Psittaciformes*)
- Turacos, cuckoos and roadrunners (*Cuculiformes*)
- Owls (*Strigiformes*)
- Nightjars, frogmouths, potoos and oilbirds (*Caprimulgiformes*)
- Swifts and hummingbirds (*Apodiformes*)
- Colies (*Coliiformes*)
- Kingfishers and allies (*Coraciiformes*)
- Trogons (*Trogoniformes*)
- Woodpeckers, barbets, honey guides and toucans (*Piciformes*)
- Perching birds (*Passeriformes*)

# Ostriches
# (*Struthioniformes*)

Family: *Struthianidae*

## Ostrich (*Struthio camelus*)

Various ostrich species can be found in Africa, both in open areas and in wooded regions. An ostrich can grow to a height of 6 to 10 feet and weigh up to 330 pounds and is, therefore, the largest bird in the world. It is also the fastest flightless bird; its long, powerful legs allow it to reach a speed of 45 miles per hour. The male is easily recognised by its black and white plumage, while the female and young animals are not only smaller, but also have a browner plumage. Its diet consists mainly of a variety of plant material, although it sometimes also likes to eat small animals. The ostrich lives in groups which usually consist of one male with several females. During the mating season, the male scratches a hole in the ground to use as a nest. The female lays 6 to 8 eggs in the nest, which weigh up to 3.5 pounds each. The male mostly incubates the eggs, although the female sometimes relieves the male during the day. The eggs hatch after approximately 41 days. The young birds are precocial and can run fast when they are only 1 month old. They reach their adult size after 6 months.

Male ostrich (*Struthio camelus*)

Female ostrich (*Struthio camelus*)

# Rheas (*Rheiformes*)

Family: *Rheidae*

## Common rhea (*Rhea americana*)

The common rhea can be found in South America, where it lives both on semi-open grassy plains and in regions with dense growth. It can grow to a height of 5.5 feet. Its diet consists mainly of plant material, but it also eats insects and other small animals. The common rhea lives in groups which sometimes consist of dozens of animals. During the mating season, however, they split into smaller groups which consist of one male and several females. The male scratches a nest in the ground and mates with the females in his group. The females lay all their eggs in the nest and the male incubates them for approximately 40 days. The male also raises the young. The young reach their adult size after 4 months, but do not reach sexual maturity until they are 2 years old.

## Darwin's rhea (*Pterocnemia penneata*)

Including its long neck and head, the Darwin's rhea can grow to a height of approximately 5.5 feet, although it only measures 3 feet to its shoulder. The Darwin's rhea can be found in South America, particularly in the Andes. Its way of life and reproduction method are almost identical to that of the common rhea (*Rhea americana*).

Darwin's rhea (*Pterocnemia penneata*)

Darwin's rhea (*Pterocnemia penneata*)

Common rhea (*Rhea americana*)

Common rhea (*Rhea americana*)

# Emus and cassowaries (*Casuariiformes*)

Families: *Casuariidae and Dromaiidae*

## Emu (*Dromaius novaehollandiae*)

The emu is found in Australia, both in forested regions and on open plains. It can reach a speed of almost 30 miles per hour and is also able to swim. An emu can grow to a height of 6 feet and weigh up to 120 pounds. There are no visible differences between the male and female. The emu reaches sexual maturity between 2 and 3 years of age. It lays an average of 9 eggs, which weigh between 1 and 1.5 pounds each. The male incubates the eggs for approximately 57 days. The young remain in the nest for the first couple of days, after which time they can walk. An emu reaches adulthood in its second year. Its diet consists mainly of a variety of plant material, but it may also eat insects.

## Double-wattled cassowary (*Casuaris casuaris*)

This bird originates from New Guinea and Northern Australia. It can grow to a height of approximately 6 feet and although it is not the largest bird, its striking colors and the helmet-like crest on the top of its head make it the most striking flightless bird. It

Emu (*Dromaius novaehollandiae*)

Emu (*Dromaius novaehollandiae*)

Double-wattled cassowary (*Casuaris casuaris*)

Double-wattled cassowary (*Casuaris casuaris*)

lives both in forested and open areas and is omnivorous. This animal lives alone outside the mating season. It lays between 3 and 6 eggs, which the male incubates for approximately 30 days in a sheltered hole in the ground. The young are precocial, but remain with their father for 4 to 6 months before going their own way.

# Kiwis (*Apterygiformes*)

Family: Apterygidae

## Common kiwi (*Apertyx australis*)

Just like the other two species of kiwis, the common kiwi is a flightless bird. Kiwis can be found only in New Zealand, where the common kiwi is the most widespread of this small family of birds. The kiwi is nocturnal and remains in a protected hideaway during the day. Its diet consists of insects, worms and berries. A common kiwi is approximately 21.5 inches long. The female weighs an average of 6.5 pounds and is heavier than the male, which weighs approximately 4.5 pounds.

Common kiwi (*Apertyx australis*)

# Tinamous (*Tinamiformes*)

Family: Tinamidae

## Elegant crested tinamou (*Eudromia elegans*)

The elegant crested tinamou can grow to a length of approximately 16 inches. The

# Penguins (*Sphenisciformes*)

Family: *Spheniscidae*

## Humboldt penguin (*Spheniscus humboldti*)

The Humboldt penguin can be found on the islands along the coast of Peru. It is approximately 25.5 inches in length and weighs approximately 9 pounds. It eats a variety of small schooling fish, as well as small cephalopods. Humboldt penguins live and hunt in groups; a school of suitable prey is enclosed by the animals. Humboldt penguins breed in colonies. The female uses a shallow hole in the sand or an alcove in the rocks as a nest in which to lay 2 white eggs, which are incubated by both parents.

## Jackass penguin (*Spheniscus demersus*)

The jackass penguin lives in colonies along the coast of South Africa. It prefers to live in a rocky habitat and uses the natural caves and crevices as both a resting area and a place to lay and incubate its eggs. Its diet consists mainly of fish which it catches by diving into the sea. This species is unable to move very fast on land, but in the water, it can reach a speed

species lives in southeast South America, where it lives mainly in semi-open areas which provide sufficient cover. It rarely flies and when in danger, it lies on the ground or runs away. The elegant crested tinamou can live by itself or in a group. Both sexes look the same. It looks for a protected hole in the ground for a nest in which the male incubates the eggs. The young are precocial and can search for food themselves almost immediately.

Humboldt penguin (*Spheniscus humboldti*)

Humboldt penguin (*Spheniscus humboldti*)

A young jackass penguin (*Spheniscus demersus*)

Jackass penguin (*Spheniscus demersus*)

Emperor penguin (*Aptenodytes forsteri*)

of up to 25 miles per hour. The jackass penguin is approximately 20 to 24 inches in height and weighs approximately 4.5 to 6.5 pounds.

## Emperor penguin
## (*Aptenodytes forsteri*)

The emperor penguin is approximately 4 feet tall and is the largest penguin in the world. It is found in the waters and pack ice along the coast of Antarctica. The female lays only one egg, which she then abandons. The male incubates the egg for approximately 64 days, during which time he does not eat. To seek protection against the cold, the males stand close together during the incubation period. The female takes over the task of looking after the young quickly after the egg has hatched.

Macaroni penguin (*Eudyptes chrysolophus*)

## Macaroni penguin
## (*Eudyptes chrysolophus*)

The macaroni penguin belongs to the genus of crested penguins (*Eudyptes*) together with less well-known species of penguins, such as the fjordland-crested penguin and the rockhopper penguin. The macaroni penguin is found along the coast of Antarctica and on the neighboring islands. The macaroni penguin grows to a height of approximately 27.5 inches and has an average weight of 9 to 11 pounds. The average incubation period for this species is between 33 and 39 days. When the eggs hatch, the animal leaves its nesting ground and goes to sea for at least 3 months.

# Grebes (*Podicipediformes*)

Family: *Podicipedidae*

## Great-crested grebe
## (*Podiceps cristatus*)

The great-crested grebe is an aquatic bird generally found throughout Europe and the bordering areas of Asia. It can grow to a length of 19 inches and eats mainly small fish, which it catches by diving into the water. Both sexes look very much the same, although the male is usually somewhat larger. The great-crested grebe has a summer and winter plumage. It builds its nest against the edge of the river and it more or less floats on the water. It lays between 4 and 6 eggs.

Great-crested grebe (*Podiceps cristatus*)

# Albatrosses, shearwaters and petrels (*Procellariiformes*)

Families: *Diomedeidae, Procellariidae, Hydrobatidae and Pelecanoididae*

## Wandering albatross (*Diomedea exulans*)

Wandering albatross (*Diomedea exulans*)

The wandering albatross is a majestic marine bird which is widely distributed — from Antarctica to Australia, South Africa and Central South America. It does not like warm weather. The wingspan of the wandering albatross is approximately 10 feet and it has a body length of approximately 3 feet. The wandering albatross does not remain in one place. It can fly hundreds of miles across the sea searching for a good feeding ground. An albatross usually forages for food at night. It eats mainly cephalopods, which it catches by diving into the sea. There are no visible differences between the male and female albatross. The bird usually mates for life and nests once every 2 years on small islands in the Pacific Ocean. It lays only one egg, which the parents take turns incubating. The egg hatches after approximately 11 weeks. The young bird is rather helpless and must be fed by its parents for at least 9 months. It takes most young birds a year to learn how to fly properly. At this age, its plumage is still a brownish color. It can take up to 9 years before the animal reaches sexual maturity. The wandering albatross is a member of the albatross family (*Diomedeidae*).

## Northern fulmar (*Fulmarus glacialis*)

The northern fulmar is very common along the coasts of Ireland and Great Britain, but can also be found across almost all of the northern half of the Atlantic and Pacific Oceans. There is no visible difference between the male and female. There are, however, many variations in the color of the plumage, which varies from white to dark grey. Its wings always have a darker color than the rest of the body. The northern fulmar eats a variety of sea animals, from fish to cephalopods and crustaceans. It is a true marine bird and rarely comes onto the land. It often stays near fishing boats where there is always food to eat. It breeds in colonies, usually on coastal rocks. It lays only one egg, which hatches after approximately 8 weeks. The young bird is looked after and fed by both parents. The young bird can more or less look after itself after approximately 2 months. An adult northern fulmar is around 18 inches in length. It is

Northern fulmar (*Fulmarus glacialis*)

Storm petrel (*Hydrobates pelagicus*)

a member of the fulmar and petrel family *Procellariidae*.

## Storm petrel
(*Hydrobates pelagicus*)

With a total length of only 6 inches, the storm petrel is one of the smallest marine birds in the world. The storm petrel can be found in the open sea to the west of Europe and in the Mediterranean. Some populations migrate in the winter to areas to the west and south of Africa. It comes onto the land only to breed and even then, it prefers to nest on an island instead of a large landmass. It breeds in colonies. Its nest can usually be found in a hole in a rock or in an abandoned underground hole. The female lays one egg, which is incubated by both parents for 5.5 to 6 weeks. The young can fend for themselves after 2 to 2.5 months. The storm petrel eats animal food which it can find in the sea, such as carrion. It is a member of the storm petrel family (*Hydrobatidae*).

# Pelicans, boobies, tropic birds, cormorants and frigate birds (*Pelecaniformes*)

Families: *Phaethontidae, Pelecanidae, Sulidae, Phalacrocoracidae, Anhingidae and Fregatidae.*

## Eastern white pelican
(*Pelecanus onocrolatus*)

The eastern white pelican is one of the most common species of pelicans kept in zoos. The eastern white pelican breeds in Europe, particularly in marshy regions, but winters in North Africa and Asia. It lives in colonies and the birds remain close together during the breeding season. It nests along the banks of the water. It usually lays 2 or 3 eggs, which hatch after approximately 5 weeks. The young are fed

Eastern white pelican (*Pelecanus onocrolatus*)

Eastern white pelican (*Pelecanus onocrolatus*)

Dalmatian pelican (*Pelecanus crispus*)

from the gular sack (throat pouch) with pre-digested fish. A young pelican can fend for itself after 3.5 months, but it often takes 3 years for it to reach sexual maturity. An adult can weigh up to 30 pounds.

quickly and can fend for themselves after 4 months. An adult Dalmatian pelican can grow to a length of more than 5 feet, has a wingspan of almost 10 feet and weighs between 15 and 30 pounds.

## Dalmatian pelican
## (*Pelecanus crispus*)

The Dalmatian pelican is found in southeast Europe and in regions further to the east, as far as China. European populations migrate to North Africa after the breeding season. Its diet consists mainly of fish. It is a gregarious bird and builds a large nest along a water bank. It usually lays 2 eggs, which are incubated by both parents for approximately 1 month, or sometimes longer. The young develop

## Northern gannet
## (*Morus bassanus*)

The northern gannet is a member of the gannet family (*Siludae*) and is found along the northern Atlantic coast. After the breeding season, it migrates southward and can then be found as far south as Africa. Its diet consists mainly of fish, which it catches by diving into the water, sometimes as deep as 100 feet below the surface. The northern gannet breeds in colonies, although the birds cannot toler-

Dalmatian pelican (*Pelecanus crispus*)

Northern gannet (*Morus bassanus*)

ate each other very well and each bird has its own small territory within the colony. It usually lays only one egg, which the parents take turns incubating and which hatches after more than 6 weeks. The color of the young is very different than the color of its parents and it can take several years before it gets its adult plumage. An adult northern gannet can grow to a length of 35 inches.

Magnificent frigate bird (*Fregata magnificens*)

## Great cormorant
## (*Phalacrocorax carbo*)

The great cormorant is a member of the family *Phalacrocoracidae*. It is an excellent flyer and swimmer, but is not so agile on land. The great cormorant can grow to a height of approximately 37 inches and weigh up to 4.5 pounds. It is found in Europe, Asia, eastern North America, Africa and Australia. Its nesting habits vary per region. For some populations, nests are built in trees or bushes, while others build them on the ground. A clutch of eggs usually consists of 3 or 4 bluish eggs, which are incubated by both parents for 24 days. The young can leave the nest when they are between 6 and 8 weeks old and 6 weeks later, most are fully independent. The great cormorant dives into the water to catch fish. It can dive to a depth of 10 feet and remain under water for approximately 30 seconds. The great cormorant not only eats fish, but also other aquatic animals and amphibians. In some countries, they are trained to catch fish. The great cormorant is a member of the cormorant family (*Phalacrocoracidae*).

Great cormorant (*Phalacrocorax carbo*)

Great cormorant (*Phalacrocorax carbo*)

## Magnificent frigate bird
(*Fregata magnificens*)

The magnificent frigate bird is found in Central and South America, as well as on the Galapagos Islands. The inflatable, bright red throat pouch is a distinguishable characteristic of this bird. This throat pouch develops only on the male during the mating season and has an important function in the courtship ritual. The magnificent frigate bird breeds in colonies. It usually builds its nest in bushes but may sometimes build it on the ground from large material. A magnificent frigate bird lays one egg, which is incubated by both parents for 6 to 7 weeks. The young remain in the nest for 4 or more months

Anhinga (*Anhinga anhinga*)

and are able to fend for themselves only 3 to 5 months later. The magnificent frigate bird eats mainly flying fish, which it catches above the surface of the water. It also steals food from other birds and eats the nestlings of other species of birds. It grows to a height of approximately 3 feet and has a wingspan of more than 6 feet. Despite its size, it does not usually weigh more than 3.5 pounds. Outside the mating season, the female can be recognised by a white band on her breast; the male does not have this band. The magnificent frigate bird is a member of the family of frigate birds (*Fregatidae*).

## Snakebird
(*Anhinga anhinga*)

The snakebird is one of two species of birds which belong to the darter family (*Anhingidae*), the other species being the oriental darter. The snakebird is found in the north of South America, Central America and several southern states in the United States. It always lives close to water where it catches its food. Its diet consists mainly of fish, which it dives deep into the water to catch, although it also eats insects and small amphibians. It breeds in colonies and builds its nest in trees along the edge of the water. On average, it lays 4 or 5 eggs, which are incubated by both parents. An adult snakebird has a total length of approximately 35 inches.

# Herons, storks, ibis and flamingos (*Ciconiiformes*)

Families: *Ardeidae, Cochlearidae, Balaenicipitdae, Scopidae, Ciconiidae, Threskiornithidae and Phoenicopteridae.*

## Grey heron (*Ardea cinerea*)

The grey heron is generally found in Europe and in large areas of northern Asia. Some northern populations migrate south for the winter. Its diet consists mainly of fish, which it catches in the water with a fast reaction from its bill. The grey heron, therefore, spends a great deal of time at the edge of the water waiting for suitable fish to come into reach. It also eats other animals besides fish, such as the larvae of the water beetle, crabs and

Grey heron (*Ardea cinerea*)

small rodents. Undigested food is regurgitated in the form of pellets. The heron broods in colonies. It usually builds its nest in trees and often returns to the same nest, although this is often extended and improved. It lays 3 to 5 eggs which have a bluish-green shell. The parents take turns incubating the eggs and they hatch after approximately 4 weeks. The young are fed regurgitated food. The young can leave the nest after one month but it usually takes another month or longer before they can fend for themselves. The grey heron reaches sexual maturity between the age of 1 and 2 years. An adult grey heron can grow to a height of more than 35 inches.

Grey heron (*Ardea cinerea*)

Cattle egret (*Ardeola/Bubulbus ibis*)

## Cattle egret (*Ardeola/Bubulbus ibis*)

The cattle egret originally comes from Africa, but has managed to spread to other continents so that nowadays, it can also be found in Australia, southern Europe, large areas of Asia, as well as North and South America. An adult cattle egret can grow to a length of approximately 19 inches. The cattle egret gets its common name from the fact that is spends a good deal of time with domesticated and wild cattle to search for its food. It eats a variety of insects, but mostly grasshoppers and eats insects from the cattle themselves, as well as a variety of aquatic animals and fish. It is not fussy when it comes to its habitat. It can be found in rainforests, on lowland plains and in urban areas. It usually builds its nest in a tree or a bush and lays 3 or 4 eggs.

Boatbill or Boat-billed heron (*Cochlearius cochlearius*)

## Boatbill or Boat-billed heron (*Cochlearius cochlearius*)

The boatbill is a member of the family *Cochleariidae* and has the shortest and widest bill of all the herons. It is found in the north of South America, as well as Central America and grows to a height of 20 inches. The boatbill is predominantly active at dusk and at night and rarely shows itself during the day. Its diet consists of fish and other aquatic animals. It builds its nest in a tree or a large bush and lays approximately 3 eggs, which are incubated by both parents.

78

Young black-crowned night heron

Young black-crowned night heron

# Black-crowned night heron
## (*Nycticorax nycticorax*)

The black-crowned night heron is a member of the heron family (*Ardeidae*) and is found throughout the world from Europe to Asia, Africa and Central and South America. It gets its common name from the fact that it usually hunts at dusk and during the night. Its diet consists of a variety of small animals, including fish, frogs, young birds and rodents. It nests in colonies. The black-crowned night heron lays an average of 4 eggs, which have a bluish-green shell and which are incubated by both parents for approximately 28 days. The color of the young bird is not the same as its parents and it can take up to 3 years before the bird receives its final coloring. An adult black-crowned night heron can grow to a length of 24 inches.

# White stork
## (*Ciconia ciconia*)

The white stork is a member of the family *Ciconiidae*. It can grow to a height of more than 3 feet and have a wingspan of more than 6 feet. It weighs between 5.5 and 9 pounds. There is little difference in appearance between the sexes. During the winter, most animals live in Africa and, to a lesser extent, in southern Asia. For the summer, however, it migrates north to Europe and northern Asia. The species is

Adult black-crowned night heron

White stork (*Ciconia ciconia*)

White stork in its nest (*Ciconia ciconia*)

found in both remote and urban areas. Its diet includes frogs, small rodents and a variety of insects, which it finds on land and in shallow water. The white stork often reaches sexual maturity between the ages of 3 and 4 years. Its nest is made from large material and is often situated high off the ground, such as in a high tree or on a chimney. It usually lays 3 to 5 eggs, which are incubated by both parents for more than a month. The young can leave the nest when they are approximately 8 weeks old, but they are unable to fend for themselves fully for another couple of weeks. After migration, the white stork usually returns to the same nest, which it alters and extends every year.

## Black stork
## (*Ciconia nigra*)

The black stork is extremely widely distributed, beginning in Central Europe and continuing through Asia to the coast of the Pacific Ocean. After the breeding season, the bird migrates southward and many black storks can then be found deep

in Africa. In contrast to the white stork, the black stork avoids human settlements and prefers forested regions. The black stork eats fish, small reptiles and amphibians. Both parents build a nest from large material, usually in a tree. It lays an average of 4 eggs, which the parents take turns incubating for approximately 4.5 weeks. The young, which initially have an almost completely white, downy plumage, are fed by both parents and leave the nest for the first time when they are approximately 2 months old.

Black stork (*Ciconia nigra*)

## Saddle-billed stork (*Ephippiorhynchus senegalensis*)

With its brightly colored bill, the saddle-billed stork is one of the most colorful species of stork. It gets its common name from the saddle-like, yellow marking on the top of its bill. Its diet consists mainly of fish, which it catches in shallow water. The adult male measures 4.5 feet, while the female is often several inches shorter. Another clear difference between the sexes is the color of the eyes; the male has brown eyes, while those of the female are yellow. The birds live in pairs and build their nests in trees. The saddle-billed stork can be found throughout Africa, but not in the northern region or in Madagascar. In contrast to most species of storks, this bird does not migrate and usually remains in the same area.

Yellow-billed stork (*Mycteria ibis*)

## Yellow-billed stork (*Mycteria ibis*)

The yellow-billed stork is a member of the stork family (*Ciconiidae*) and is found on the island of Madagascar and in tropical Africa. It lives in marshy regions, where it rummages for food in shallow water and mud. It eats a variety of animals which it finds in and near the water, such as

Saddle-billed stork (*Ephippiorhynchus senegalensis*)

Marabou stork (*Leptoptilos crumeniferus*)

worms, amphibians, crustaceans and small fish. The yellow-billed stork breeds in colonies. An adult has a total length of approximately 40 inches.

## Marabou stork
## (*Leptoptilos crumeniferus*)

The marabou stork has a typical throat sack, which gets larger as the animal becomes older. It is found in Africa, where it lives both in vast unpopulated areas, as well as close to humans. It usually eats carrion, but sometimes catches small, living animals as well. Because of its close relation to the stork and its eating habits, the marabou is sometimes also called the scavenging stork. Furthermore, it also eats non-animal food, which it finds in and around human settlements.

Marabou stork (*Leptoptilos crumeniferus*)

The marabou stork breeds in colonies. It builds its nest in a tree and lays 2 or 3 eggs, which hatch after approximately 1 month. The marabou stork can live for approximately 70 years. An adult marabou stork is approximately 5 feet tall, has a wingspan of 10 feet, but weighs only 11 pounds. The marabou stork is a member of the stork family (*Ciconiidae*). The typical manner of sitting adopted by the marabou stork is also adopted by other birds, such as the crane.

## Scarlet ibis
## (*Eudocimus ruber*)

The scarlet ibis is found in South America, particularly close to the northeast coast. It eats a variety of small animals, which it rummages for in the shallow water of marshes and along riverbanks. It lives and breeds in colonies. It builds an untidy nest from large material which is usually found in trees. It lays approximately 2 eggs, which hatch after 3 weeks. The young are fed and cared for by both parents. The young are often able to leave the nest after 3 weeks, but it can take 2 years for them to reach sexual maturity. The scarlet ibis is a member of the ibis and spoonbill family (*Threskiornithidae*).

Scarlet ibis (*Eudocimus ruber*)

Puna ibis (*Plegadis ridgwayi*)

Waldrapp ibis (*Geronticus eremita*)

The nest is often no more than a hole in the ground or a sheltered place in a crack in the rocks, which both parents cover with plant material. It lays an average of 3 eggs, which hatch after approximately 4 weeks. Both parents incubate the eggs, in addition to feeding and raising the young. It can take a long time before a waldrapp ibis reaches sexual maturity; the waldrapp ibis often does not have the urge to mate before it is 5 years old. In the past, the waldrapp ibis was a common bird, even in Central Europe, but nowadays, only a small number of birds are found in a limited number of areas of North Africa and Asia. Some populations migrate south when the temperature falls but there are also populations which do not migrate.

## Puna ibis
## (*Plegadis ridgwayi*)

The puna ibis is found in the mountainous regions of Bolivia and Peru. Its diet consists mainly of small (aquatic) animals, worms and insects which live in the mud or shallow water. Therefore, it relies on the close proximity of water for its food. It is a gregarious bird and prefers to live and breed in groups. There is no visible difference between the male and female, although the female often has a lighter build than the male. The puna ibis is a member of the ibis and spoonbill family (*Threskiornithidae*).

Sacred ibis (*Threskiornis aethiopicus*)

## Waldrapp ibis
## (*Geronticus eremita*)

The waldrapp ibis lacks feathers on its head and neck. It eats mainly a variety of living animals, such as insects and worms, but may also eat larger prey. The species prefers to breed on rocks near water and is often found close to human settlements.

## Sacred ibis
### (*Threskiornis aethiopicus*)

In ancient Egypt, the sacred ibis was considered to be a holy bird and this is where it gets its common name. Mummified examples of this bird have been found and it has also been depicted in ancient Egyptian drawings. The sacred ibis can be found in a large part of Africa. It is omnivorous and is not particularly fussy about what it eats. It lives and breeds in groups and is seldom found alone. The bird builds its nest in a low bush, a tree or in a sheltered location on the ground. The sacred ibis can grow to a length of 30 inches.

White spoonbill (*Platalea leucorodia*)

Lesser flamingo (*Phoenicopteridae minor*)

## White spoonbill
### (*Platalea leucorodia*)

The white spoonbill gets its common name from its typical spoon-like bill. The sensitive bill is used to search shallow water for food. The white spoonbill usually eats small fish, crayfish and water insects. It prefers to live in marshy regions, where the water level is low and where there is an abundance of food. The white spoonbill lives and breeds in groups. Nests are often built close together in low bushes. The bird lays 3 or 4 eggs, which hatch after 3.5 weeks. An adult white spoonbill can have a wingspan of approximately 4 feet. Despite its size, it often does not weigh more than 3.5 pounds. The bird can live for 25 years. The white spoonbill is found in Europe, North Africa and Asia, and as far as Japan. It stays in northern regions during the summer and migrates south for the winter. The white spoonbill is a member of the ibis and spoonbill family (*Threskiornithidae*).

## Flamingo
### (*Family Phoenicopteridae*)

The flamingo is a large, pinkish white bird which is found both in the Old and New Worlds. A typical characteristic of this bird is its bill, which it uses as a sieve to filter its food out of the water. Most

Greater flamingo (*Phoenicopteridae ruber*)

flamingos eat small aquatic crustaceans and other small aquatic animals but the James' flamingo (*Phoenicoparrus jamesi*) eats mainly algae. It usually builds its nest atop a mound of mud. The female lays one egg, which is incubated by both parents for approximately 4 weeks. The young bird is fed by both parents with a special, bright-red colored liquid which is made in the gullet and the stomach. The young bird usually leaves the nest after

Chilean flamingo (*Phoenicopteridae chilensis*)

a week and joins the rest of the group with its parents. After time, it develops a sieve in its bill so that it can collect its own food out of the water. The color of its plumage changes over time and it reaches its adult color only when it is approximately 3 years old. There are about 5 different species of flamingo. The best-known is the Greater flamingo (*P. ruber roseus*), which is found in certain regions of Africa, Europe and Asia. It grows to a height of 4 feet and is the largest species of flamingo. Another well-known species is the Chilean flamingo (*P. chilensis*), which grows to a height of more than 3 feet. The lesser flamingo (*P. phoeniconaias minor*) is the smallest species of flamingo. It grows to a height of only 31 inches and is found in South Africa.

# Screamers and wildfowl (*Anseriformes*)

Families: *Anhimidae and Anatidae*

## Crested screamer (*Chauna torquata*)

The crested screamer is a member of the screamer family (*Anhimidae*). It is found in certain areas of South America, including Bolivia and Uruguay. Outside the mating season, it lives in large colonies, particularly in marshy regions, but always close to water. Its large nest is built in shallow water or on a water bank. It lays an average of 5 eggs, which are incubated by both parents. The young are precocial. The crested screamer eats weeds, roots and corn. Although its appearance would not initially suggest so, the crested screamer is an excellent flier. An adult crested screamer grows to a total length of 35 inches and does not usually weigh much more than 5.5 pounds.

## Magpie goose (*Anseranas semipalmata*)

The magpie goose is found in Australia, Tasmania and a part of New Guinea, where it lives mainly in marshy regions. It

Magpie goose (*Anseranas semipalmata*)

Crested screamer (*Chauna torquata*)

prefers to live in colonies and eats mostly grasses and (aquatic) plants. There is almost no difference in the appearance of the male and female, although the bump on the forehead is less prominent on the female. As with most wildfowl, this species also builds its nest in shallow water or on a water bank. The number of eggs laid varies from 4 to 12 and these hatch after 35 days. An adult grows to a length of approximately 33 inches. The magpie goose is a member of the duck, goose and swan family (*Anatidae*).

## Mallard (*Anas platyrhynchos*)

Various subspecies of mallard are found in the moderate to subtropical areas of the northern hemisphere. Its great ability to adapt is demonstrated by the large num-

White is one of the color mutations of the mallard.

A male mallard (*Anas platyrhynchos*)

Pintail (*Anas acuta*)

A female mallard (*Anas platyrhynchos*)

mately 2 months. An adult mallard grows to a length of approximately 23 inches.

## Pintail (*Anas acuta*)

The pintail is found in large parts of Europe, North America and northern Asia. It migrates south for the winter, as far as Central America and Central Africa. The difference between the male and female of this species can be deciphered by the color of the tail feathers; the tail of the male is much more colorful than the brownish tail of the female. The tail feathers on the male are longer and this is where the bird gets its common name. The sexes also differ in size; the female is approximately 22 inches in length and the male is approximately 4 inches longer. It builds its nest along the edge of the water. The female lays around 8 eggs, which she incubates for approximately 22 to 24 days.

Hottentot teal (*Anas punctata*)

ber of (semi-)tame ducks found in city parks. There are countless color mutations. White is the best-known color, although there are also several white spotted combinations. As with most ducks, the different sexes of this species can be distinguished easily by the color. The male has a green head and black feathers on its tail, which curl upwards. The mallard eats mainly plant material, but may also eat small animal food. Its bill acts as a sieve which it uses to filter food particles from the water. In its search for food, the mallard scrapes the shallow water bed with its bill so that only the rear part of its body remains visible. It builds its nest in a sheltered location on the ground or in a hollow tree. It lays 8 to 12 greenish eggs, which are incubated by the female for approximately 4 weeks. The young are precocial and can swim with their mother fairly soon after hatching. The young remain with their mother for approxi-

## Hottentot teal
### (*Anas punctata*)

The Hottentot teal is a small species of duck found in the south, south-east and east of Africa, as well as in Madagascar. It grows to a length of 13 inches and is the smallest of the dabbling ducks. It is also one of the quietest. There is only a marginal visible difference between the sexes. The female's marking on the breast looks more like a spot than a stripe, but for the rest, both sexes look exactly alike. It builds its nest from a variety of plant material, usually in the thick overgrowth along a water bank or in very shallow water. It lays approximately 6 eggs, which hatch after about 3 weeks. The bird is seldom found in groups and usually lives in pairs.

Cape teal (*Anas capensis*)

## Cape teal
### (*Anas capensis*)

The cape teal is often found in the south and east of Africa. There is no visible difference between the male and female of this species. It is predominantly herbivorous. It nests in a hole in the ground, which it lines with down feathers. It lays an average of 8 eggs, which are incubated by the female. The Cape teal has a total length of approximately 16 inches.

Canvasback (*Aythya valisineria*)

Smew (*Mergus albellus*)

Common shelduck (*Tadorna tadorna*)

## Canvasback
## (*Aythya valisineria*)

During the breeding season, the canvasback is found in the northwestern part of North America, including Alaska and the Yukon. After the breeding season, some populations migrate southward along the coast and further inland in the southern part of the United States. Some groups migrate further, even as far as Mexico. It is predominantly herbivorous, but supplements its diet with small aquatic animals and insects. There is a clear difference between the male and female; the brown-silver plumage of the male is more colorful than that of the female. It builds a large nest along the edge of the water and lays an average of 8 eggs, which hatch after approximately 4 weeks. An adult canvasback grows to a length of approximately 21 inches.

## Smew (*Mergus albellus*)

The smew is a member of the merganser family. Its toothed bill makes it easy for the bird to hold fish, its main food source, which it hunts for under water. It breeds in Scandinavia, Russia and Siberia and migrates to more southern countries, such as the Netherlands, Japan and even Northern India, for the winter. The difference between the sexes can be seen by both the markings and the color. The

male is black and white and has a black eyespot on a white head which extends to the bill. The smew usually builds its nest in a hollow tree or in another sheltered location. It lays approximately 8 eggs, which are incubated by the female for about a month. An adult smew grows to a length of around 16 inches.

## Common shelduck
## (*Tadorna tadorna*)

The common shelduck is native to certain parts of Asia and Europe. Some common shelducks migrate south for the winter. It can grow to approximately 24 inches in length. It eats mainly small aquatic animals, fish, spat and crustaceans but may also eat soft aquatic plants and algae. The male of this species can be recognised by its brighter colors and the lump on its bill. The common shelduck is monogamous; once it forms a pair, it remains with the same partner for life. A peculiarity of this species is that it builds its nest in an underground hole, usually an abandoned rabbit burrow. Sometimes, however, it builds its nest on the ground or in a hollow tree. It usually lays between 7 and 11 eggs, which are incubated by the female for more than 4 weeks.

Ruddy shelduck (*Tadorna ferruginea*)

## Ruddy shelduck
(*Tadorna ferruginea*)

The ruddy shelduck is found in the most diverse habitats of Central Asia. Some populations migrate after the mating season, some as far south as Korea and some as far west as Southern Europe. Some populations of ruddy shelduck are found in Spain, which breed and spend the winter there. It is active mostly at dusk and during the night and is predominantly herbivorous. The male can be distinguished from the female by its black breast band, which the predominantly more pale- colored female does not have. The bird grows to a length of approximately 24 inches.

## Radjah shelduck
(*Tadorna radjah*)

The radjah shelduck is found in New Guinea and on the Molucca Islands and is also called the Moluccan radjah shelduck. It grows to a length of 20 inches. There is no visible difference between the sexes. This species of bird lives either alone or in pairs. It builds a nest in a hollow tree during the breeding season and apart from some down, virtually no nest material is used. It lays between 6 and 12 eggs, which are incubated exclusively by the female for approximately 30 days. The radjah shelduck eats mainly a variety of small animals, such as molluscs, although a small part of its diet consists of plant material.

## African pigmy goose
(*Nettapus auritus*)

The African pigmy goose is a member of the perching ducks family and lives in the forested, marshy regions of Africa and Madagascar. It eats aquatic plants and small aquatic animals. It usually lives in small groups or in pairs. The difference between both sexes can easily be seen by the difference in color. The female, which is generally not as brightly colored as the male, does not have a green mark on her neck. It usually builds its nest in a hollow tree using several different kinds of grass,

Radjah shelduck (*Tadorna radjah*)

A male African pigmy goose (*Nettapus auritus*)

A female African pigmy goose (*Nettapus auritus*)

but the way the nest is built may vary. It lays approximately 6 eggs, which are incubated by the female. The African pigmy goose is approximately 12 inches in length.

## Fulvous whistling duck (*Dendrocygna biocolor*)

The fulvous whistling duck gets its common name from its whistling call. It is found in parts of America, Asia and Africa, where it lives in marshy areas. It is predominantly nocturnal and grows to a length of 19 inches. There are no visible differences between the male and female. It eats a variety of seeds and grains, as

Fulvous whistling duck (*Dendrocygna biocolor*)

well as insects and other small (aquatic) animals. It lays between 5 and 16 eggs, which are incubated by both parents. The eggs hatch after approximately 25 days.

## White-faced whistling duck (*Dendrocygna viduata*)

The white-faced whistling duck is found in Africa, Madagascar and in tropical regions of South America. It always lives in groups and is mostly active at dusk and at night. It builds its nest from grass in a hollow tree or in a sheltered location on the ground. It lays an average of 10 eggs, which the parents take turns incubating for 4 weeks. The white-faced whistling duck is omnivorous. It finds its food both on land and in the water and often scrapes the bottom of a shallow river for crayfish and worms. It also eats plant

White-faced whistling duck (*Dendrocygna viduata*)

Some ducks dabble (*Dendrocygna viduata*)

Mandarin duck (*Aix galericulata*)

material, such as grasses and aquatic plants. The white-faced whistling duck grows to a length of approximately 18 inches.

## Mandarin duck
## (*Aix galericulata*)

This small and colorful species of duck is mostly found in eastern Asia, particularly in the forested regions of Japan and China. The species has also been introduced in Great Britain. The Mandarin duck is omnivorous and eats a variety of (aquatic) animals and plant material, such as rice, nuts and seeds. It is easy to distinguish between both sexes; the female is much less colorful than the male. They usually mate for life. The Mandarin duck prefers to brood in a hollow tree, but may also build its nest in a sheltered location on the ground. If it uses a hollow tree as a nesting place, the nest may be located

several feet above the ground. A Mandarin duck covers a suitable location in down and does nothing further to build its nest. It lays an average of 10 eggs, which are incubated by the female for approximately 30 days. The female takes full responsibility for raising the young. Young Mandarin ducks develop very quickly and can fend for themselves after 1.5 to 2 months. An adult measures approximately 12 inches.

## Eider
## (*Somateria mollissima*)

The eider is found mostly along the north and northwest coast of Europe, in places such as Scotland, Scandinavia, Iceland, the Netherlands and Germany, but has also been observed further inland. It always lives in relatively large groups and breeds in colonies on land. The nest is often no more than a hollow in the ground covered in down. The female lays between 4 and 6 eggs, which hatch within 4 weeks. The young are precocial and can swim with their mother shortly after hatching. The eider is carnivorous and mostly eats small mussels, including the shell. It grows to a length of 23 inches.

A male eider (*Somateria mollissima*)

A female eider (*Somateria mollissima*)

Greylag goose (*Anser anser*)

## Greylag goose
(*Anser anser*)

Emperor goose (*Anser canagicus*)

The greylag goose is one of the best-known species of geese. It is found in certain regions of Europe and in the northwest of Asia and lives both in salt and fresh water. The greylag goose migrates south for winter and always lives in groups. Both sexes look very similar to each other except for their size; the male is larger than the female. A male greylag goose can grow to a height of 33 inches. The greylag goose is herbivorous and eats grasses and fruit but if necessary, will also eat turnips and carrots. In contrast to many other species of geese, the greylag goose does not, as a rule, live in colonies. The birds form small groups during the breeding season, but the pairs usually separate from the group. It builds its nest on the ground. It lays approximately 6 eggs, which are incubated by the female for about 4 weeks. The young are precocial and can walk with their mother and rummage for food soon after they hatch. The young often remain with their mother until she lays a new clutch of eggs. It reaches sexual maturity at an age of 3 years.

## Emperor goose
(*Anser canagicus*)

An adult emperor goose measures approximately 26 inches. It eats mostly sea lettuce, algae and sea grasses, as well as grasses which grow on land and small animals. It lives in small groups which usually contain between 10 and 45 animals.

The emperor goose is found along the coast of Alaska and the northeast coast of Siberia. During the breeding season, it searches for small streams and small expanses of water in marshy regions further inland, where it incubates its eggs. It lays between 4 and 6 eggs, which are incubated by the female for approximately 25 to 27 days. The emperor goose migrates southward for the winter after the breeding season.

## Bar-headed goose
## (*Anser indicus*)

The bar-headed goose is found in India and in the regions to the north and northeast of India, as far as the Himalayas. In the winter, it lives in the southern regions of its natural habitat. It lives in groups which can vary in size from dozens to hundreds or thousands of birds. It also breeds in colonies. There is no visible difference between the sexes. The female lays an average of 4 eggs, which hatch within 4 weeks. The diet of both the young and adult birds consists of a variety of grasses and aquatic plants, as well as berries and grain. The bird rests during the day and

Red-breasted goose (*Branta ruficollis*)

usually searches for food at dusk and during the night. An adult bar-headed goose measures approximately 29.5 inches.

## Red-breasted goose
## (*Branta ruficollis*)

With a maximum length of 22 inches, the red-breasted goose is one of the smallest species of goose. The red-breasted goose lives mainly on the northern Siberian tundra and on the Black Sea in Romania. It prefers to migrate south for the winter. It is herbivorous and eats grasses and bulbs. There is no visible difference between the male and female. It breeds in colonies. It builds its nest on the ground and lays an average of 5 eggs, which are incubated by the female for about 25 days.

Bar-headed goose (*Anser indicus*)

Nene or Hawaiian goose (*Branta sandvicensis*)

## Nene or Hawaiian goose (*Branta sandvicensis*)

One of the most striking characteristics of this initially not very spectacular species of goose is that it has small webbed feet and can walk much more quickly and smoothly than other geese; it does not waddle. In contrast to other species of geese, it spends a large amount of time on land. It is not dependent on water being nearby and eats a variety of berries, grasses and grain that it can find on land. There were once large numbers of nene in Hawaii and the neighboring island of Maui, but because of over-hunting and cultivation of its breeding ground, this species was on the verge of extinction. Birds bred in captivity were returned to their natural habitat in the 1960s and the animal is no longer in danger. It lays 4 or 5 eggs, which hatch after approximately one month.

## Barnacle goose (*Branta leucopsis*)

The barnacle goose is found along the coasts of Greenland, Spitsbergen and northern Siberia and spends the winter along the coastal regions of northwest Europe, particularly Scotland and the Netherlands. It is herbivorous and eats grasses and the stalks of white clover. The male and female have the same coloring

Barnacle goose (*Branta leucopsis*)

Mute swan (*Cygnus olor*)

and markings. The barnacle goose breeds in colonies. It builds its nest on the ground, close to the water. It usually lays 4 eggs, which hatch after approximately 25 days. The young are raised by both parents and can usually fly when they are between 1.5 and 2 months old. An adult barnacle goose is between 24 and 28 inches long.

## Mute swan (*Cygnus olor*)

The mute swan is the largest living swan and a male can grow to a length of 5 feet. The male is larger than the female and this is the only visible difference between the sexes. It prefers to build its nest in reeds, which it makes from the reeds themselves. To build its nest, it breaks the stems of the reeds and stacks them to create a firm base. It lays between 4 and 7 greyish-green eggs, which are incubated exclusively by the female. The male always remains close to the female and the nest and acts as the protector. The eggs hatch after 35 days. The young are precocial and can soon swim with their mother and quickly learn how to forage for their food. It takes a relatively long time, however, before they are independent and they only reach sexual maturity between the age of 4 and 5 years. The mute swan is found in Europe and parts of Asia and has also been introduced in Australia and the United States. Some populations migrate south for the winter and others, including many almost domesticated birds, remain in the same area during the winter. The mute swan usually lives on stationary or slow-flowing fresh water. Its diet consists of aquatic plants and, to a lesser extent, small animals.

## Black swan
## (*Cygnus atratus*)

The black swan originates from Australia and Tasmania. Its diet consists mainly of aquatic plants and algae. It reaches sexual maturity between the age of 4 and 5 years. The black swan breeds in small colonies. It usually builds its nest from a variety of large plant material in reeds or in shallow water, which it covers in down. It lays approximately 6 green eggs, which the parents take turns incubating for about 5 weeks. An adult black swan can grow to a length of 4.5 feet.

Black swan (*Cygnus atratus*)

## Bewick's swan
## (*Cygnus bewickii*)

The Bewick's swan can grow to a length of more than 3 feet. It is a migratory bird. It spends the summer in northern regions, such as northern Russia and Scandinavia and migrates south for the winter. The Bewick's swan usually lives in small groups where the members are usually related to each other. It is herbivorous and eats a variety of aquatic plants, and grasses. Both the male and female of this species reach sexual maturity between the ages of 4 and 5 years. When two birds form a pair, they normally stay together for life. It builds its nest on a water bank and lays an average of 4 eggs, which are incubated by the female for 5 to 6 weeks.

Black swan (*Cygnus atratus*)

Bewick's swan (*Cygnus bewickii*)

# Birds of prey
## (*Falconiformes*)

Families: *Cathartidae, Sagittarriidae, Accipitridae, Pandionidae* and *Falconidae*.

## King vulture
## (*Saracoramphus papa*)

The king vulture is a member of the New World vultures (*Cathartidae*). It is found in Central America and in several of the northern countries of South America. It mostly lives in forested regions, but has also been observed on plains. The king vulture can grow to a length of 32 inches. Not only does it eat carrion, which it can spot with its excellent sense of smell, but it sometimes also hunts for living animals. It lays its eggs in a sheltered location, usually in a hollow tree, and they are incubated by both parents. It can take 2 years

Turkey vulture (*Cathartes aura*)

for the magnificent colors of its head, neck and bill to develop fully.

## Turkey vulture
## (*Cathartes aura*)

The turkey vulture is widely distributed throughout South and Central America, as well as North America, but not in the northern states. It eats carrion, as well as

King vulture (*Saracoramphus papa*)

Turkey vulture (*Cathartes aura*)

Griffon vulture (*Gyps fulvus*)

waste vegetation. The female usually lays 2 eggs, which hatch after around 5.5 weeks. An adult turkey vulture has a wingspan of 6 feet and weighs 6.5 pounds. The turkey vulture can live to be very old and if the conditions are favorable, it can live for as long as 45 years.

## Griffon vulture (*Gyps fulvus*)

The griffon vulture is an impressive bird. Its wingspan can measure up to 9 feet and it can weigh as much as 20 pounds. The griffon vulture was once very common in southern Europe, North Africa, southeast Asia and parts of the Middle East. Its numbers have since declined considerably, particularly in southern Europe. There are currently projects in which animals bred in zoos are released in southern Europe. The griffon vulture breeds in colonies. It lays only one egg, which hatches in 7 to 8 weeks. Its diet consists of carrion. In zoos, the griffon vulture lives for as long as 50 years.

## Black vulture (*Coragyps atratus*)

The black vulture is found in South and Central America, as well as in several of the southern United States. It lives in groups which can consist of dozens or even thousands of birds. It eats carrion

Black vulture (*Coragyps atratus*)

and finds its food using its sense of smell, which is very well developed. It also eats other kinds food, and birds which live near slums may sometimes eat the waste produced there.

## Bearded vulture
## (*Gypaetus barbatus*)

The bearded vulture, or lammergeier, is widely distributed. It is found in southern Europe, North Africa, the Middle East and in several Asian countries, as far as Tibet. Like most vultures, the bearded vulture eats mainly carrion. It builds its nest in a sheltered location, usually in an alcove in a rock. It lays an average of 2 eggs, which in most instances, are incubated exclusively by the female, although sometimes both parents incubate them. The eggs hatch after approximately 52

Bearded vulture (*Gypaetus barbatus*)

days and the birds can leave the nest about 3.5 months later.

## Egyptian vulture
## (*Neophron percnopterus*)

The Egyptian vulture grows to a length of approximately 27 inches, weighs approximately 4.5 pounds and has a wingspan of 5 feet. It is found in Africa, southern Europe, the Middle East and the bordering countries of Asia. The species is found mainly in desert regions and high up in the mountains. It usually builds its nest in a sheltered alcove in a rock from a variety of material, including the carcasses of dead animals. It usually lays 2 eggs, which are incubated by both parents for approximately 6 weeks. The young can fly when they are between 2.5 and 3 months old.

## Andean condor (*Vultur gryphus*)

The Andean condor is found in the Andes and the lowland plains of Peru. It eats mainly animal carcasses but sometimes catches its own prey. It usually has a fixed habitat, but may fly many miles a day in search of food. The Andean condor lays

Egyptian vulture (*Neophron percnopterus*)

Andean condor (*Vultur gryphus*)

The bald eagle has a wingspan of approximately 6.5 feet

while flying by moving its claws toward its beak. The bald eagle breeds once a year. It lays 2 or 3 eggs, which hatch after 5 or 6 weeks. An adult bald eagle has a wingspan of approximately 6.5 feet and is around 30 inches tall. It weighs relatively little; the male weighs approximately 9 pounds and the female 13 pounds. The bald eagle is a member of the family *Accipitridae*.

one egg every 2 years. It does not build a nest, but rather lays the egg on a suitable surface, often high up on a rock. The young remain dependent on their mother for a considerable time. The Andean condor can grow to a length of 51 inches and has a wingspan of almost 10 feet.

## Bald eagle
## (*Haliaeetus leucocephalus*)

The bald eagle appeals to many people's imagination and is the national bird of the United States. Despite its large popularity, the species is not as abundant nowadays as it once was, due to agricultural pesticides and culling. Not so long ago, there was a reward in Canada for each dead bald eagle. The bald eagle eats a variety of animals, such as rodents, rabbits and (flying) fish. It can eat its prey

## White-tailed sea eagle
## (*Haliaeetus albicalla*)

The white-tailed sea eagle is found along the coast of northern Europe and more inland to the east in Siberia, as well as in Greenland. It always remains close to water, but this does not necessarily have

White-tailed sea eagle (*Haliaeetus albicalla*)

Bald eagle (*Haliaeetus leucocephalus*)

to be salt water. It eats mainly fish and a variety of aquatic birds, but may also eat carrion. It lays 2 or 3 eggs, which are incubated by the female and hatch within 6 weeks. The white-tailed sea eagle lives in pairs in its own territory. The female has a wingspan of approximately 8 feet and is larger than the male of the species, which usually has a wingspan which is about 10 inches shorter. The female is also often a couple of pounds heavier than the male and can, therefore, catch larger prey. The white-tailed sea eagle is a member of the family *Accipitridae*.

## Common caracara (*Polyborus plancus*)

The common caracara grows to a length of more than 20 inches. It is found in the south of the United States, as well as in Central and South America. This bird eats a variety of small animals, but mainly car-

Common caracara (*Polyborus plancus*)

rion. Its large nest is built by both partners and can be situated either in a tree or on the ground. It lays 2 or 3 eggs, which are light brown with dark speckles. Both parents incubate the eggs for approximately 4 weeks. The young sometimes leave the nest when they are 2 months old, but this can also take a month longer. The common caracara is a member of the caracara and falcon family (*Falconidae*).

## Secretary bird (*Sagittarius serpentarius*)

The secretary bird can grow to a height of 3 feet and have a wingspan of almost 6.5 feet. It runs extremely fast and rarely flies. It lives in Africa where it eats mainly reptiles and, more specifically, snakes, which it kills with its deadly claws. The secretary bird lives alone or in pairs. During the mating season, it builds a very large nest with a diameter of up to 6.5 feet. It generally lays 2 or 3 eggs, which are usually incubated by the female for 6 weeks. The young leave the nest when they are approximately 3 months old.

Northern goshawk (*Accipiter gentilis*)

Secretary bird (*Sagittarius serpentarius*)

## Northern goshawk (*Accipiter gentilis*)

The northern goshawk and various subspecies are found in Europe, North America and Asia. The sexes can be distinguished by their size. The female grows to a length of 24 inches, has a wingspan of more than 40 inches and is larger than the male, who usually grows to a length of 20 inches and has a wingspan of less than 40 inches. Northern goshawks hunt for warm-blooded prey, such as pheasants, doves, hares and rabbits. It has its own territory where no birds of the same species are allowed. The northern goshawk builds its nest in a tree and lays an average of 4 eggs, which are incubated mostly by the female and which hatch after 5 to 6 weeks. The young leave the nest when they are older than 5 weeks. The northern goshawk is a member of the family *Accipitridae*.

Saker falcon (*Falco cherrug*)

# Saker falcon
## (*Falco cherrug*)

The saker falcon is a member of the family *Falconidae* and is found in areas from Eastern Europe to Central Asia. Saker falcon usually live in pairs. The saker falcon eats birds and small mammals, which it catches both on land and in the air. The saker falcon often uses a nest which has been built by a different species of bird, but sometimes also builds its own nest either in an alcove in a rock or high up in a tree. It usually lays 4 eggs, which are generally incubated by the female for one month. The young leave the nest when they are approximately 6 to 7 weeks old but they still remain close to their parents for quite some time. The saker falcon is a member of the caracara and falcon family (*Falconidae*).

The saker falcon is one of the species of birds traditionally used for hunting.

# Peregrine falcon
## (*Falco peregrinus*)

The peregrine falcon and various subspecies are found throughout the world. It is common in North America, Europe, Central and southern Africa, northern Asia and in Australia. Birds which live in northern regions migrate south after the mating season, while other birds are sedentary. The female peregrine falcon grows to a height of approximately 19 inches and is larger than the male. The female can weigh up to 2 pounds, while the male is usually a third lighter. The peregrine falcon is one of the fastest birds in the world. While diving, it can reach a speed of more than 200 miles an hour

Peregrine falcon (*Falco peregrinus*)

Eurasian kestrel (*Falco tinnunculus*)

European black kite (*Milvus migrans*)

and it can still catch its prey when travelling at this speed. The peregrine falcon eats other birds almost exclusively, which it catches in flight. It nests on rocks, in trees and even on the ground. If it nests in a tree, it usually takes over an abandoned nest. It generally lays 3 eggs, which are usually incubated by the female.

## Eurasian kestrel (*Falco tinnunculus*)

Of all the members of the caracara and falcon family (*Falconidae*), the Eurasian kestrel is the most widespread and the most abundant. It is found throughout Europe, in a large part of Asia and in many places in Africa, particularly in the north. It measures between 13 and 14 inches and eats mainly (field) mice. The male can be distinguished from the female by its color. The male has more contrast on its back covering and a grey head. The male is also somewhat smaller than the female. The Eurasian kestrel is not very fussy about where it builds its nest; it may be in a tree or on the ledge of a house. It lays an average of 5 eggs, which are incubated by the female for almost a month. Young Eurasian kestrels grow quickly and are reasonably independent after only one month.

## Black kite (*Milvus migrans*)

The black kite is widely distributed and, together with several subspecies, can be found throughout Europe, Africa, certain areas of Asia and Australia. Birds which live in southern regions are sedentary, while northern populations migrate south after the mating season for the winter. In

Honey buzzard (*Pernis apivorus*)

contrast to most birds of prey, this bird is seldom territorial. Nests are often built close together and the birds are often found in groups. The black kite eats a variety of animals. It catches its own prey but if given the opportunity, will also eat carrion. It normally builds its nest in a tree, but sometimes takes over an abandoned nest built by a different species of bird. It lays 2 to 3 eggs, which are usually incubated by the female. The male brings the female food during the incubation period so that she does not have to leave the nest. The eggs hatch after a month and the young leave the nest 6 weeks later. An adult black kite grows to a length of approximately 22 inches.

## Honey buzzard
## (*Pernis apivorus*)

The honey buzzard is found in an area which covers a great deal of Asia and extends as far as the western coast of Europe. It is rarely found on the Iberian peninsula, northern Scandinavia, southern Italy, Great Britain or Ireland. Most honey buzzards spend the winter in Africa and the Middle East. Its diet consists mainly of wasps and their larvae. It may also eat other insects, but never eats other animal species. The honey buzzard usually builds its nest high up in a tree. It sometimes builds its own nest, but may take over an abandoned nest if one is available. It lays between 1 and 3 eggs, which are incubated by both parents. The eggs hatch after one month and the young leave the nest when they are just 1.5 months old. The female honey buzzard is approximately 23 inches in length and has a wingspan of approximately 5 feet. The male is an inch or so smaller. It can live between 25 and 30 years. The honey buzzard is a member of the family *Accipitridae*.

A bird handler with a red-tailed hawk (*Buteo jamaicensis*)

Harris' hawk/Bay-winged hawk (*Parabuteo unicinctus*)

## Red-tailed hawk
## (*Buteo jamaicensis*)

This buzzard hawk gets its common name from the color of its tail. It is found in North and Central America along with several of its subspecies, both in dense forest regions and on open plains. It eats a variety of small animals, such as rodents, birds, amphibians and insects. The male of the species is approximately 17 inches in length and has a wingspan of 43 inches. The female is quite a bit larger, is approximately 25 inches in length and has a wingspan of 57 inches. It builds its nest in a variety of locations. The female lays between 2 and 5 eggs, which hatch after approximately 4.5 weeks.

## Harris' hawk or Bay-winged hawk
## (*Parabuteo unicinctus*)

The female of this species grows to a length of approximately 23 inches, while the male is usually about 4 inches smaller. The female has a wingspan of more than 40 inches. The bird is found in the southwest of the United States and in Central America, as far south as Chile. It usually eats small mammals. It lays 3 or 4 eggs, which hatch after approximately 28 days. It is a member of the family *Accipitridae*.

## Eurasian sparrowhawk
## (*Accipiter nisus*)

The Eurasian sparrowhawk eats mainly small birds, which it catches in flight. The female of the species is considerably larger than the male. The female grows to a length of almost 16 inches, while the male measures only 12 inches. It usually builds its nest in a conifer tree. It lays approximately 5 eggs, which are incubated by the female for 5 weeks. The Eurasian sparrowhawk is found throughout Europe, North Africa and Central and western Asia. Some populations migrate south for the winter after the mating season. The Eurasian sparrowhawk is a member of the family *Accipitridae*.

Eurasian sparrowhawk (*Accipiter nisus*)

# Grouse, pheasants, quail and turkeys (*Galliformes*)

Families: *Tetraonidae, Phasianidae, Numididae, Meleagrididae, Opisthocomidae, Cracidae and Megapodiidae.*

## Crested wood partridge (*Rollulus roulroul*)

The crested wood partridge lives in the dense forests on the islands of Borneo and Sumatra. Its diet includes a variety of seeds, berries, insects and worms, which it forages for on the ground. The crested wood partridge lives in small groups, the members of which form pairs and remain together for life. The male can be recognised by its crest, which the female does not have. It builds an ingenious nest with an opening at the front. It lays between 4 and 6 eggs, which are incubated by the female for approximately 18 days. Although the young can walk fairly soon after hatching, they remain in the nest at night for the first couple of weeks. An adult crested wood partridge grows to a length of approximately 10 inches.

## Ocellated turkey (*Agriocharis ocellata*)

The ocellated turkey lives mainly on the ground but rests and sleeps in trees. It is

A female crested wood partridge (*Rollulus roulroul*)

A male crested wood partridge (*Rollulus roulroul*)

found in Yucatan, Central America. It lays between 8 and 12 eggs, which hatch after 28 days. An adult can weigh up to 11 pounds. The ocellated turkey is a member of the turkey family (*Meleagrididae*).

Ocellated turkey (*Agriocharis ocellata*)

# Brush turkey
## (*Alectura lathami*)

The name of this bird is somewhat misleading, as it is not a turkey, but rather a member of the family of megapodes (*Megapodiidae*). The brush turkey lives in east Australia. The hen lays between 12 and 16 eggs in a mound of rotting vegetation, which the male has collected. The eggs are then covered and abandoned by both parents. The eggs are incubated by the warmth of the sun, which makes the mound extremely hot. The length of time it takes for the eggs to hatch depends on the heat that is produced, but usually takes about 7 weeks. Once the young have hatched, they work themselves out of the mound and have to fend for themselves. The hen of this species can be recognised by the wider and brightly colored yellow neck band.

# Black grouse
## (*Lyrurus tetrix*)

The black grouse is found in the coniferous forests in certain parts of Europe (particularly in Scandinavia) and further east as far as Siberia. It is the largest living grouse. The male can grow to a length of 35 inches and often weighs between 11 and 13 pounds or more. The hen sometimes weighs half as much. It has an unusual mating ritual. The cocks and hens live separately, but during the mating season, the hens of the region are attracted by the courtship display of the cock. After mating, the hens go their own way again. It does not make a nest but lays between 6 and 11 eggs in a hole in a sheltered location. The eggs hatch after approximately 4 weeks. The young animals are precocial and can rummage for their own food, although they initially need their mother to keep them warm. As soon as the young can fully care for themselves, usually after 2 months, they form small groups consisting of only male or female birds. The young black grouse is predominantly carnivorous and eats insects and worms, but becomes herbivorous when it reaches adulthood. The black grouse is a member of the grouse family (*Tetraonidae*).

# Eurasian black grouse
## (*Tetrao tetrix*)

The Eurasian black grouse is found in the north of Great Britain, northeast Europe and north Asia. Like the black grouse, the

Black grouse (*Lyrurus tetrix*)

Eurasian black grouse (*Tetrao tetrix*)

Vulturine guinea fowl (*Acryllium vulturinum*)

Eurasian black grouse does not form pairs. During the mating season, the cocks congregate in a certain location and perform a mating ritual to attract hens. The hen then searches for a place on the ground to build a nest in which to lay and incubate her eggs. The cock plays no further part. The Eurasian black grouse lays between 6 and 11 eggs, which hatch after approximately 26 days. The young are precocial and remain with their mother for between 1 and 1.5 months before they can fend for themselves. Young birds eat mainly small animals, such as insects and worms, while adult Eurasian black grouse are herbivorous. The Eurasian black grouse is a member of the grouse family (*Tetraonidae*).

## Vulturine guinea fowl
## (*Acryllium vulturinum*)

There are several species of guinea fowl which are found only in Africa. The vulturine guinea fowl is by far the most colorful and striking of these. Although its bald head and neck imply that it is a scavenger, the bird is predominantly herbivorous, however it does supplement its diet

with snails, worms and insects. It is found in Ethiopia, Somalia and Kenya. The vulturine guinea fowl lives in loose groups in which close couples are formed. Although it has excellent flying abilities, it seldom excersises them. It grows to a length of approximately 24 inches.

## Grey partridge
## (*Perdix perdix*)

The grey partridge originally comes from large parts of Europe, except for the south-west, and also from West and Central Asia, but has now also been introduced in the United States. It eats weeds and seeds and, to a lesser extent, insects. It nests in a hole in a sheltered location, often in tall grass on the edge of farmland. The grey partridge is a productive bird; the female can lay as many as 20 eggs. The

Grey partridge (*Perdix perdix*)

eggs are a greyish-green color and are incubated by the female for approximately 24 days. The male remains with the female and the young. The male does not incubate the eggs, but acts as a protector. The young remain with their parents for a considerable time, often until the end of the winter or early spring of the following year when they split up and form their own pairs. An adult grey partridge measures approximately 12 inches and is a member of the family *Phasanidae*.

## Gambel's quail
## (*Lophortyx gambelli*)

The Gambel's quail is also called the desert quail. It is a member of the pheas-

ant family (*Phasianidae*) and the genus *Lophoryx*, which also includes the well-known California quail (*L. californica*). The Gambel's quail is found in Mexico and in the southeast of the United States and grows to a length of approximately 9 inches. It builds its nest on the ground, usually in a sheltered location. The female lays approximately 15 eggs, which take about 3 weeks to hatch. The young are precocial and predominantly carnivorous. As they grow older, they become predominantly herbivorous.

## Common pheasant
## (*Phasianus colchicus*)

The common pheasant is very widely distributed. It originally comes from Asia, but man has since introduced it into Europe, North America and New Zealand. It tends to live near agricultural land, at the edge of woodland and in areas with sufficient undergrowth. The cock is not only larger than the hen but also more colorful. The cock can grow to a length of up to 35 inches, while the hen does not usually grow larger than 24 inches. It eats a variety of vegetation and small animals. It usually remains on the ground, although it will fly short distances close to the ground if disturbed. A cock pheasant has more than one hen and will protect its territory and its females against male intruders. The hen lays an average of 10

Gambel's quail (*Lophortyx gambelli*)

Common pheasant (*Phasianus colchicus*)

Golden pheasant (*Chrysolopus pictus*)

eggs in a shallow hole in the ground, which she incubates for 22 to 26 days. The young birds are precocial and can walk around with their mother soon after hatching. The young develop very quickly; they can fly a bit after 2 weeks and can often fend for themselves after 6 weeks. The cock neither incubates the eggs nor helps to raise the young. Like many other birds in this order, the young pheasant is predominantly carnivorous. As an adult, it becomes herbivorous and eats seeds and weeds.

## Golden pheasant
## (*Chrysolopus pictus*)

The golden pheasant is one of the most colorful species of pheasant known to man. It is found in mountainous regions in China with a good deal of undergrowth and has been introduced in Great Britain. The golden pheasant eats small animals, such as snails and worms, as well as plant material. The sexes can be distinguished easily; the male is much more colorful and heavier than the brown-black female and is much larger. During the breeding sea-

son, the cock has several females and does not allow any other males to come close. Outside the breeding season, the animals live together peacefully in groups. The female builds an untidy nest in a sheltered location on the ground in which she lays approximately 8 eggs. The eggs hatch after approximately 3 weeks.

## Crested fireback
## (*Lophura ignita*)

Various subspecies of the crested fireback are found in the forests of Sumatra, Borneo and Malaysia. The bird gets the second part of its common name from the bright red feathers on its back which appear only during the breeding season. Crested pheasants are usually found in pairs. On average, the crested fireback lays 5 or 6 creamy white eggs, which take approximately 24 days to hatch. The bird shown in the picture is a male Delacour's crested fireback (*L. ignita macartneyi*), which is a subspecies of the crested fireback and is found in South East Sumatra.

Delacour's crested fireback

A female blue peacock (*Pavo cristatus*)

# Great argus
# (*Argusianus argus*)

The great argus is a solitary bird which is found in the forests of Malaysia, Borneo and Sumatra. Excluding the long tail of the male, it measures approximately 27 inches. It eats both animal and plant food which it finds on the ground. During the mating season, the male performs a vocal mating ritual to attract far-away females. The female builds her own nest and also incubates the eggs and raises the (precocial) young.

Great argus (*Argusianus argus*)

# Blue peacock
# (*Pavo cristatus*)

The blue peacock originates from India and Sri Lanka but has been successfully bred and held in captivity throughout the world. It is omnivorous and eats insects, snails and worms, as well as berries and seeds. Although it spends most of its time on the ground, it can fly if necessary. It usually spends the night in a tree or a bush. It is easy to distinguish the sexes; the male has the familiar train of tail feathers which it displays during the mating ritual. Furthermore, the breast of the male is bright blue, while the female is more of a brown color. The male blue peacock usually gathers several females around him, which he attracts through his courtship behavior and call. After a female has been fertilised, she goes off by herself. The male takes no further part in caring for the eggs or the young. The female usually lays 5 eggs, which she has incubated for approximately 28 days. An adult male can grow to a length of more than 6.5 feet, including its tail, while the female is smaller than 3.5 feet. The blue peacock is a member of the family *Phasanidae*.

A male blue peacock (*Pavo cristatus*)

# Cranes, rails, coots, seriemas and bustards (*Gruiformes*)

Families: *Mesitornithidae, Turnicidae, Pedionomidae, Gruidae, Aramidae, Psophiidae, Rallidae, Heliornithidae, Rhynochetidae, Eurypygidae, Cariamidae and Otididae.*

## Common gallinule (*Gallinula chloropus*)

This species of bird is found throughout the world, except in Australia. It has striking green feet and legs and a red bill with a yellow end. It lives close to still or slow-flowing fresh water. It is omnivorous and eats fruit, berries and aquatic plants, as well as small animals. Both parents build a nest, usually in a sheltered location along the edge of the water, using a variety of material. On average, it lays between 7 and 9 eggs, which are incubated by both parents for approximately 3

An immature common gallinule (*Gallinula chloropus*)

Common gallinule (*Gallinula chloropus*)

weeks. The young are precocial. Another clutch of eggs is usually laid once the young have been raised. The young from the first nest are not driven away, but usually stay with their parents. An adult common gallinule measures approximately 12 inches. It is a member of the rail family (*Rallidae*).

# Sunbittern
# (*Eurypyga helias*)

The sunbittern grows to a length of approximately 18 inches. Various subspecies are found in the northeast of South America and in Central America. This bird is always found near water, where it catches its main food source, small aquatic animals, by wading in the shallow water. It builds a large nest in a tree or bush in which it lays 2 or 3 eggs. The eggs are incubated by both parents and hatch after

Sunbittern (*Eurypyga helias*)

European coot (*Fulica atra*)

approximately 28 days. The young remain in the nest for at least 3 weeks, during which time they are fed by both parents. The sunbittern is a member of the family of sunbitterns (*Eurypygidae*).

# European coot
# (*Fulica atra*)

The European coot is very widely distributed. It is common throughout Europe, in large parts of Asia, North America and Australia. The European coot usually builds its nest along a water bank or sometimes in shallow water. The nest, which is built by both partners, is constructed mostly from reeds. It lays between 5 and 8 eggs, which the parents take turns incubating for 3 weeks. The European coot often breeds twice in one season. Sometimes, the second clutch of eggs is laid so soon after the first that the young from the first clutch are still dependent on their parents. This, however, does not cause a problem because the young from the first clutch are always accepted by the nest and can count on help from their parents. Older immature birds often help to look after their younger brothers and sisters. Nestlings of this species can be recognised by their black plumage and the bold, light red head and neck. The European coot grows to a length of approximately 15 inches and is a member of the rail family (*Rallidae*).

An immature European coot (*Fulica atra*)

A coot often builds its nest along the bank or in shallow water.

## Sarus crane
## (*Grus antigone*)

The sarus crane is found in South-East Asia and northeast Australia, where it prefers to live on open grassland plains. It eats berries and grain, as well as insects and small vertebrates (amphibians). The sarus crane lives either in pairs or in groups. In a group, however, it lives monogamously with a mate that it stays with for life. It builds its nest on the ground from a variety of vegetation. It usually lays 2 eggs, which are incubated by the female and hatch after approximately 1 month.

## White-naped crane
## (*Grus vipio*)

The white-naped crane lives in family groups. Like the sarus crane, this bird is a member of the crane family (*Gruidae*). The bird is omnivorous. Its breeding ground is in Southern Russia, in the area to the east of Mongolia, and in Western China. It spends the winter in China, Japan or Korea. As with all cranes, the white-naped crane returns each year to

Sarus crane (*Grus antigone*)

White-naped crane (*Grus vipio*)

the same location where it bred the previous year. It usually lays 2 eggs, which both parents take turns incubating. The eggs hatch after approximately 1 month. The young are precocial and are soon able to walk with their parents. The young birds can fly when they are approximately 2.5 months old. The white-naped crane grows to a height of approximately 4 feet.

## Demoiselle crane
## (*Antropoides virgo*)

The demoiselle crane is the smallest species of crane. It is usually found in parts of Russia, China and Mongolia but is also found, to a lesser extent, in North Africa and Europe. The demoiselle crane is predominantly herbivorous and eats weeds and seeds but may sometimes also eat animals. It always lives in groups and

breeds close to other birds. Its nest is a hole in the ground in which it lays 2 eggs. The eggs are incubated by the female and hatch after approximately 4 weeks. The young birds are precocial.

## African crowned crane
## (*Balearica pavonina*)

The African crowned crane is the best-known crane (*Gruidae*). It gets its common name from the typical decoration on the top of its head, which is present on both the male and female bird. There is no visible difference between the sexes. It is found in the marshy regions of tropical Africa. The African crowned crane is omnivorous and eats grain and soft plant matter, as well as insects, worms and amphibians, which it searches for on the ground. It searches only for a branch sit-

A young white-naped crane (*Grus vipio*)

Demoiselle crane (*Antropoides virgo*)

uated above ground level when in danger or at rest. An adult African crowned crane can grow to a length of more than 3 feet.

## Kori bustard
## (*Ardeotis kori*)

The kori bustard is a member of the bustard family (*Otididae*) and more specifically is of the paauw genus. An adult bird can grow to a length of 4 feet. The kori bustard is found on the savannahs of East Africa. It spends most of its time on the ground, even at night, although it can fly when in danger. The kori bustard is omnivorous and eats mice, frogs, insects, seeds, soft grasses and other plant material. A well-known characteristic of this species is the mating ritual of the male, during which the throat expands up to four times its normal size. When doing so,

African crowned cranes (*Balearica pavonina*)

the male makes a low, heavy, long-range noise. The kori bustard is monogamous and once a pair is formed, it usually stays together for life. It lives in pairs.

African crowned crane (*Balearica pavonina*)

Kori bustard (*Ardeotis kori*)

# Plovers, sandpipers, gulls, terns and auks (*Charadriiformes*)

Families: *Jacanidae, Rostratulidae, Haematopodidae, Charadriidae, Scolopacidae, Ibidorhynchidae, Recurvirostridae, Phalaropodidae, Dromadidae, Burhinidae, Glareolidae, Thinocoridae, Chionididae, Stercorariidae, Laridae, Rhynchopidae and Alcidae.*

## Ruff (*Philomachus pugnax*)

The ruff gets its common name from the collar or ruff which the male acquires during its courtship display to attract females. The male mates with the female during the mating season, but the birds do not form pairs. After mating, the female builds a nest in a hole in the ground, which she covers with a variety of nesting material. She lays an average of 4 eggs, which hatch after approximately 3 weeks. There are large differences in color between ruffs; no two birds are the same. Only the male has the striking, protruding feathers around the neck and head during the mating season. The ruff is omnivorous and eats small animals and plant material which it rummages for on the ground. It is found in Europe and northwest Asia. It is a member of the family *Scolopacidae.*

Eurasian lapwing (*Vanellus vanellus*)

A male ruff during the mating season (*Philomachus pugnax*)

## Eurasian lapwing (*Vanellus vanellus*)

The Eurasian lapwing is a member of the plover family (*Charadriidae*) and is found in parts of Europe and Asia. The northern and eastern populations found in Europe are migratory and migrate south in the autumn, sometimes even earlier, and return in February or March. The bird lives on grassland plains, fields and other flat areas, always close to water. Its diet consists mainly of a variety of insects, but it may sometimes eat worms and other small animals. The sexes can be distinguished by the crest, which is longer on the male than on the female. It nests in a small hole in the ground, often in the middle of a field or meadow, which is usually prepared by the female. It generally lays 4 speckled eggs that are round on one side and pointed on the other. The eggs are incubated by both parents and hatch after approximately 26 days. Both parents feed the young. The young develop quick-

Spur-winged lapwing (*Vanellus spinosus*)

ly and most can fly usually after only 1.5 months. An adult Eurasian lapwing is approximately 11 inches long.

## Spur-winged lapwing (*Vanellus spinosus*)

The spur-winged lapwing is a member of the plover family (*Charadriidae*). The species is most widespread in Africa, but is also found in the southern portion of the Balkans, parts of Asia and the Middle East. It prefers to live in marshy regions, but is always found close to water. Like the Eurasian lapwing, the spur-winged lapwing lays 3 to 4 eggs in a hole in the ground, which it only slightly covers with nesting material. The diet of the young and adult birds consists mainly of insects and, to a lesser extent, worms.

Cayenne lapwing (*Vanellus cayanus*)

## Cayenne lapwing (*Vanellus cayanus*)

The cayenne lapwing is found in open or semi-open areas in South America. It shares a striking characteristic with the spur-winged lapwing, namely the long, sharp spurs on the front of its wings. An adult bird measures approximately 14 inches. The cayenne lapwing is a member of the plover family (*Charadriidae*).

## Masked lapwing (*Vanellus miles*)

The masked lapwing is often found in Australia, where it is just as common as the Eurasian lapwing is in Europe. It is also found to a lesser extent in New Guinea and New Zealand. The masked lapwing prefers to live in open areas, such as farmland. Its main diet is a variety of

Masked lapwing (*Vanellus miles*)

Blacksmith plover (*Anitibyx armatus*)

insects and worms. It lays an average of 3 or 4 eggs in a hole in the ground, which hatch after 4 weeks. The masked lapwing has a wingspan of approximately 29 to 31 inches and can live for up to 12 years.

## Blacksmith plover (*Vanellus armatus*)

The blacksmith plover is found in dry regions in Africa, but always within flying

Pied avocet (*Recurvirostra avosetta*)

A pied avocet in its nest (*Recurvirostra avosetta*)

distance of water. It lives in pairs or small groups and eats insects, insect larvae and worms. It nests in a hole in the ground in which it lays approximately 3 eggs which hatch after 4 weeks. The young leave the nest after approximately 4 weeks. The blacksmith plover grows to a length of approximately 12 inches and is a member of the plover family (*Charadriidae*).

## Pied avocet (*Recurvirostra avosetta*)

The pied avocet is found in Europe and certain parts of Asia. Some populations spend the winter in Africa and China and the animal prefers to live on sandy soil near water. It uses its unusually shaped bill to look for small aquatic animals in shallow water. It breeds in colonies and builds its nest in a small hole in the ground, which it poorly covers with a variety of nesting material. It lays 4 eggs, which are incubated by both parents and hatch after approximately 24 days. The pied avocet is a member of the family *Recurvirostridae*.

## Black-winged stilt (*Himantopus himantopus*)

The black-winged stilt is a cosmopolitan bird and is found on many continents, from Europe to Australia. A completely

Black-winged stilt (*Himantopus himantopus*)

black subspecies is found in New Zealand, the *H.h. novaseelandiae*. Its diet consists of small aquatic animals. For this reason, it is always found close to water, although this can be brackish, fresh or salt water. The black-winged stilt breeds in colonies. It digs a hole in the ground for a nest in which it usually lays 4 speckled eggs. Both parents incubate the eggs, which hatch after approximately 26 days. An adult black-winged stilt measures 14 inches in total.

Palaearctic oystercatcher (*Haematopus ostralegus*)

## Palaearctic oystercatcher (*Haematopus ostralegus*)

The Palaearctic oystercatcher is between 16 and 17 inches in length and weighs approximately 1 pound. It is common along the coasts of Europe and Africa, North and South America and even New Zealand and Australia. There are also populations which live inland, but these always live close to water. It normally migrates to warmer regions after the breeding season, but some populations have become sedentary. This bird lives in large groups outside the mating season, but during the mating season, the pairs separate themselves from the other birds. The breeding ground is usually a constant factor in the bird's life and most birds return to the same familiar location each year. It usually lays 3 eggs in a covered hole in the ground. The eggs are incubated by both parents and hatch after 4 weeks. The young birds are precocial. The diet of the adult bird depends both on the location and the amount of food available. Birds which live along the coast usually eat mussels, snails and (lug)worms.

## Snowy or Kentish plover (*Charadrius alexandrinus*)

The snowy plover is a small coastal bird which is widely distributed. It can be

A male snowy/Kentish plover (*Charadrius alexandrinus*)

A female snowy/Kentish plover

Ruddy turnstone (*Arenaria interpres*)

found along almost all the coasts of Europe, Asia, North Africa and North and South America. After the mating season, it migrates southward for the winter. Its diet consists of small insects and other small animals which it finds along the tideline and on the beach. The sexes can be distinguished by the color of the head; the top of the head is brown on the male and grey on the female. It nests in a hollow which it covers with a variety of hard material. It usually lays 3 eggs, which are incubated by both parents. The eggs hatch after approximately 24 days and the young can fly when they are only one month old.

## Ruddy turnstone
### (*Arenaria interpres*)

The ruddy turnstone is a member of the family *Scolopacidae*. It is a coastal bird and outside the mating season, it is found throughout the world, as far as Australia.

It breeds, however, in the Arctic. The ruddy turnstone is approximately 9 to 10 inches in length. In the summer, the bird has a plumage of three colors but in the winter, it becomes less colorful. The ruddy turnstone's diet consists mainly of a variety of insects and worms, which it finds between and under stones.

## Bush thick-knee
### (*Burhinus grallarius*)

The bush thick-knee is a member of the stone curlew family (*Burhinidae*) and is found in Australia, where it prefers to live in open areas close to water. It is nocturnal and is not seen during the day. It is predominantly carnivorous and eats insects, snails, small reptiles and rodents. It uses its sharp vision to search for food. It nests in a hole in the ground which it digs using its feet. The nest is sometimes covered with small stones, although not all bush thick-knees take the trouble to do this. It usually lays 2 eggs, which hatch after approximately 25 days. An adult bush thick-knee has a total length of approximately 16 inches.

Bush thick-knee (*Burhinus grallarius*)

Crocodile bird (*Pluvianus aegyptius*)

## Crocodile bird (*Pluvianus aegyptius*)

The crocodile bird is a member of the courser and pratincole family (*Glareoli-*

Common puffin (*Fratercula arctica*)

*dae*). It is found in several regions in tropical Africa, including Zaire, the Sudan and Ghana. It prefers to live along the banks of larger rivers where it can forage for its food. It is predominantly insectivorous. It gets its common name from the fact that it rummages for food in the open mouths of crocodiles. Crocodiles accept the presence of this bird, probably because it does them a service. The crocodile bird lives either in pairs or in family groups. There is no visible difference between the male and female. An adult bird has a total length of approximately 8 inches.

## Common puffin (*Fratercula arctica*)

The common puffin is a sea and coastal bird and is mainly found along the coasts of Scandinavia, Iceland, Great Britain, Greenland, Spitsbergen and the northeastern coast of North America. The com-

123

Inca tern (*Larosterna inca*)

it is abandoned. After a couple of days, the young bird also leaves the nest and is then able to fend for itself. The common puffin is a member of the auk family (*Alcidae*).

## Inca tern
## (*Larosterna inca*)

This bird is very noticeable, due to its dark grey plumage, bright red webbed feet, striking red beak and white plumes under its eyes. This very active bird is found along the east coast of South America, where it lives in groups. It actively hunts for surface fish, which it catches by diving into the water. It breeds in a sheltered location on rocks along the coast. The young birds do not look like their parents; they do not have the red beak and feet and their wings are marked. The inca tern is approximately 16 inches long and is a member of the gull and stern family (*Laridae*).

mon puffin has a parrot-like beak and dives into the sea to catch fish, its main food source. It breeds in colonies. It always lays only one egg, which can be laid in a sheltered alcove in a rock or on land in an abandoned rabbit burrow. The egg hatches after 40 days and the young bird is fed for approximately the same length of time by both parents, after which

## Black-headed gull
## (*Larus ridibundus*)

The black-headed gull is common throughout Europe (but not in the southern countries) and a large part of central and western Asia. The black-headed gull is omnivorous and eats fish, worms, snails and even small rodents, as well as plant material. The typical dark marking on its head appears only in the summer. The marking disappears during the winter, but a darker spot always remains visible behind the ear. Young birds do not look much like their parents; they have a white plumage which is mixed with brown. It builds its nest on the ground in which it usually lays 3 green, dark speckled eggs. The eggs are incubated by both parents and hatch after approximately 24 days. Both parents look after the young birds. An adult black-headed gull measures

Black-headed gull (*Larus ridibundus*)

New gull (*Larus canus*)

approximately 14 inches and is a member of the gull and stern family (*Laridae*).

## New gull (*Larus canus*)

The new gull is distributed throughout a large part of Europe, North Africa, the Middle East, north and Central Asia, as well as the north-west of North America. It is also regularly observed on the west coast of the southern part of North America. During the breeding season, birds which live more inland move to the coast to breed in colonies. There is no visible difference between the sexes. Young birds can be recognised by the darker markings on their plumage. An adult is white and its wings and back are grey. The bird is omnivorous and grows to a length of 16 inches.

Herring gull (*Larus argentatus*)

## Herring gull (*Larus argentatus*)

This sturdy species of gull is found throughout the northern hemisphere and is a common coastal bird. During the summer months, it lives in northern regions, such as Siberia, Greenland and Canada. In the winter, it migrates southward to Central America, Africa or south Asia, although there are also populations which do not migrate. The bird has adapted to increasing urbanisation and is often seen further inland, even in the middle of cities, where it also breeds. It is carnivorous but is not particular about what it eats and, if hungry enough, may even catch an adult puffin in flight. There is no visible difference between the sexes. The herring gull prefers to breed in colonies. It can build its nest in any location, such as on a building, on a rock, in a tree or even on the ground. It usually lays 3 eggs, which are incubated by both parents and hatch after approximately 4 weeks. The young develop quickly and can fly quite well after only 1.5 months. At that age, they do not yet have their final color, but have a brownish plumage with grey markings. They reach sexual maturity at an age of 3 years, or sometimes even later. The herring gull grows to a length of 25 inches. It is a member of the family *Laridae*.

## Common tern (*Sterna hirundo*)

The common tern is very widely distributed and is found along the coast and inland throughout Europe, west and central Asia, North America and North Africa. It spends the winter in southern regions, which are sometimes thousands of miles from its breeding ground. The common tern always lives near large lakes, rivers or the sea. There is a striking difference between the bird's summer and winter coloring. In the summer, the bird

Common tern (*Sterna hirundo*)

catches in the water; on land, however, it also eats insects and other similar animals. The common tern usually breeds in colonies and generally builds a small nest on the ground. The female lays approximately 3 eggs, which are incubated mostly by the female herself. The eggs hatch after approximately 3 weeks and the young are fed and cared for by both parents. The common tern is a member of the gull and tern family (*Laridae*).

## Wattled jacana (*Jacana jacana*)

To a layman, this species of bird looks a great deal like a lightly built moorhen. The birds are not related and the wattled jacana is classified in a different order. It is a member of the jacana family together with the other species of jacanas, the lotus bird and the water pheasant. The wattle jacana is not a very good swimmer and prefers to waddle in shallow water or walk on aquatic plants, between which it searches for food. The species is found in South America, mainly in northern regions and to the east of the Andes. An adult measures approximately 10 inches.

has a characteristic black hood on its head which extends to its neck. In the winter, the black between the beak and above the eyes becomes white. The beak is bright red with a black point in the summer but becomes almost completely black in the winter. The common tern is approximately 9 inches long. It eats mainly small fish and other aquatic animals, which it

The wattled jacana likes to walk on aquatic plants (*Jacana jacana*)

Wattled jacana (*Jacana jacana*)

126

# Pigeons and doves (*Columbiformes*)

Family: *Columbidae*

## Rock dove (*Columba livia*)

Rock dove (*Columba livia*)

The rock dove is the wild ancestor of all the domesticated dove species and the well-known homing pigeon. This species originates from southern Europe, the Middle East, North Africa and the bordering regions of Asia, but due to human intervention, wild rock doves are now found throughout the world. The original rock dove builds its nest in alcoves and on protruding rocks, but the wild dove is so accustomed to living close to humans that it lays its eggs on the ledges of buildings. It breeds in colonies and builds a poorly constructed nest from large pieces of plant and animal material. It lays 2 eggs, which hatch after approximately 18 days. The young birds leave the nest when they are one month old. An adult bird grows to a length of approximately 12 inches. Its diet consists mainly of seeds, but it may also eat small animals. The species is one of the fastest doves; it can fly at a speed of 100 miles an hour.

## Stock dove (*Columba oenas*)

The stock dove is found throughout Europe and prefers to live in semi-open forested regions. It eats a variety of seeds, nuts and fruit, as well as insects and similar small animals. The female usually lays her eggs in an abandoned woodpecker nest. The eggs are incubated by both parents and hatch after approximately 17 days. The young birds leave the nest when they are 3 or 4 weeks old. An adult stock dove is approximately the same size as a rock dove.

## Wood pigeon (*Columba palumbus*)

The wood pigeon is approximately 16 inches long and is the largest species of pigeon found in Europe. It lives in forested regions or close to large trees and is often found living close to humans. The wood pigeon is widely distributed. It is native to Europe, northwest Africa and a large part of northwest Asia. As with almost all species of pigeons, its nest is poorly constructed. It builds its nest in a tree in which it lays 2 white eggs. The eggs are incubated by both parents and

Wood pigeon (*Columba palumbus*)

Stock dove (*Columba oenas*)

Speckled pigeon (*Columba guinea*)

Crested pigeon (*Ocyphaps lophotes*)

## Crested pigeon
## (*Ocyphaps lophotes*)

The crested pigeon is a very common species of pigeon found in Australia. It always lives in pairs and is found in urban areas as well as in regions far from human settlements. The crested pigeon mainly eats seeds. It prefers seeds of the locust tree, although it also eats berries, fruit and soft herbaceous parts of plants. There is no noticeable difference between the sexes, although the color of the female is a little duller. It lays 2 eggs, which are incubated by the female and hatch after approximately 18 days. The young birds leave the nest when they are 3 weeks old, although they are still fed and accompanied by their parents for some time. An adult crested pigeon measures 13 inches.

## Collared dove
## (*Streptoptelia decaocto*)

Although the collared dove is distributed across a large part of Asia and almost all of Europe, it was not found in Western Europe until about 70 years ago. It is (still) not known whether the collared dove was introduced by humans or whether it found its own way there. Its diet consists mainly of seeds. During the winter, it usually lives in groups from which it finds a partner and forms a pair. The birds which form pairs remain very

hatch after approximately 16 days. During the first week, the young are fed crop milk and later receive more solid food from their parents. The wood pigeon usually breeds more than once in a single season.

## Speckled pigeon
## (*Columba guinea*)

The speckled pigeon is approximately 14 inches long. It and several subspecies are found in certain parts of Africa, where it often lives and breeds in cities and villages. It eats a variety of plant material ranging from seeds and nuts to weeds and berries, although it may sometimes also eat small animals. As with many pigeons, there is no visible difference between the male and female. Its nest is poorly constructed from large material. It lays 2 eggs, which hatch after 15 or 16 days. The young birds leave the nest when they are approximately 3 weeks old.

Collared dove (*Streptoptelia decaocto*)

White-winged dove (*Melpelia asiatica*)

close for the rest of the year and often raise between 4 and 5 broods. The pair occupies a territory in which no other pigeons are permitted. It builds a poorly constructed nest in which it lays 2 white eggs. The eggs are incubated by both parents and hatch after approximately 16 days. The young birds leave the nest when they are between 2 and 3 weeks old and often reach sexual maturity when they are only 4 months old. The collared dove is sedentary. It does not migrate and lives in the same area throughout the year, which can be a wooded area, an urban park or a garden. An adult collared dove is approximately 12 inches long.

## White-winged dove
## (*Melpelia asiatica*)

This dove, with its striking blue-rimmed eyes, is found in a part of Mexico and the south-west of the United States. It grows to a length of approximately 12 inches. It eats a variety of seeds which it finds on the ground, but may also eat weeds and berries. The white-winged dove is gregarious. During the mating season, it builds a poorly constructed nest from large material close to other nests in the shelter of trees and bushes. The white-winged dove lays 2 eggs. The eggs are mainly incubated by the female and hatch after approximately 18 days. The young birds develop quickly and leave the nest when they are 2.5 weeks old.

## Bleeding heart pigeon
## (*Gallicolumba luzonica*)

The bleeding heart pigeon gets its common name from its lugubrious and very peculiar red breast markings, the shape and color of which make it appear as if the bird has been wounded in the heart. The bleeding heart pigeon is found almost exclusively on a small number of Philippine Islands, where it usually lives on the ground in the protection of thick forests. It rarely flies, but can if necessary. It eats a variety of small food, ranging from seeds to larvae. It builds its nest in a tree or bush and lays 2 eggs. The eggs are incubated by both parents and hatch after approximately 2 weeks. The bleeding heart pigeon is approximately 12 inches long, but is sturdier than the collared dove.

## Diamond dove
(*Geopelia cuneata*)

This Australian species of dove is usually not much bigger than 7 inches. It is difficult to distinguish between the sexes, although the ring around the eyes of the male is said to be more brightly colored during the mating season. It usually lives in pairs. It lays 2 eggs, which are incubated by both parents and which hatch after 2 weeks. For the first few days of their lives, the young are fed only crop milk by the female but later the male helps to feed the young. The young leave the nest when they are between 12 and 14 days old but are still fed and helped by their parents for another week before they can fend for themselves.

## Green-winged dove
(*Chalcophaps indica*)

Many subspecies of the green-winged dove are found in southern Asia, New Guinea and Australia. It is a strikingly colored dove and is approximately 10 inches long, although this varies between the subspecies. It prefers to live in thickly forested regions and searches for seeds, fruit and insects on the ground. As with many doves, this dove is not particularly skilled in building its nest. It lays 2 eggs, which hatch after approximately 2 weeks. The young birds leave the nest after 2 weeks and are able to fend for themselves a couple of weeks later. The green-winged dove usually breeds more than once in a single season.

Bleeding heart pigeon (*Gallicolumba luzonica*)

Diamond dove (*Geopelia cuneata*)

Green-winged dove (*Chalcophaps indica*)

Scheepmarker's crowned pigeon

Scheepmarker's crowned pigeon

## Pied imperial pigeon (*Ducula bicolor*)

This sturdy pigeon grows to a total length of 16 inches. It and several subspecies are found in southern Asia and Australia, where it lives predominantly in forests. Its diet consists mainly of nutmeg, although it also eats other fruits and berries. In contrast to many other pigeons, this species does not lay 2 eggs, but only 1 per brood, and it takes approximately 26 days to hatch.

## Common crowned pigeon (*Goura cristata*)

The various crowned pigeon species look very similar and are undoubtedly the most

Pied imperial pigeon (*Ducula bicolor*)

Victoria crowned pigeon

striking and largest of the pigeon species. The common crowned pigeon is one of these birds. This species is found in the forested regions of New Guinea. It is approximately 31 inches long and weighs around 5 pounds. The common crowned pigeon is a very quiet, intimate pigeon. It usually remains on the ground, where it forages for its food. Although it can fly short distances, it rarely does so. It builds its nest in a tree and lays one egg, which hatches after 4 weeks. The young bird leaves the nest when it is 1 month old, although it usually takes another 1.5 months before it can fend for itself. During this time, the young bird is still fed and accompanied by its parents. The common crowned pigeon can live to be quite old–there have been reports of common crowned pigeons which have lived in excess of 40 years.

# Parrots (*Psittaciformes*)

Family: *Psittacidae*

## Blue-and-yellow macaw (*Ara ararauna*)

The blue-and-yellow macaw is found in Central America and the in the northern part of South America and is approximately 33 inches long. There is no visible difference between the male and female. It is a very social bird and prefers to live in large groups. The blue-and-yellow macaw lays between 2 and 4 eggs, which are incubated by the female for 24 to 28 days. The young are fed by both parents and, as a rule, do not venture outside the nest before they are 2.5 to 3 months old.

Blue-and-yellow macaw (*Ara ararauna*)

Green-winged macaw (*Ara chloroptera*)

## Green-winged macaw (*Ara chloroptera*)

The green-winged macaw is found in the northern part of South America, where it lives in large groups. It grows to a length of approximately 33 inches. There is no visible difference between the sexes. It can take 4 years or longer before the bird reaches sexual maturity. The female lays an average of 4 eggs, which she incubates for 24 to 28 days. The young leave the nest when they are between 3 and 4 months old, although they are then still unable to fend for themselves and are helped by their parents for some time longer.

## Sulphur-crested cockatoo (*Cacatua galerita*)

The sulphur-crested cockatoo measures approximately 14 inches. The sulphur-

Sulphur-crested cockatoo (*Cacatua galerita*)

A male cockatiel in the foreground(*Nymphicus hollandicus*)

crested cockatoo is found in Indonesia, where it lives in groups. The sexes can be distinguished by the iris, which is black on the male and a reddish brown on the female. A sulphur-crested cockatoo reaches sexual maturity at an age of 4 or 5 years. It lays 2 or 3 eggs in the hollow of a tree, which the male and female take turns incubating. The eggs hatch after 26 to 30 days. The young birds leave the nest when they are 2 months old. They are unable to fend for themselves at that age, so the parents still look after the young birds for a little longer. The sulphur-crested cockatoo can live for 40 years.

## Cockatiel
## (*Nymphicus hollandicus*)

The cockatiel is found in the Australian outback and measures between 11 and 13 inches. The male bird has a yellow head and yellow cheeks, in contrast to the female, which has hardly any yellow col-

Hawk-headed parrot (*Derotyus acciptrinus*)

133

oring. The cockatiel is a very social and good-natured bird which lives in groups. It is predominantly herbivorous and eats mainly seeds which it prefers to forage for on the ground. It lays between 3 and 9 white eggs. The eggs are incubated by both parents and hatch after 18 to 21 days, although the female does most of the brooding. The young are cared for mostly by their mother. They leave the nest when they are one month old and it takes another month before they are independent of their parents. The cockatiel is very popular as a pet and there are now a large number of color mutations which are quite different from the color of the birds found in the wild.

## Hawk-headed parrot
## (*Derotyus acciptrinus*)

The hawk-headed parrot is almost the same size as the grey parrot. It has a brightly colored collar around its neck, which it displays when it is disturbed or feels threatened. It is found in the northeastern part of South America, particularly in Columbia and Venezuela, as well as in Brazil. The hawk-headed parrot lives in groups or in pairs. There is no visible difference between the sexes.

## Red-winged parrot
## (*Aprosmictus erythropterus*)

The red-winged parrot is a very colorful bird found in Australia and New Guinea. It prefers to live in eucalyptus forests and likes to eat the seeds of eucalyptus and locust trees. It also eats fruit, nectar and, to a lesser extent, insects and larvae. This bird lives in groups outside the mating season, but during the mating season, pairs of birds separate from the group to nest. It builds its nest in a hollow tree and the nest can sometimes be several meters below the entrance. It lays between 3 and

6 eggs, which hatch after 3 weeks. Including its tail, an adult red-winged parrot measures approximately 13 inches.

## Grey parrot
## (*Psittacus erithacus*)

Just like almost all other species of parrot, the grey parrot is a social bird and lives in groups. The grey parrot mates for life. It is found in tropical West Africa. There is no visible difference between the sexes. The grey parrot nests in a hollow tree in which it lays between 3 and 5 eggs. The eggs are incubated by the female and hatch after approximately 1 month. The young birds leave the nest when they are between 2 and 3 months old, although they are still fed and accompanied by their parents for a further 1 to 1.5 months. The grey parrot is herbivorous and eats seeds, nuts and fruit. It is approximately 14 inches long

Red-winged parrot (*Aprosmictus erythropterus*)

and can live to be very old; if kept as a pet and cared for and fed correctly, a grey parrot can live for 70 years or more.

Blue-fronted Amazon (*Amazona aestiva*)

Grey Parrot (*Psiltacus erithacus*)

# Blue-fronted Amazon (*Amazona aestiva*)

The blue-fronted Amazon is found in Brazil and Argentina and is approximately 14 inches long. There is no visible difference between the sexes. Some blue-fronted Amazons have very little blue or yellow coloring on the head, while others have a great deal. This is a natural variation and has nothing to do with the sex. The blue-fronted Amazon is a very social bird which lives in large groups. It eats a variety of seeds and fruits. Like almost all parrots, it is an excellent climber and flier. It nests in a hollow tree in which it lays 2 to 4 eggs. The eggs are incubated by the female for 4 weeks, during which time she is fed by the male. The young birds can leave the nest when they are 1.5 to 2 months old and can fend for themselves when they are 3 to 4 months old. The bird reaches sexual maturity when it is approximately 5 years old.

The yellow-fronted parakeet is very closely related to the blue-fronted Amazon.

Kea (*Nestor notabilis*)

## Kea (*Nestor notabilis*)

This species of parrot is only found on the southern island of New Zealand. It always lives in groups consisting of several females and a single male. The group occupies a territory and the male defends the territory and his females against intruders of the same species or sex. The

Senegal parrot (*Poicephalus senegalus*)

kea eats insects, larvae and other small animal food, although it may also eat soft fruits, weeds, pollen and nectar. There is no visible difference between the male and female. It nests in a hollow tree or rock crevice and covers its nest with plant material and twigs that have been bitten into small pieces. It usually lays 2 to 4 eggs, which are incubated by the female for 3 to 4 weeks. An adult kea is approximately 19 inches long.

## Senegal parrot
## (*Poicephalus senegalus*)

This parrot is found in West Africa and grows to a length of approximately 9 inches. Its diet includes seeds. There is no visible difference between the male and female. It lays 3 or 4 white eggs, which are incubated by the female for approximately 28 days. The young birds leave the nest when they are approximately 8 to 10 weeks old and are able to fend for themselves 2 weeks later.

## Conure
## (*Cyanoliseus patagonus*)

The conure is found in Chile and Argentine where it lives in very large, noisy groups, usually on rocks. The conure is an excellent climber, as well as a good flier. Its diet consists mainly of a variety of seeds and berries. The conure breeds in

Conure (*Cyanoliseus patagonus*)

Princess parrot (*Polytelis alexandrae*)

## Princess parrot (*Polytelis alexandrae*)

The Princess parrot inhabits the dry regions of the western Australian outback and grows to a length of 18 inches. The male is more colorful than the female and its tail feathers are longer. It eats a variety of seeds and berries. Like many species of parrots, this bird does not build a nest. It searches for a suitable hollow in a tree in which it lays 4 to 6 white eggs. The female incubates the eggs for 3 weeks. The young are fed by both parents and leave the nest when they are 5 weeks old.

## Fischer's lovebird (*Agapornis fischeri*)

Fischer's lovebird is found in northern Tanzania and is approximately 6 inches long. It is a very lively bird and is an excellent climber and flier. It eats a variety of seeds and fruit. There is no visible difference between the male and female. It lives

colonies. It builds its nest in a small, sheltered crevice or alcove in the rocks and usually lays 2 eggs. The eggs are incubated by the female and hatch after approximately 24 days. The young birds leave the nest when they are 2 months old, but it takes another 2 months before they can fend for themselves. An adult conure is approximately 18 inches long.

Peach-faced lovebird (*Agapornis roseicollis*)

Fischer's lovebird (*Agapornis fischeri*)

in groups, but during the mating season the pairs separate from the group to breed. It builds a nest from large plant material in which the female lays 3 to 5 eggs. She incubates the eggs for about 3 weeks. The young birds leave the nest when they are approximately 6 weeks old.

## Peach-faced lovebird (*Agapornis roseicollis*)

This lovebird is found in Africa, where it lives in noisy groups. It measures approximately 7 inches. There is no visible difference between the male and female. In contrast to most other birds of this order, the peach-faced lovebird makes its own nest from large twigs which it bites into narrow strips. It lays an average of 4 eggs, which are incubated by the female for 18 to 22 days. The young birds leave the nest when they are between 1 and 1.5 months old. The nestling is paler than its parents

and has a black beak. The peach-faced lovebird eats seeds, weeds and fruit.

## Budgerigar (*Melopsittacus undulatus*)

The budgerigar is a very social bird and great swarms inhabit the grass plains of Australia. Its diet consists mainly of (grass) seeds. It is easy to see the difference between the male and female adult bird: the male has a blue nose shell, while the nose shell of the female is of a browner color. The budgerigar does not build a nest, but searches for a suitable hollow in a tree. It lays 4 to 6 white eggs, which are incubated by the female for approximately 18 days. The young are fed by both parents and they can fend for themselves when they are 5 to 6 weeks old. An adult budgerigar is approximately 7 inches long. It is a very popular pet. As many color mutations have taken place, there are now

Budgerigar (*Melopsittacus undulatus*)

A budgerigar nestling.

Barred parakeet (*Bolborhynchus lineola*)

many different colors of budgerigar, such as blue, yellow, albino and multi-colored birds.

## Bourke's parrot
## (*Neophema bourkii*)

The Bourke's parrot inhabits the dry plains of central and southern Australia. It grows to a length of approximately 9 inches and its diet consists mainly of (grass) seeds. The Bourke's parrot is a very social, tolerant bird, which usually lives in groups on the ground. The female is usually slightly smaller than the male and has a smaller head. Only the male has the front blue head feathers. Once a pair is formed, the birds usually remain together for life. The Bourke's parrot lays 3 to 6 eggs on a soft, slightly damp base in the hollow of a tree. The eggs are incubated by the female for 18 to 20 days. The young birds can fend for themselves when they are 6 weeks old. The Bourke's parrot is

a productive bird and a single pair usually raises more than one brood each year. The young bird receives its adult color when it is approximately 8 months old.

## Barred parakeet
## (*Bolborhynchus lineola*)

This small parakeet, found in Central and South America, is a very social bird and lives in groups. It eats a variety of seeds and fruit. The male and female are not easily distinguished from each other, but the female is generally of a lighter green color and has less contrasting markings on her wings and quill feathers. It uses a hollow in a tree as a nest in which it lays an average of 4 eggs. The eggs are incubated by the female and take approximately 3 weeks to hatch. The male feeds his partner during this period so that she does not have to leave the eggs. The young leave the nest when they are approximately one month old. An adult barred parakeet is approximately 6.5 inches long.

Bourke's parrot (*Neophema bourkii*)

# Turacos, cuckoos and roadrunners (*Cuculiformes*)

Families: *Musophagidae and Cuculidae*

## Common cuckoo (*Cuculus canorus*)

The common cuckoo gets its common name from the unusual call of the male. It is a member of the family *Cuculidae* and is native to most of Europe and to Asia and North Africa. This solitary bird usually lives in wooded regions. In the spring, it migrates northward to lay its eggs. The female common cuckoo lays at least 8 eggs, each of which she lays in a different nest of a smaller species of (perching) bird. This typical characteristic is called brood parasitism. As soon as the young bird hatches, usually after approximately 12 days, it pushes any nestlings or eggs belonging to the host bird out of the nest so that it is the only bird in the nest which must be fed. This is necessary, because the young bird is usually much larger than the host parents and they have a lot of work keeping "their" hungry young bird happy. A young common cuckoo develops quickly and can fly when it is approximately 3 weeks old, although it is still cared for by its host parents for another week or two.

A young common cuckoo

The common cuckoo is predominantly insectivorous and grows to a length of approximately 13 inches. The common cuckoo is one of many species of birds which belong to the cuckoo family (*Cuculidae*).

## Roadrunner (*Geococcyx californianus*)

The roadrunner is native to the north of Central America and several of the southern US states, where it lives exclusively in vast semi-arid regions. The roadrunner can grow to a length of approximately 22.5 inches and weighs 1 pound. There is no visible difference between the male and the female. Once a pair is formed, the birds usually remain together and occupy a territory where no other birds of the same species are tolerated. As its common name suggests, it lives on the ground. It can fly, but prefers to run quickly when hunting or in danger. Its diet consists mainly of insects (mostly grasshoppers) and small reptiles, which it rummages for on the ground. Although it is a member of the cuckoo family (*Cuculidae*), it does not display the unusual characteristic of brood parasitism. It builds its own nest, usually in

Roadrunner (*Geococcyx californianus*)

a cactus or prickly bush and rears its own young.

## White-crested turaco (*Tauraco leucolophus*)

The white-crested turaco is, together with the other species of turacos, a member of the turaco family (*Musophagidae*). All turacos are found in Africa. The white-crested turaco is mostly found in Central Africa, where it lives in the trees of dense forests. It is unable to fly very well. An adult bird measures 18 inches, including its tail. The white-crested turaco eats mainly various types of fruit.

White-crested turaco (*Tauraco leucolophus*)

# Owls (*Strigiformes*)
Families: *Tytonidae and Strigidae*

## Eurasian pygmy owl (*Glaucidium passerinum*)

The Eurasian pygmy owl is distributed across an area which stretches from northern and Eastern Europe, through Russia, to China. It prefers to live in coniferous forests, where it hunts for small birds and mice at dusk and during the day. Once a pair is formed, the birds remain together, even outside the mating season. It builds its nest in the hollow of a tree, usually an abandoned woodpecker's nest. It lays approximately 6 eggs, which are incubated by the female for about 4 weeks. The

Eurasian pygmy owl (*Glaucidium passerinum*)

female rarely leaves the nest and is fed by the male, even after the eggs have hatched. The male then flies back and forth with food, which he gives to the female so that she can feed the young. The young pygmy owls leave the nest when they are approximately 1 month old. An adult pygmy owl grows to a length of approximately 6 inches and the female is heavier than the male. The Eurasian pygmy owl is a member of the owl family (*Strigidae*).

## Long-eared owl
## (*Asio otus*)

The long-eared owl is native to Europe, North America, Asia and Northern Africa. During the day, it remains hidden in the foliage, but at dusk and at night, it hunts for food. Its diet consists of a variety of small animals, including insects, moles, rodents, bats, reptiles and birds. It lives in groups outside the breeding season. It usually nests in an existing bird nest, but nests of long-eared owls have also been found in sheltered locations on the ground. It usually lays 5 eggs, which hatch after approximately 4 weeks. The young birds can fend for themselves when they are about 2 months old. An adult long-eared owl grows to a length of 15.5 inches. The long-eared owl is a member of the owl family (*Strigidae*).

Long-eared owl (*Asio otus*)

Great grey owl (*Strix nebulosa*)

## Great grey owl
## (*Strix nebulosa*)

The great grey owl is one of the largest and most noticeable species of owl and is only about an inch smaller than the Eurasian eagle owl. The great grey owl is found not only in northern Scandinavia, but also in many parts of northern Asia and northern regions of North America. It not only hunts for its food at night, but also during the day. Its diet consists almost entirely of mice. There is no visible difference between the male and female. The great grey owl sometimes nests in a nest abandoned by another species of bird or in the hollow of a tree. It lays an average of 4 eggs, which are incubated by the female for 1 month. The young birds remain with their parents for a long time, often until winter.

Spectacled owl (*Pulsatrix perspicillata*)

Milky eagle owl (*Bubo lacteus*)

## Spectacled owl (*Pulsatrix perspicillata*)

The spectacled owl grows to a length of approximately 17.5 inches and is found in Central America, as well as in South America in the region to the west of the Andes. It is not found in the southern parts of South America. The spectacled owl is a true forest dweller and hunts for food only at night. It eats a variety of live animals, such as amphibians, insects, small mammals and birds.

Eurasian eagle owl (*Bubo bubo*)

## Milky eagle owl (*Bubo lacteus*)

The milky eagle owl is also known by the name *Verreaux eagle owl*. It is found in parts of Africa (including Ethiopia), particularly in areas where many locust trees grow. This owl is active at dusk and at night. Its prey consists mainly of snakes and lizards. An adult measures between 23.5 and 25 inches.

Eurasian eagle owl (*Bubo bubo*)

Young Eurasian eagle owls (*Bubo bubo*)

## Eurasian eagle owl (*Bubo bubo*)

The Eurasian eagle owl grows to a length of approximately 28.5 inches and has a wingspan of approximately 67 inches and is one of the largest species of owl. The male is usually smaller than the female and has a lighter build. Although its main food source is rodents, its large size allows it to catch much larger prey as well. It is found in parts of Europe, North Africa and throughout Asia, except in Siberia and the southern peninsulas. It is a territorial bird. It builds its nest in a crack in a rock or in a hole in the ground. It lays 2 or 3 eggs, which hatch after 1 month. The young birds can fly when they are approximately 32 days old, but often remain with their parents until they are about six months old when they then leave their birthplace to search for their own territory.

## Hawk owl (*Surnia ulula*)

The hawk owl gets its common name from the fact that it looks like a hawk. It is widely distributed and is found in the northern parts of North America, Europe and Asia. In contrast to most species of owl, this bird is active during the day. Its diet consists mainly of mice, but it may catch small birds in flight. The hawk owl grows to a length of approximately 15 inches.

Hawk owl (*Surnia ulula*)

Snowy owl (*Nyctea scandiaca*)

## Snowy owl
## (*Nyctea scandiaca*)

The snowy owl inhabits the Arctic tundras in northern Scandinavia, Iceland, Greenland, Russia and Canada. With its predominantly white plumage, it is scarcely noticeable in the snowy regions where it lives. The feathers not only cover its body, but also a large part of its beak and feet so that it is well protected against the extreme cold. Besides its feathers, the bird has another form of protection—a layer of fat directly under the skin. The layer of fat not only works to keep the warmth in, but can also be drawn upon when food is scarce. The snowy owl eats lemmings and other small animals and will also eat carrion and birds during difficult times. Unlike most species of owl, it does not build its nest in a tree, but rather in a sheltered hole in the ground. The number of

eggs laid by the female can vary from 4 to 13. The eggs hatch after approximately 33 days. An adult snowy owl measures approximately 23 inches.

## Common barn owl
## (*Tyto alba*)

The common barn owl is widely distributed and is found throughout Europe, in many parts of Africa, India and several Asiatic islands, Australia, North and South America and in a large part of the United States. Measuring 15.5 inches, it is not a large species of owl. The color of the bird varies and it is darker in some regions than in others. The bird shown in the picture is a light variant, as found on the British Isles. The common barn owl is carnivorous and eats mainly small mammals. It often nests in a hollow tree, but

Common barn owl (*Tyto alba*)

# Nightjars, frogmouths, potoos and oilbirds (*Caprimulgiformes*)

Families: *Steatornithidae, Podargidae, Nyctibiidae, Aegothelidae and Caprimulgidae*

## Tawny frogmouth (*Podargus strigoides*)

The tawny frogmouth is a very striking inhabitant of the forested regions of Australia and Tasmania and is a member of the frogmouth family (*Podargidae*). It is nocturnal and hides in the foliage during the day. It eats a variety of animals, such as beetles, lizards and small rodents. If it is threatened, it assumes an unusual posture pointing its neck upwards, holding its beak upright and closing its eyes so that it can be easily overlooked. The bird

Tawny frogmouth (*Podargus strigoides*)

also lives near human settlements and is often seen breeding in church towers and barns. The common barn owl does not build a nest. It lays an average of 5 eggs, which are incubated exclusively by the female. The eggs hatch after one month and the young birds can already fly reasonably well when they are 2 months old. Like most species of owl, the common barn owl is nocturnal. It is the best-known member of the barn owl family (*Tytonidae*), which consists of approximately 14 different birds.

Common swift (*Apus apus*)

# Swifts and hummingbirds (*Apodiformes*)

Families: *Apodidae, Trochilidae and Hemiprocnidae*

## Common swift (*Apus apus*)

often sleeps in this position. The tawny frogmouth builds a large nest from twigs high in a tree. It lays between 2 and 4 eggs, which the female incubates for approximately 25 to 30 days. The young are fed by both parents and leave the nest when they are 5 weeks old. An adult tawny frogmouth has a total length of approximately 18 inches.

The common swift is found in Europe, parts of Asia, Siberia, and various parts of Africa, including Madagascar. It is a member of the swift family (*Apodidae*). It eats insects, which it catches in flight. It breeds in colonies and nests in a sheltered location, such as an alcove in a rock or a hollow tree. It lays 2 or 3 eggs, which are incubated by both parents for approximately 19 days. The young are fed and cared for by both parents and they leave the nest when they are approximately 6 weeks old. An adult bird is approximately 6 inches long.

## Common nightjar (*Caprimulgus europaeus*)

The common nightjar is the most common member of the large family of nightjars (*Caprimulgidae*) and is found in Europe, Africa and west Asia. As its common name suggests, it is a nocturnal bird. It eats a variety of insects, which it catches in flight. The common nightjar grows to a total length of approximately 10.5 inches. The easiest way to distinguish the male from the female is by the wings: the male has a white marking on the underside of the flight feathers which the female does not have. Its nest is often nothing more than a hole in the ground. The female lays 2 eggs, which are incubated by both parents. The eggs hatch after approximately 18 days and the young birds leave the nest 18 days later. When conditions are favorable, the common nightjar breeds twice in a single season.

Common swift (*Apus apus*)

Sparkling violet-ear (*Colibri coruscans*)

## Sparkling violet-ear
### (*Colibri coruscans*)

This species of hummingbird grows to a total length of 4.5 to 5.5 inches. As with most hummingbirds, this bird is very active during the day searching for, and collecting food. Its diet consists mainly of nectar, although it often catches insects in flight. This species of hummingbird is territorial and is only found alone or in pairs. It lays 2 eggs, which are incubated by both parents for approximately 16 days. The sparkling violet-ear is found in South America in a region which runs from Venezuela southward, through Bolivia, to northern Argentina. This species is a member of the hummingbird family (*Trochilidae*).

## Violet-bellied hummingbird
### (*Damophila julie*)

The violet-bellied hummingbird is found in open areas and at the edges of rain forests in a region stretching from the lowland plains of Panama to western Ecuador. It avoids heights. An adult violet-bellied hummingbird measures 3 inches. The female is somewhat smaller than the male and her belly is paler and lighter in color. It eats flower nectar. It usually lives alone and only looks for a mate during the breeding season which, depending on the region, lasts from March to June.

Violet-bellied hummingbird (*Damophila julie*)

# Kingfishers and allies
# (*Coraciiformes*)

Families: *Alcedinidae, Todidae, Momotidae, Meropidae, Coraciidae, Brachypteraciidae, Leptosomatidae, Upupidae, Phoeniculidae* and *Bucerotidae*

## Kookaburra
### (*Dacelo novaeguinae*)

The kookaburra is a member of the kingfisher family (*Alcedinidae*) and its length of approximately 17.5 inches makes it the largest member of this family. The kookaburra is found in Australia, where it lives in both urbanised and rural areas. Its diet consists mainly of small vertebrates, such as lizards, snakes, nestlings and rodents, although it may sometimes eat insects and also catches fish by diving into the water.

Kookaburra (*Dacelo novaeguinae*)

Blue-winged kookaburra (*Dacelo leachii*)

It usually builds its nest in a hollow tree, or sometimes in a hole at the edge of the water or in a termite nest. It lays 2 to 4 eggs, which hatch after approximately 25 days. The kookaburra is known for its very loud, laughing call.

## Blue-winged kookaburra (*Dacelo leachii*)

The blue-winged kookaburra is also a member of the kingfisher family. It is found in northern Australia, Southern New Guinea and in Tasmania. Its diet consists of animals, such as birds and amphibians. An adult bird measures approximately 16 inches.

## Common kingfisher (*Alcedo atthis*)

This member of the family *Alcedinidae* is found in certain areas of Europe, North Africa and certain parts of Asia. The common kingfisher usually lives near water in wooded areas. Its diet consists mainly of

small fish and other aquatic animals, which it catches with a well-aimed dive into the water from an overhanging branch, but it may also eat insects. It is a solitary bird. There is no visible difference between the male and female. It

Common kingfisher (*Alcedo atthis*)

149

builds its nest, which has a long entrance, in a hole along the edge of the water. It lays an average of 6 to 8 white eggs, which the parents take turns incubating. The eggs hatch after approximately 3 weeks. The young birds develop very quickly and are often independent when they are only one month old. The common kingfisher raises 2 or 3 broods per season. It grows to a length of approximately 6 inches.

## Abyssinian ground hornbill (*Bucorvus abyssinicus*)

The Abyssinian ground hornbill is a member of the hornbill family (*Bucerotidae*) and lives in various African countries, including Gambia and Kenya. It eats a variety of small and larger animals, such as large grasshoppers, snakes and small rodents. The female usually lays 2 eggs, which hatch after 28 days. The young birds usually remain in the nest for 3

Trumpeter hornbill (*Ceratogymna bucinator*)

Abyssinian ground hornbill (*Bucorvus abyssinicus*)

Wrinkled hornbill (*Aceros corrugatus*)

months until they can reasonably fend for themselves. An adult Abyssinian ground hornbill can be more than 3 feet in height and weigh between 7.5 and 11 pounds.

## Wrinkled hornbill (*Aceros corrugatus*)

The wrinkled hornbill is a member of the hornbill family (*Bucerotidae*) and is found in Malaysia, Borneo and Sumatra. This bird lives in pairs outside the mating season, although the various pairs spend a good deal of time together during this period. The wrinkled hornbill eats a variety of fruit and seeds, but during the mating season, it also eats insects and nestlings. Like most members of this bird family, the wrinkled hornbill makes its nest in a hollow tree. The opening is covered well with clay and dung so that only a very small opening through which the male feeds the female remains. The wrinkled hornbill usually lays 2 or 3 eggs. The female always sits on the eggs and even after the eggs have hatched, some 4 weeks later, she will still have not left the nest. The male continues to feed the young until they leave the nest. An adult wrinkled hornbill is approximately 25.5 inches long and weighs 3 pounds.

## Trumpeter hornbill
### (*Ceratogymna bucinator*)

The trumpeter hornbill is a member of the hornbill family (*Bucerotidae*) and lives in small groups in the dense forests of East and Central Africa. Its diet consists mainly of fruit, but it may also eat insects and similar animals, which it catches in trees. An adult measures 23.5 inches on average.

## Great Indian hornbill
### (*Buceros bicornis*)

The great Indian hornbill is found in southeast Asia, where it usually lives in dense forests. It is omnivorous. The sexes can be distinguished not only by their size–the female is smaller and has a smaller bill–but also by the color of the iris. The iris of the male is red, while that of the female is light blue. The male great Indian hornbill can grow to a total length of 55 inches, including its tail and enormous

A male great Indian hornbill (*Buceros bicornis*)

A female great Indian hornbill (*Buceros bicornis*)

bill. The female great Indian hornbill searches for a hollow in a tree to lay her eggs and covers the opening as much as possible with clay and her own dung. The male then feeds the female through the small opening that remains. The great Indian hornbill lays 1 to 3 eggs, which are incubated by the female for approximately one month.

## Red-billed hornbill
### (*Tockus erythrorhynchus*)

The red-billed hornbill is found on the savannahs in the west, east and southeast of Africa. Just like the great Indian hornbill, this bird is a member of the hornbill family. The red-billed hornbill has excellent flying abilities but spends a lot of time on the ground rummaging for food. It eats large insects, such as beetles and grasshoppers, but will sometimes also rob nests. It builds its nest and raises its young

in the same way as the wrinkled hornbill. It lays an average of 4 eggs, which hatch after 24 days.

## Pied hornbill
## (*Tockus fasciatus*)

The pied hornbill is found in Africa, particularly in Zambia and Angola. It eats fruit, insects and other small animals. The pied hornbill is a hole-nesting bird and builds its nest from plant material in a hole in a tree. The entrance to the nest is almost completely covered so that only a small crack remains. The female remains in the nest while the male brings her food.

## Common hoopoe
## (*Upupa epops*)

This crested bird is carnivorous and eats small animals, such as caterpillars, grass-

Common hoopoe (*Upupa epops*)

hoppers and worms. The common hoopoe is found in large parts of Europe, Asia and almost all of Africa. During the mating season, this striking bird lives in the northern regions of its habitat and spends the winter in southern Asia and Africa. It builds its nest in the hollow of a tree or a rock in which it lays an average of 5 eggs. The female incubates the eggs for 15 or 16 days, during which time the male supplies her with food. The young birds leave the nest when they are approximately one month old. An adult bird measures approximately 12 inches. The common hoopoe is the only member of the hoopoe family (*Upupidae*).

Pied hornbill (*Tockus fasciatus*)

# Woodpeckers, barbets, honey guides and toucans (*Piciformes*)

Families: *Galbulidae, Bucconidae, Capitonidae, Indicatoridae, Ramphastidae and Picidae*

## Toco toucan (*Ramphastos toco*)

The toco toucan is the largest living species of toucan; an adult measures approximately 23.5 inches. It is found in eastern South Africa and is a member of the family *Ramphastidae*. Its enormous bill is undoubtedly the most striking characteristic of this forest inhabitant. The toco toucan lives in small groups and eats mainly a variety of fruits, as well as insects, molluscs, eggs and nestlings. Like other toucans, the toco toucan tends to lay its eggs in the same place each year, usually in a hole in a tree far from the ground. Both parents incubate the eggs. The young toco toucans develop rather slowly; they often remain in the nest for 8

Toco toucan (*Ramphastos toco*)

to 9 weeks. The toco toucan is a member of the toucan family (*Ramphastidae*).

## Red-billed toucan (*Ramphastos tucanus*)

The colorful red-billed toucan is found in the northeast of South America, where it usually lives in pairs in dense forests. It has a very varied diet and eats nuts and fruits, as well as eggs, nestlings and birds,

Red-billed toucan (*Ramphastos tucanus*)

European great spotted woodpecker (*Dendrocopos major*)

small reptiles and a variety of insects. The red-billed toucan grows to a length of approximately 20.5 inches.

A female black-cheeked woodpecker (*Melanerpes pucherani*)

## European great spotted woodpecker (*Dendrocopos major*)

The European great spotted woodpecker is a member of the woodpecker family (*Spicidae*) and is found throughout Europe, in a large part of Asia and in the northwest of Africa. Some populations spend the winter in their breeding ground, while others migrate southward. The European great spotted woodpecker eats mainly pinecone seeds, but also eats insects which live on tree trunks. It uses its strong beak to chop a suitable hole in a tree trunk for a nest. The female lays 4 to 7 eggs, which are incubated by both parents for approximately 16 days. The young birds leave the nest when

A male black-cheeked woodpecker (*Melanerpes pucherani*)

A male black woodpecker (*Dryocopus martius*)

A female black woodpecker (*Dryocopus martius*)

they are approximately 3 weeks old. The top of the bird's head is red in infancy, but this later turns completely black on the female, while a red speck remains on the back of the male's head. The European great spotted woodpecker is approximately 9 inches long.

## Black-cheeked woodpecker
## (*Melanerpes pucherani*)

The black-cheeked woodpecker is a small, active species of woodpecker which eats a variety of insects and their larvae. It searches for its food between the bark of trees. It is an exception to the woodpecker family, because almost all other species of woodpecker search for food by drilling straight through the bark of trees. The black-cheeked woodpecker drills through the bark only to build its nest. Although insects and their larvae are its main food source, the black-billed woodpecker also eats berries and nectar. It lays an average of 3 eggs, which hatch after about 2 weeks.

The black-cheeked woodpecker is found in Central America and several northern countries in South America. It is approximately 7.5 inches long.

## Black woodpecker
## (*Dryocopus martius*)

The black woodpecker is a member of the woodpecker family (*Picidae*). This fairly large species of woodpecker is found mainly in Europe and Asia, as far away as Mongolia. It lives in wooded areas and eats a variety of animals that it finds in and on the bark of trees. The sexes can be distinguished easily by the red marking on the top of the head. On the male, the marking extends to the tip of the beak, while only the back of the female's head is red. The nest is dug out of a tree trunk in which it lays an average of 4 eggs. Both parents incubate the eggs for approximately 2 weeks. The young birds leave the nest when they are approximately one month old.

155

# Perching birds
## (*Passeriformes*)

Families: *Eurylaimidae, Dendrocolaptidae, Furnariidae, Formicariidae, Conopophagidae, Rhinocryptidae, Contingidae, Pipridae, Tyrannidae, Oxyruncidae, Phytotomidae, Pittadae, Acanthisittidae, Philepittidae, Menuridae, Atrichornithidae, Alaudidae, Hirundinidae, Motacillidae, Campephagidae, Pycnonotidae, Irenidae, Laniidae, Vangidae, Bombycillidae, Dulidae, Cinclidae, Troglodytidae, Mimidae, Prunellidae, Turdidae, Timaliidae, Chamaeidae, Paradoxornithidae, Picathartidae, Polioptilidae, Sylviidae, Regulidae, Maluridae, Ephthianuridae, Acanthizidae, Monarchidae (subfamily; Rhipidurinae), Platysteiridae, Muscicapidae, Eopsaltriidae, Pachycephalidae, Aegithalidae, Remizidae, Paridae, Hyposittidae, Daphoenositttiae, Tichodromadidae, Sittidae, Certhiidae, Salpornithidae, Rhabdornithidae, Climactheridae, Dicaeidae, Zosteropidae, Nectariniidae, Promeropidae, Meliphagidae, Emberizidae, Catamblyrhynchidae, Cardinalidae, Thraupidae, Tersinidae, Coerebidae, Cyclarhidae, Vireolaniidae, Vireonidae, Parulidae, Drepanididae, Icteridae, Fringillidae, Estrildidae, Viduinae, Ploceidae, Sturnidae, Priolidae, Dicruridae, Callaeidae, Grallinidae, Artamidae, Cracticidae, Ptilonorhynchidae, Paradisaeidae and Corvidae.*

## Black-billed magpie
## (*Pica pica*)

The black-billed magpie is a member of the crow family (*Corvidae*). It is found throughout Europe, Canada, the northern

Black-billed magpie (*Pica pica*)

Black-billed magpie (*Pica pica*)

United States, parts of Asia and North Africa. It can grow to a length of 21.5 inches, including its tail. The black-billed magpie eats mainly nestlings, amphibians, insects and worms, but also eats fruit and similar food. It builds a nest in a tree during the breeding season. The female lays approximately 6 eggs, which are incubated mostly by her for about 17 days. During this period, she hardly leaves the nest and is fed by her partner. The young birds leave the nest when they are 3 to 4 weeks old, but often remain close to their parents for quite some time. Most young birds leave only at the start of the breeding season the following year.

## Eurasian jay
## (*Garrulus glandarius*)

The Eurasian jay is found throughout Europe, North Africa and a large part of Asia. It inhabits mainly deciduous forests but is often also found in gardens and parks. Its diet consists of insects, worms, small mammals, eggs, nestlings, fruit, seeds and berries. A typical characteristic of this bird is that it sometimes buries non-perishable food so that it will have something to eat when food is scarce. The Eurasian jay is solitary outside the mating season. It builds a nest in the shelter of a large tree in which it lays an average of 5 to 7 eggs. The eggs are incubated by the female for about 18 days. The young are fed by both parents and can often fend for themselves when they are 4 weeks old. An adult Eurasian jay measures approximately 13 inches. The Eurasian jay is a member of the crow family (*Corvidae*).

## Jackdaw
## (*Corvus monedula*)

The jackdaw is also a member of the crow family (*Corvidae*). It is found throughout Europe, but not in northern Scandinavia. It is also common in large parts of Asia and certain areas in North Africa. Certain populations, particularly those which live in northern regions, migrate southward before the winter sets in. Other populations remain at their breeding ground throughout the winter. The jackdaw lives in groups and is not fussy about its habitat. It is found in a variety of locations, ranging from abandoned mountain slopes to busy cities. The bird is not fussy about its nest, either; it may build its nest in a tree, on a rock or on a building. The nest, which can be quite large, is built by both parents using twigs, leaves, animal hair and similar material. It lays approximately 5 eggs of a light greenish-brown color with dark speckles, which are incubated by the female for 2 to 3 weeks. Both

Eurasian jay (*Garrulus glandarius*)

parents feed the young. They grow quickly and leave the nest after one month. The jackdaw is omnivorous. It adapts to conditions and can eat seeds and berries, as well as insects, nestlings and carrion. There is no visible difference between the male and female. An adult jackdaw is approximately 13 inches long.

Jackdaw (*Corvus monedula*) collecting nesting material.

Jackdaw (*Corvus monedula*)

## Rook (*Corvus frugilegus*)

The rook is approximately 19.5 inches long and weighs between 1 and 1.5 pounds. It is predominantly carnivorous and its diet varies from worms and insects to small mammals, although it may also eat seeds and nuts. The rook breeds in colonies and builds its nest in tall trees, sometimes with dozens of grouped nests. It lays an average of 4 eggs, which are incubated by the female for approximately 18 days. During this period, the male feeds the female so that she does not have to leave the eggs. The young birds leave the nest when they are approximately 5 weeks old. The rook is found throughout Europe and a large part of Asia. After the breeding season, it migrates southward in groups. A rook can live for as long as 20 years. It is a member of the crow family (*Corvidae*).

## Nutcracker (*Nucifraga caryocatactes*)

The nutcracker lives mainly in the Russian taiga but small populations are also found in certain parts of Europe. The bird always looks for the shelter of coniferous trees. It lays an average of 4 eggs, which hatch after approximately 17 days. The young birds are almost fully independent when they are 4 weeks old. The nutcracker eats a variety of seeds and insects, but gets its common name from the nuts which make up most of its diet when they are in season. The nutcracker is a member of the crow family (*Corvidae*).

## Carrion crow (*Corvus corone*)

The carrion crow is a very common bird in Europe, particularly in Central and Western Europe. It prefers to live on open arable land and in urban areas. The carrion crow is omnivorous and eats grain and berries, as well as eggs and carrion. There is no visible difference between the male and female. The carrion crow reaches sexual maturity when it is about 4 years old. It builds a large nest from all sorts of raw material in a high tree in which it lays an average of 5 eggs. The eggs are incubated exclusively by the female and hatch after almost 3 weeks. The young are fed by both parents and leave the nest when they are approximately 4 to 5 weeks old. Independent young birds form (large) groups until they are old enough to breed.

Carrion crow (*Corvus corone*)

## Superb starling
## (*Lamprotornis superbus*)

The superb starling is found in eastern Africa and grows to a length of approximately 7.5 inches. There is no visible difference between the male and female. Its diet consists of berries, fruit and a variety of insects and worms. It lays an average of 3 to 4 eggs with a bluish-green shell, which hatch after approximately 13 days. The young are fed by both parents. They leave the nest when they are approximately 3 weeks old and can fend for themselves when they are 5 to 6 weeks old. The superb starling is a member of the starling family (*Sturnidae*).

## Golden-breasted starling
## (*Cosmopsarus regius*)

This brightly colored, gregarious starling is found in eastern Africa. It is omnivorous and eats insects, molluscs, fruit, berries and seeds. There is no difference in color between the male and female, although the male is somewhat larger and has a longer tail. It lays an average of 3 eggs, which are incubated mainly by the female. The eggs hatch after approximately 2 weeks. The young are fed mainly with insects and insect larvae. The young birds leave the nest after 3 weeks, but are still accompanied by the parents for some

Golden-breasted starling (*Cosmopsarus regius*)

Superb starling (*Lamprotornis superbus*)

The young of a superb starling (*Lamprotornis superbus*)

time. An adult golden-breasted starling measures 12.5 to 14 inches.

## Hill mynah
## (*Gracula religiosa*)

Various subspecies of the hill mynah are found in Asia, including Indonesia, China, India and Sri Lanka. The main difference between the subspecies is their size; the largest species measures 12 inches and the smallest is 10 inches. There is no visible difference between the male and female of this gregarious bird. Its diet consists of insects and fruit. It usually lays 2 bluish-green eggs with light brown speckles. The eggs hatch after 2 weeks and the young birds leave the nest when they are

Hill mynah (*Gracula religiosa*)

4 weeks old. The hill mynah is a member of the starling family (*Sturnidae*).

## Common starling (*Sturnus vulgaris*)

The common starling is common in Europe and temperate areas of western Asia. It spends the winter in more southern areas. The species has also been introduced in various countries, including Australia, South Africa and North America. It searches for insects and worms on the ground. It is a very active bird. It is social, but splits off into pairs during the breed-

Common starling (*Sturnus vulgaris*)

ing season. It builds its nest in a (tree) hollow in which it lays approximately 5 light blue eggs. The eggs are incubated by both parents and hatch after approximately 13 days. An adult common starling measures approximately 8 inches.

## Bali mynah (*Leucopsar rothschildi*)

With its snow-white plumage, its black wings and tail end and the bright blue rings around its eyes, the Bali mynah is undoubtedly the most colorful species of the alredy colorful starling family. The Bali mynah is found in Indonesia, where it mainly lives in dense forests. Its diet consists of fruit and insects. Outside the breeding season, the males and females live harmoniously in large groups, but during the breeding season, the birds split

Bali mynah (*Leucopsar rothschildi*)

off into pairs. There is no visible differ-ence between the male and female. It builds its nest in the hollow of a tree in which it usually lays 3 to 5 eggs. An adult Bali mynah is approximately 10 inches long.

## Fairy bluebird
## (*Irena puella*)

The fairy bluebird is approximately 10 to 10.5 inches long and is a member of the iora, leafbird and fairy bluebird family (*Irenidae*). This species is found in parts of Asia, particularly in the southeast and, just like the Bali mynah, is a true forest dweller. The sexes can be distinguished easily by the color of the feathers. The male is a deep black with shiny blue plumage, while the female does not have any black markings and the blue is of

A female fairy bluebird (*Irena puella*)

a different shade. The fairy bluebird eats soft fruit and honey. It builds a nest in a tree using a variety of soft plant materi-al in which it lays an average of 2 eggs.

## White-eared catbird
## (*Ailuroedus buccoides*)

The white-eared catbird is a member of the bowerbird family (*Ptilonorhynchi-dae*). It is found in the dense rain forests of New Guinea and the neighboring islands. The white-eared catbird eats fruit and small animals and lays between 1 and 3 eggs.

A male fairy bluebird (*Irena puella*).

White-eared catbird (*Ailuroedus buccoides*)

Golden oriole (*Oriolus oriolus*)

## Golden oriole
## (*Oriolus oriolus*)

The golden oriole is a very brightly colored bird and is a member of the golden oriole and fig-bird family (*Oriolidae*). It is found in Europe, western Asia and North Africa. It is not found in cold northern regions and spends the winter in Africa and Southern Asia. The golden oriole prefers to live in the protection of large groups. It eats insects, fruit and berries. The male can be recognised by its brightly colored yellow plumage and the contrasting brown and black markings on its wings. The female is somewhat smaller and less spectacularly colored. Its nest is an ingenious construction which practically hangs from a branch. It lays an average of 4 eggs, which are incubated by the female for 2 weeks. The golden oriole is approximately 8.5 inches long.

## Bohemian waxwing
## (*Bombycilla garrulus*)

The Bohemian waxwing is a member of the waxwing family (*Bombycillidae*). Its natural habitat lies in the most northern coniferous forests of Asia, Europe and North America, where it finds an abundance of mosquitoes and berries, which form its main food source. The nest is built by the male and female in a tree or bush. It lays 4 to 6 eggs, which are incubated exclusively by the female for approximately 13 days. The young are fed by both parents for 2 or more weeks with small flying insects, particularly mosquitoes. The Bohemian waxwing is approximately 8 inches long, including the tail.

## Blue-faced honeyeater
## (*Entomyzon cyanotis*)

The blue-faced honeyeater is an active and inquisitive bird and is a member of the honeyeater family (*Meliphagidae*). With a length of 12.5 inches, it is one of the largest honeyeaters found in Australia. Besides eastern Australia, this bird is also found in certain regions of New Guinea. The blue-faced honeyeater is often found in or close to towns and villages. It eats mainly nectar, which it easily extracts from flowers using its bristly tongue. It also eats fruit and insects. The female lays 1 or 2 eggs, which hatch after 2 weeks.

Bohemian waxwing (*Bombycilla garrulus*)

Blue-faced honeyeater (*Entomyzon cyanotis*)

Seven-coloured tanager (*Tangara fastuosa*)

## Seven-colored tanager (*Tangara fastuosa*)

The seven-colored tanager is a member of the tanager family (*Thraupidae*). It is found in eastern Brazil where it prefers to live in trees. It eats mainly nectar and fruit. The male of this species can be recognised by its brighter colors. Seven-colored tanagers often build their nests close to each other. It lays an average of 3 eggs, which hatch after 3 weeks and another 3 weeks later, the young birds leave the nest. An adult measures approximately 7.5 inches, including the tail.

## Common swallow (*Hirundo rustica*)

The common swallow is a member of the swallow family (*Hirundinidae*). It spends the winter in southern regions, such as South Africa and southern Asia and breeds in northern regions, as far north as Russia, Canada and Scandinavia. It often builds its ingenious nest under the eaves of a building using clay. The common swallow lays an average of 5 eggs, which are incubated by the female for 2 weeks. The young are fed by both parents and they leave the nest when they are 3 weeks old. The young birds are then helped for about another week before they can fend for themselves. The common swallow usually nests twice in a single year, although it may nest three times if conditions are favorable. It eats a variety of insects, most of which it catches in flight.

Common swallow (*Hirundo rustica*)

163

White-spotted laughing thrush (*Garrulax ocellatus*)

## White-spotted laughing thrush (*Garrulax ocellatus*)

The white-spotted laughing thrush is a member of the babbler family (*Timaliidae*) and can grow to a length of approximately 12.5 inches. It is seldom seen in the open and prefers to remain in wooded regions, although it is not a particularly shy bird. Its natural habitat stretches from China to the Himalayas. The white-spotted laughing thrush is a social bird and eats a variety of food, including fruit, seeds, insects and worms. There is no visible difference between the male and female.

## Red-billed leiothrix (*Leiothrix lutea*)

This perching bird is found in southeast Asia and is approximately 6 inches long.

Red-billed leiothrix (*Leiothrix lutea*)

The sexes cannot be distinguished easily, although the female is sometimes not as colorful as the male. The male can always be recognised, however, by his song. The red-billed leiothrix eats a variety of insects and their larvae, as well as eggs, worms, berries and soft fruit. It is a very active bird, which prefers to live in foliage. It lives in small groups outside the breeding season. It builds its nest in a thick bush in which it lays approximately 3 or 4 light blue-green eggs with brown speckles. Only the female incubates the eggs, which hatch after approximately 12 days. The young red-billed leiothrixes leave the nest when they are approximately 14 days old, but can fend for themselves only when they are 5 or 6 weeks old. The bird gets its final coloring when it is approximately 3 months old. The red-billed leiothrix is a member of the babbler family (*Timaliidae*).

## European nuthatch (*Sitta europaea*)

The European nuthatch is a small, active bird which eats insects and seeds. There is no visible difference between the male and female. It builds its nest in a cavity,

European nuthatch (*Sitta europaea*)

White wagtail
(*Motacilla alba*)

which can be either a tree hollow or a suitable bird box. The cavity is filled with soil and tree bark, so that the nest is enclosed on all sides, except for a small opening at the front. The female lays approximately 6 eggs, which she incubates for about 2 weeks. The European nuthatch is a sedentary bird and is found in large parts of Europe and Asia. An adult European nuthatch measures approximately 5.5 inches. It is a member of the nuthatch family (*Sittidae*).

## White wagtail
## (*Motacilla alba*)

The white wagtail is only one of the many species of wagtail found in Europe and it is distributed far into Asia and North Africa. During the winter, some populations can be found in southern regions (its regional habitat), while others are sedentary. The species is a member of the wag-

Great tit (*Parus major*)

tail and pipit family (*Motacillidae*). The white wagtail is not fussy about its habitat and is found both in dense woodland and in open, developed areas. During the breeding season, a pair occupies a territory in which no other wagtail is permitted. The nest is built by both parents from a variety of plant and animal material, usually in a protected, partially covered, location. It lays an average of 5 eggs, which are incubated by the female for 14 days. The young are fed by both parents and leave the nest when they are approximately 2 weeks old.

## Great tit
## (*Parus major*)

The great tit is a small, brightly colored bird belonging to the titmouse family (*Paridae*). The sexes can be distinguished by the broad black strip which runs from the throat to the tail on the male–it is smaller and shorter on the female. It nests in a cavity. In urban regions, the bird sometimes nests in a small, closed bird box in a garden; otherwise, it nests in a hole in a tree. The great tit lays a large number of eggs, sometimes as many as 14, which are incubated by the female for approximately 14 days. During this period, she does not leave the nest and the male flies back and forth with food, which consists mainly of a variety of small insects and seeds. The young birds can fend for themselves when they are 4 to 5 weeks old. The great tit is found in Europe, North Africa and Asia. Some populations migrate southward after the breeding season, although most great tits are sedentary.

## Zebra finch
## (*Poephila guttata*)

The zebra finch is found in Australia and is approximately 4 inches long. The male can be recognised by the orange-brown markings on its cheeks. It is a very social bird and lives in large flocks. It is predominantly herbivorous and eats food such as grass seeds. It lays 4 to 6 very light green eggs, which hatch after 12 to 13 days. The young birds can fend for themselves when they are 5 weeks old. The zebra finch is one of the most popular aviary birds and breeders have produced dozens, if not hundreds, of color variations. The original common name no longer suits this domesticated bird since it refers to the black-and-white stripes on the tail of the wild bird. The zebra finch is a member of the waxbill family (*Estrildidae*).

Zebra finch (*Poephila guttata*)

A zebra finch nestling (*Poephila guttata*).

Star finch (*Neochmia ruficauda*)

## Star finch
## (*Neochmia ruficauda*)

The star finch is found in northern Australia. It is a gregarious bird and eats mainly seeds. The sexes can be distinguished easily by the mask and the color of the belly; the male has a slightly larger face and its belly has a darker color. It builds a nest in a sheltered bush in which it lays 4 or 5 eggs. The eggs are incubated by both parents and hatch after 12 days. Both parents feed the young. They can fly when they are 3 weeks old, but cannot fend for themselves for another 2 weeks. An adult star finch measures 4 to 4.5 inches.

## Red-billed fire finch
## (*Lagonosticta senegala*)

The red-billed fire finch is found mainly in West Africa. Its diet primarily consists of small seeds, but it sometimes also eats insects. The male is a deep red color, while the female has a paler, beige to brown plumage. It usually builds a small nest in a sheltered bush in which it lays 3 to 4 eggs. The eggs are incubated by both parents and hatch after approximately 11 days. The young are fed by both parents. An adult measures 4 inches, including the tail. The red-billed fire finch is a member of the waxbill family (*Estrildidae*).

Red-billed fire finch (*Lagonosticta senegala*)

Long-tailed finch (*Poephila acuticauda*)

## Black-throated finch (*Poephila cincta*)

The black-throated finch is found on the grass plains in the north-east of Australia and is approximately 4.5 inches long. It is difficult to distinguish the sexes, although the markings on the throat are slightly more elongated on the female. The black-throated finch eats mainly grass seeds, but may sometimes also eat small insects. It lays 6 eggs on average, which hatch after 11 or 12 days. The young birds leave the nest when they are 3 weeks old, but can

fend for themselves only when they are approximately 5 weeks old.

## Long-tailed finch (*Poephila acuticauda*)

This Australian waxbill lives in large groups. It mainly eats a variety of grass seeds, but may sometimes supplement this with small insects. There is no noticeable visible difference between the male and female, although the black band on the male is somewhat larger and the tail is

Black-throated finch (*Poephila cincta*)

often somewhat longer. It builds a nest in a sheltered bush or tree in which it lays an average of 5 eggs. The eggs are incubated by both parents and hatch after approximately 11 days. The young leave the nest when they are 3 weeks old, although they still need their parents' help and must be fed until they can fend for themselves when they are 5 to 6 weeks old. The long-tailed finch can grow to a length of approximately 6 inches.

## Green-winged pytilia
## (*Pytilia melba*)

The green-winged pytilia originates from Africa and is approximately 5 inches long. Like most waxbills, the green-winged pytilia eats mainly seeds, but supplements its diet with insects. The male of this species can be recognised by the red on the top of its head and throat. The bird builds a nest in a sheltered bush in which it lays an average of 4 eggs. The eggs are incubated by both parents for approximately 12 days. The young leave the nest when they are approximately 3 weeks old. The young birds have a paler plumage than their parents and their bill is not yet red. It gets its final coloring when it is approximately 6 months old.

Green-winged pytilia (*Pytilia melba*)

## Java sparrow
## (*Padda oryzivora*)

The Java sparrow is found in Indonesia, South China and the Philippines. The bird is usually 5 to 5.5 inches long. It is sometimes also called the ricebird because it has a fondness for rice, which makes up most of its diet. There is no visible difference between the male and female. The nest is built mostly by the male. The female lays 4 to 6 white eggs, which are incubated by both parents for approximately 13 days. The young are fed by both parents with plant and animal matter. The young birds leave the nest after 28 to 32 days, but can fend for themselves only 2 weeks later. The Java sparrow is a member of the waxbill family (*Estrildidae*).

Java sparrow (*Padda oryzivora*)

Orange-cheeked waxbill (*Estrilda melpoda*)

A young black-headed Gouldian finch (*Chloebia gouldiae*)

## Orange-cheeked waxbill (*Estrilda melpoda*)

The orange-cheeked waxbill is approximately 4 inches long and lives in large groups in Africa. There is no visible difference between the male and female. It builds its nest either on or close to the ground. It lays an average of 4 to 6 white eggs, which are incubated by both parents for approximately 12 days. The young birds leave the nest when they are about 2 weeks old and can fend for themselves when they are 5 weeks old.

An adult red-headed Gouldian finch (*Chloebia gouldiae*).

## Gouldian finch (*Chloebia gouldiae*)

The Gouldian finch is a very colorful bird which is a well-known aviary bird, like many of the small birds belonging to the waxbill family. Flocks of Gouldian finches inhabit northern Australia, where they eat a variety of grass seeds. There are three different colors of Gouldian finch, one with a black head, a red head and an orange head. Despite the difference in color, they are all of the same species and they even crossbreed with each other. The black-headed variant is the most common. Through careful observation, the female can be distinguished from the male by her duller plumage. Furthermore, the female's bill is dark grey during the breeding season. It builds a small nest either on or under the ground. It lays 4 to 8 eggs, which hatch after 14 days or so. The

Common waxbill (*Estrilda astrild*)

Serin (*Serinus serinus*)

young birds leave the nest when they are older than 3 weeks. An adult Gouldian finch is approximately 5 inches long.

## Common waxbill
## (*Estrilda astrild*)

This species is found in Ethiopia, where it lives either on the grassland plains, in wooded regions or close to humans. The common waxbill lives in small to very large groups. Its diet consists mainly of grass seeds. It builds a pear-shaped nest in a sheltered location in the foliage. It lays approximately 5 eggs, which are incubated by both parents for 11 to 13 days. The young are fed mainly small insects and they leave the nest when they are approximately 3 weeks old. The common waxbill is approximately 4 inches long.

## Serin
## (*Serinus serinus*)

The serin is approximately 4 to 4.5 inches long and is found throughout North America and Europe, except in Scandinavia and the British Isles. It spends the summer in the northern regions of its habitat and migrates southward after the breeding season, usually in October. Its diet consists mainly of grass seeds and the seeds of weeds. It builds a semi-open, circular nest from a variety of fine material in a sheltered location in a tree. It lays an average of 4 eggs, which are incubated mainly by the female. The eggs hatch after approximately 13 days and the young birds leave the nest another 13 days later. The serin often breeds twice in a single year. The serin is a member of the chaffinch family (*Fringillidae*).

## Yellow-fronted canary
## (*Serinus mozambicus*)

This gregarious bird is approximately 4 inches long and is found in tropical Africa. Its diet consists mainly of seeds. The female can be distinguished from the male by her chain-like dark breast markings, which the male does not have. The

Yellow-fronted canary (*Serinus mozambicus*)

yellow-fronted canary builds a nest in a sheltered location in which it usually lays 3 eggs. The eggs are a white to light blue color with red-brown speckles. The eggs are incubated mostly by the female and hatch after 13 days. The young are fed by both parents and leave the nest when they are 3 weeks old. The yellow-fronted canary is a member of the chaffinch family (*Fringillidae*).

## Common bullfinch
## (*Pyrrhula pyrrhula*)

The common bullfinch grows to a length of 5.5 to 6.5 inches. It eats a variety of seeds, flower buds and berries, but may sometimes also eat small insects. The sexes can be distinguished easily: the male has a bright pinkish-red breast, while the female has a far more modest color. Only the male sings. The common bullfinch lives in pairs and the parents become very devoted to each other. The female builds a bowl-shaped nest in which she lays 4 to 5 light blue to light greenish-brown, speckled eggs. The eggs hatch after approximately 12 to 14 days. The young birds leave the nest when they are approximately 14 days old. Various subspecies are found in large parts of the world, from Europe to deep into Asia. The common bullfinch is a member of the chaffinch family (*Fringillidae*).

## Red crossbill
## (*Loxia curvirostra*)

The red crossbill gets its common name from its unusual bill which has evolved to facilitate the eating of its main food source: pinecone seeds. It is found in the coniferous forests of Europe, North America and Asia. The sexes can be distin-

Common bullfinch (*Pyrrhula pyrrhula*)

Red crossbill (*Loxia curvirostra*)

guished by their color. The male is red, while the female is yellow-green. The red crossbill builds a very large nest with thick walls in which it lays approximately 3 eggs. The female incubates the eggs for about 2 weeks, during which time she does not leave the nest and is fed by her partner. The young birds leave the nest when they are 3 weeks old, or younger. The red crossbill is a member of the chaffinch family (*Fringillidae*).

## European goldfinch
## (*Carduelis carduelis*)

The European goldfinch is found in Europe, West and central Asia and North America. It prefers to eat thistle seeds, but also eats other seeds, berries and insects. Both sexes look the same and both sing, although the song of the male is richer. It lays 3 to 6 light blue eggs with brown specks. The eggs are incubated by the female and hatch after approximately 14 days. The young birds leave the nest after 2 to 3 weeks, but are fed and accompa-

nied by their parents for a further 3 weeks. Depending on the subspecies, an adult goldfinch is between 4.5 to 6.5 inches long.

## Chaffinch
## (*Fringilla coelebs*)

The chaffinch is native to Europe, North Africa, parts of the Middle East and temperate areas of Asia. During the breeding season, the sexes can be distinguished easily by their color. The male, with its

Chaffinch (*Fringilla coelebs*)

European goldfinch (*Carduelis carduelis*)

Ultramarine grosbeak (*Cyanocompss/Passerina brissoni*)

silver-grey and rust colored markings, is much more colorful than the predominantly brown female. Only the male of this species sings. The chaffinch grows to a length of 6 to 6.5 inches. It is a territorial bird and fiercely protects its territory from intruders, particularly during the mating season. Its diet consists of small insects, (weed) seeds, berries and fruit. The female chaffinch makes an ingenious nest in which she lays an average of 3 to 4 eggs. The eggs are incubated mainly by the female and hatch after 11 to 13 days. The young are fed by both parents with small insects, such as fruit flies and greenflies. The young birds leave the nest when they are 12 to 17 days old.

## Yellow grosbeak
## (*Pheucticus chrysopeplus*)

The yellow grosbeak is a member of the cardinal family (*Cardinalidae*) and is 8 inches long. The adult male has an intense yellow color with black and white accents, although it can take 3 years before it gets this adult coloring. The parts which are black on the male are usually brown on the female. The yellow grosbeak tends to live in pairs. Its bowl-shaped nest is usually located several feet above the ground in a bush. It lays 3 to 4 eggs, which hatch after approximately 12 days. The young birds leave the nest when they are

10 to 12 days old. Its diet consists of seeds and insects which it cleverly catches in the air. The species is found in many areas between Mexico and Colombia, both in dense forests and close to human settlements.

## Ultramarine grosbeak
## (*Cyanocompss/Passerina brissoni*)

There are few birds which have such an intense deep blue color as the male ultramarine grosbeak. The female is brown, often with a few blue feathers or blue markings on her head. The ultramarine grosbeak is closely related to the blue grosbeak. The main difference is in the color, which is much deeper in the ultramarine grosbeak, although it also has a softer song. The ultramarine grosbeak eats mainly seeds and other plant material, but may also eat small insects. It mea-

Yellow grosbeak (*Pheucticus chrysopeplus*)

A male black-headed weaver (*Ploceus cucullatus*).

Red-billed quelea (*Quelea quelea*)

A female black-headed weaver (*Ploceus cucullatus*).

black-headed weaver is a member of the weaver family (*Ploceidae*). The members of this family are known for their large ingenious hanging nests.

## Red-billed quelea (*Quelea quelea*)

The red-billed quelea is found in West and Central Africa, where it forms extremely large groups. Its diet consists mainly of seeds. During the mating season, the bird is found mainly in southern Africa, where it breeds in colonies. The male builds a typical weaver's nest in a tree. The female lays 2 or 3 eggs, which hatch after approximately 12 days. The young are fed by both parents and leave the nest when they are only 12 to 14 days old. The red-billed quelea is approximately 5 inches long and is a member of the weaver family (*Ploceidae*).

sures approximately 6 inches, including its tail. It lays 3 or 4 eggs, which hatch after approximately 12 days. The young birds often leave the nest when they are only 10 days old. The ultramarine grosbeak is found in northern Venezuela, eastern Brazil, Argentina, Paraguay and Bolivia. It is a member of the cardinal family (*Cardinalidae*).

A male house sparrow (*Passer domesticus*).

## Black-headed weaver (*Ploceus cucullatus*)

The black-headed weaver measures approximately 7 inches. The sexes can be distinguished easily: the male is much more colorful than the female. The black-headed weaver is found in many parts of Africa, where it lives in almost any habitat. This bird always lives and breeds in colonies. Its diet consists of seeds and insects. The

A female house sparrow (*Passer domesticus*).

## House sparrow (*Passer domesticus*)

A young house sparrow (*Passer domesticus*)

Few species of birds have adapted to humans as well as the house sparrow. This bird is found in urban areas throughout the entire world. The bird is not fussy at all about where it builds its nest and it can be found on eaves, in trees, nesting boxes, rocks and even nests abandoned by other birds. The nest is round and has an opening on the side. The house sparrow lays approximately 5 eggs which can vary greatly in color, even in the same nest. This is not unique to the house sparrow and occurs in other species of birds as well, including the Chinese pigmy quail. The eggs are incubated by both parents and hatch after approximately 12 days.

The young are fed mostly insects, while an adult's diet consists mainly of seeds. An adult house sparrow is approximately 6 inches long. The house sparrow is a member of the weaver family and related birds (*Ploceidae*).

Chiffchaff (*Phylloscopus collybita*)

## Chiffchaff (*Phylloscopus collybita*)

The chiffchaff is a small, inconspicuously colored bird which is found throughout Central and northern Europe and a large part of northern Asia. It spends the winter in southern areas, such as Africa and southern Europe. There is no visible difference between the male and female, although only the male sings. The chiffchaff builds its round nest in a bush, often close to the ground. It lays approximately 6 white eggs, which are incubated by the female for about 2 weeks. The young are fed only by the female, although the male always remains close by to ward off enemies. The young birds can fend for themselves when they are 3 to 4 weeks old. The chiffchaff is a member of the family *Sylviidae*.

## European blackbird (*Turdus merula*)

The European blackbird is found throughout Europe, parts of Asia and North Africa. Some populations are migratory and migrate southward after the breeding season, while others are sedentary. Many European blackbirds prefer to live close to humans and inhabit gardens and parks. The bird grows to a length of 9.5 to 10 inches. The sexes can be distinguished easily: the male is black with a yellow beak, while the female is brown and has a grey beak. Only the male sings. The European blackbird is territorial and usually lives in pairs or alone. It eats insects, worms, berries, fruit and seeds. It builds a bowl-shaped nest in foliage in which it lays approximately 5 light green-blue eggs with reddish-brown speckles. The eggs are incubated by the female and hatch after approximately 2 weeks. During this period, the male keeps watch and remains close to the nest. The young are fed by both parents and are reasonably independent when they are approximately 5 weeks old, although they leave the nest when they are only 3 weeks old. The European blackbird generally breeds 2 or 3 times in a single season. The European

A male European blackbird (*Turdus merula*).

A female European blackbird bathing

Song thrush (*Turdus philomelos*)

blackbird is a member of the large thrush family(*Turdidae*).

## Song thrush (*Turdus philomelos*)

The song thrush is closely related to the European blackbird and is found throughout Europe and a large part of Asia. Some populations migrate southward after the breeding season, while others remain at their breeding ground. The song thrush prefers to remain in the shelter of foliage and usually builds a nest in the fork of a branch. It lays 4 or 5 eggs, which are incubated by the female for approximately 12 days. An adult song thrush is approximately 9 inches long.

## European robin (*Erithacus rubecula*)

The European robin is a member of the thrush family (*Turdidae*) and is found throughout Europe, North Africa and parts of Asia. Some populations migrate southward before winter, while others are sedentary. The European robin is mainly found in deciduous forests, but also likes to build its nest in parks and quiet, sheltered gardens. During the breeding season, the male and female occupy a territory in which no other European robin is permitted. The nest, which is usually built close to or on the ground, is made from small plant material and often finished off using horsehair. The European robin lays an average of 5 eggs, which the female incubates for approximately 2 weeks. The young are fed by both parents, mainly with small insects, and leave the nest when they are approximately 14 days old. An adult European robin eats insects and berries. The male and female are the same color, but only the male sings. The European robin is approximately 5.5 inches long.

## Nightingale (*Luscinia megarhynchos*)

The nightingale is a member of the thrush family (*Turdidae*). During the breeding season, it is found throughout Europe (except in the most northern regions), North Africa, the Middle East and parts of Asia and it spends the winter in southern regions. It is found mostly in dense woodland areas. The nightingale eats small animals as well as plant material, such as fruit. Both sexes have the same color and markings, but only the male sings. It builds its nest in a sheltered location, usually

European robin (*Erithacus rubecula*)

Nightingale (*Luscinia megarhynchos*)

close to the ground in a bush. The eggs are light to dark brown and are incubated by the female for almost 2 weeks. An adult nightingale is 6 to 6.5 inches long.

## Oriental white-eye (*Zosterops palpebrosus*)

This lively bird gets its common name from the striking white rings around its eyes and is found in India and Sri Lanka. The oriental white-eye is gregarious, but splits off into pairs to nest during the breeding season. There is only a small difference between the male and female; the female has a duller color. It builds a bowl-shaped nest in foliage in which it lays an average of 3 light blue-green, speckled eggs. The eggs are incubated by both parents and hatch after 11 or 12 days. The young are almost exclusively fed live food. The young birds leave the nest when they are 10 to 14 days old. The oriental white-eye eats insects and their larvae, berries, fruit and nectar. It is approximately 4 inches long and is a member of the white-eye family (*Zosteropidae*).

## Hooded pitta (*Pitta sordida*)

The hooded pitta is a member of the pitta family (*Pittidae*) and lives in the dense forests stretching from the Himalayas to New Guinea. Although the bird can fly, it prefers to remain on the ground. It searches for its food, which consists of a variety of insects and molluscs, on the ground in the forest.

Oriental white-eye (*Zosterops palpebrosus*)

Hooded pitta (*Pitta sordida*)

## Blue-crowned pitta
## (*Pitta soror*)

This species of bird is found throughout southeast Asia as far as southern China. It eats a variety of snails, worms and insects, which it finds on the ground in dense, humus forests. Its spherical nest is strikingly large. Although it is usually built on the ground, the nest can sometimes be built in a bush or a small tree. It lays an average of 4 eggs.

## Golden-collared manakin
## (*Manacus vitellinus*)

The golden-collared manakin is a member of the manakin family (*Pipridae*). This species is found in Columbia, where it lives in the undergrowth of the rain forest. The golden-collared manakin eats insects and fruit. The male can be recognised by its golden-yellow breast and collar, as well as the black on the top of its head, while the female is a very inconspicuous brown color. It grows to a length of approximately 4 inches.

Blue-crowned pitta (*Pitta soror*)

Golden-collared manakin (*Manacus vitellinus*)

Eastern black-and-white colobus (*Colobus guereza*)

# 4 Mammals (Class *Mammalia*)

Mammals are warm-blooded animals. This means that, unlike reptiles and amphibians, they can maintain or control a constant body temperature. The body temperature and metabolism of cold-blooded animals changes to a certain extent according to the surrounding temperature, so that these animals require less food during cold periods. Warm-blooded animals, such as mammals, have a constant body temperature; the need for food, therefore, increases when it becomes colder because the body needs more energy to maintain a constant temperature. This adaptation means that mammals are found throughout the world, even at the North and South Poles, where cold-blooded animals have no chance of survival.

Mammals are predominantly terrestrial animals, but many of them also live partly on land and partly in the water. Relatively few mammals live exclusively in water. Most mammals have hair on their skin, although there are exceptions to this rule. The density and length of the hair can vary according to the surrounding temperature; mammals which live in a moderate climate often develop a summer and winter coat. Sometimes, the colors of the winter and summer coats differ. Several carnivores, lagomorphs and rodents which inhabit northern regions have a white winter coat which provides excellent camouflage in the snow.

All mammals' milk teeth are replaced by their permanent teeth, which they keep

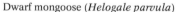
Dwarf mongoose (*Helogale parvula*)

Harbour seal (*Phoca vitulina*)

Great grey kangaroo (*Macropus giganteus*)

Alaskan bear

African elephant

for the rest of their lives. For some mammals, the incisor teeth have adapted for constant chewing and they grow continuously. However, when a tooth falls out of the jaw, a new tooth does not grow in its place, not even in rodents. This is a significant difference between mammals and, for example, snakes, which can always grow new (venomous) fangs.

Communication usually takes place through sound, body posture, facial expressions and smell. Most mammals can make many different noises, they have a well-developed sense of smell, they have excellent hearing and their vision is usually good. However, the development of the various senses differs between species and this is related to the environment in which the animal lives, its enemies and food source. Lagomorphs and several kinds of rodents, for example, have developed excellent eyesight so that they can

see their enemies approaching in time. For the same reason, the sense of smell is above average in some animals, while others like bats, have excellent hearing.

The lungs, heart and vascular systems of mammals are extremely well developed. Oxygen enters the lungs via the nose or mouth, where it is passed on to fine blood vessels which transport the oxygen throughout the entire body.

The reproduction organs are also well developed. Mammals have internal fertilization and the fetus develops in the body of the mother. The fetus of nearly all mammals receives nutrients from the blood of the mother through a placenta. Mammals differ in this respect from ovoviviparous reptiles and fish, since the fetus of these animals is fed by the nutrients in the yoke of the egg. All mammals are viviparous, except for the platypus and echidna (*Monotremata*). Mammals get their name

Okapi (*Okapia johnstoni*)

Black-tailed prairie dog (*Cynomys ludovicianus*)

from the way the female feeds her young with milk from her mammary glands, which are usually located on the underside of the animal. The number of glands varies per species and often depends on the number of young that the species produces per litter.

The care of the young is usually very advanced in mammals. The mother and sometimes the father protect the young against enemies. Some mammals dig a hole in which the young are protected until they can fend for themselves. For other mammals which do not have a fixed habitat or territory, the young can walk almost immediately after birth so that they can move with the herd, although they still require milk from the mother for some time. There is always a strong mater-

nal bond and the young depend a great deal on their mother until they can fend for themselves.

The adult size of mammals varies greatly. The largest living mammal is the blue whale, which can measure up to 100 feet and the smallest mammals are the small species of shrews, which have an adult length of only two inches. It is striking that small mammals require proportionally more food to maintain a constant body temperature than large mammals. A shrew has a relatively larger body surface area than a blue whale and, accordingly, loses more heat than the blue whale.

There are approximately 4,600 different species of mammals, subdivided into 26 orders.

Slender-tailed meerkat (*Suricata suricatta*)

Blue wildebeest (*Connochaetes taurinus*)

Giraffe (*Giraffa camelopardalis*)

Mouflon (*Ovis aries*)

# The following orders are included in the class of mammals:

- Platypus and echidnas (*Monotremata*)
- (*Didelphimorphia*)
- (*Paucituberculata*)

- (*Microbiotheria*)
- (*Dasyuromorphia*)
- (*Peramelemorphia*)
- (*Notoryctemorphia*)
- (*Diprotodontia*)
- (*Xenarthra*)
- Shrews, moles, hedgehogs, tenrecs and solenodons (*Insectivora*)
- (*Scandentia*)
- Colugo (*Dermoptera*)
- Bats (*Chiroptera*)
- Primates (*Primates*)
- Carnivores (*Carnivora*)
- Whales, dolphins and porpoises (*Cetacea*)
- Dugong and manatees (*Sirenia*)
- Proboscideans (*Proboscidae*)
- Perissodactyl (*Perissodactyla*)
- Hyraxes (*Hyracoidea*)
- Aardvarks (*Tubulidentata*)
- Artiodactyls (*Artiodactyla*)
- Edentates and pangolins (*Pholidota*)
- Rodents (*Rodentia*)
- Lagomorhps (*Lagomorpha*)
- (*Macroscelidae*)

Hippopotamus (*Hippopotamus amphibius*)

# Platypus and echidnas (*Monotremata*)

Families: *Ornithorhynchidae and Tachyglossidae*

## Duck-billed platypus (*Ornithorhynchus anatinus*)

The duck-billed platypus is a member of the platypus family (*Ornithorhynchidae*). The species is found in Tasmania and Australia and can grow to a length of approximately 26 inches, including its tail. The duck-billed platypus looks like several different animals stuck together; the shape of its bill looks like that of a duck, the tail looks very much like that of a beaver, its cheek pouches used to transport food easily resemble those of a hampster and, at first sight, its feet look like those of a terrapin. Both sexes are poisonous when young, but the poison glands remain only on adult males. Its poison can be harmful to humans, but is usually not fatal. The duck-billed platypus is active only at dusk and is not seen at night or in broad daylight, when it remains hidden in a network of tunnels dug with its strong claws. The duck-billed platypus prefers to remain in water, where it forages on the bottom for its food, crustaceans and small fish. It is oviparous and

Short-nosed echidna (*Tachyglossus aculeatus*)

lays its eggs in a sheltered hole. When the eggs hatch, the young are breastfed until they are old enough to fend for themselves.

## Short-nosed echidna (*Tachyglossus aculeatus*)

The short-nosed echidna is a member of the echidna family (*Tachyglossidae*). It is also called the spiny anteater because its diet consists mainly of ants and termites and because its body is covered with spines which make it look like a hedgehog. It can role up its body when in danger like a hedgehog. It has a horny, beaklike mouth. In contrast to the duck-billed platypus, the short-nosed echidna is predominantly diurnal. It likes to rest at night, half-buried in the ground. It has a very peculiar way of reproducing; shortly before mating, the female develops

Duck-billed platypus (*Ornithorhynchus anatinus*)

a pouch which contains the mammary glands. The female lays eggs, which she carries with her in her pouch. The young which hatch from the eggs remain in the pouch and feed from the milk until they grow spines. The short-nosed echidna can grow to a length of approximately 20 inches.

# Didelphimorphia

Family: *Didelphidae (subfamilies; Caluromyinae and Didelphinae)*

## Virginia opossum
### (*Didelphis virginiana*)

The Virginia opossum is very widely distributed in an area which extends from central and eastern North America to Central America. The Virginia opossum is territorial. It lives alone outside the mating season and prefers to inhabit grassland plains and wooded regions. It is omnivorous, although the largest part of its diet consists of animal matter, such as insects. The body of the Virginia opossum can grow to a maximum length of approximately 19 inches. The length of the tail can vary but is 15 inches long on average.

Virginia opossum (*Didelphis virginiana*)

The Virginia opossum weighs an average of 4.5 pounds. Once or twice a year, the female gives birth to between 5 and 8 young, which, like all opossums, remain in the pouch for a long time after they are born, often for longer than 2 months. It reaches sexual maturity when it is approximately 8 months old. Although the Virginia opossum has more than one litter per year, it will never raise more than three. The Virginia opossum is a member of the opossum family (*Didelphidae*).

# Paucituberculata

Family: *Caenolestidae*

## Rat opossum
### (*Caenolestes obscurus*)

The rat opossum is a member of the rat opossum family (*Caenolestidae*), which is the only family of this order. It is a small, mouse-like animal with a body length of approximately 4 inches or slightly longer and an almost hairless tail which is just as long as the body. The rat opossum is found in the wooded regions of Venezuela and Columbia. It is active at dusk and at night and is seldom seen during the day. Its diet consists of small insects and worms, but it may also eat plant material.

Rat opossum (*Caenolestes obscurus*)

# Microbiothera

Family: *Microbiotheriidae*

## Monito del monte
(*Dromiciops gliroides*)

The monito del monte is found in the Andes in Chile. It is a nocturnal forest dweller and eats insects and other small animals, with a clear preference for insect larvae. The species is found mostly where Chilean bamboo grows and it builds its nest entirely from the leaves of this plant. Outside the mating season, the female lives more or less close to her young (although it is not a close relationship), while the male lives alone. The monito del monte has one litter of between 1 and 5 young per year. The young spend some time in the pouch of the mother and are then carried around on her back. It reaches sexual maturity when approximately 2 years old. The monito del monte can grow to a length of approximately 5 inches, excluding its shorthaired tail. The tail is just as long as the body and has the important function of storing fat for hibernation. The monito del monte weighs only between 0.5 and 1 ounce.

# Dasyuromorhia

Families: *Thylacinidae, Myrmecobiidae* and *Dasyuridae*

## Banded anteater
(*Myrmecobius fasciatus*)

The banded anteater, or numbat, is the only species of the numbat family (*Myrmecobiidae*). It is diurnal and is found only in certain regions of Australia. It can grow to a length of approximately 16 inches, including its tail, which is slightly shorter than its body. A numbat eats ants and termites exclusively. This animal has a special adaptation to reach its food more easily; its tongue is very long and thin and releases a sticky substance. Its long, thin tongue allows it to search the outer tunnels of termite hills for food. The banded anteater has no pouch. The young hold on to the hair around the mother's nipples. In 1982, this species was considered to be one of the most endangered species in the world, but its numbers have now increased and it is no longer threatened with extinction.

Monito del monte (*Dromiciops gliroides*)

Banded anteater (*Myrmecobius fasciatus*)

## Tasmanian devil
## (*Sarcophilus harrisii*)

The Tasmanian devil is a member of the carnivorous marsupial family (*Dasyuridae*). The species is found only in Tasmania, where it lives mostly in the wooded regions, usually close to water. The Tasmanian devil is an excellent swimmer. It is predominantly nocturnal and usually remains hidden during the day. It eats a variety of live prey and its scientific name refers to this fact: *Sarco* means meat and *philus* means fondness. In theory, it eats all the animal food that it comes across, even carcasses. Its not-so-flattering common name is by no means applicable to its behavior. It is generally a friendly animal and has a large repertoire of noises to let members of the same species, and other animals, know its intentions. Although it does not reach sexual maturity until the age of 2, the Tasmanian devil lives only for approximately 7 years. A female Tasmanian devil gives birth to between 2 and 4 young per year. As with all marsupials, the young spend only a short time in the womb. The underdeveloped young crawl into the mother's pouch and when they are big enough, they are placed in a den, where they stay until they can fend for themselves. Both the mother and the father protect the young animals. A male Tasmanian devil can grow to a length of approximately 29.5 inches and weigh between 20 and 25 pounds, although the female is somewhat smaller. It is a legally protected animal in its land of origin, although its survival is not threatened and there is a healthy population in Tasmania.

# *Peramelemorphia*

Families: *Peramelidae and Peroryctidae*

## Greater bilby
## (*Macrotis lagotis*)

There are 19 different species of bilbies in Australia and New Guinea and the greater bilby, which is found only in Australia, is one of these. The animal digs and hides in a network of underground tunnels during the day and appears at dusk to search for food. The greater bilby is carnivorous and eats mainly insects and their larvae, although its preferred food is termites. It can grow to a length of approximately 27.5 inches, including its long tail. The female gives birth to an average of 3

Greater bilby (*Macrotis lagotis*)

Tasmanian devil (*Sarcophilus harrisii*)

young, which remain in her pouch for about 2 months.

# Notoryctemorphia

Family: *Notoryctidae*

## Marsupial mole
## (*Notoryctes typhlops*)

The marsupial mole is a member of the only family in this order, the marsupial mole family (*Notoryctidae*), which consists of only two species. The marsupial mole is found in southwest Australia. It grows to a length of approximately 6 inches, but adults can vary in size. It has a short, bald tail. The animal has many similarities with other species of moles which do not belong to the marsupials; it is totally blind (almost lacking eyes) and has strong, very large claws on its front feet which it uses to dig a network of tunnels. In contrast to other moles, this animal does not dig tunnels, but buries itself just below the surface. The way it moves is very unusual; it moves partly above the ground and partly underground, just below the surface. It does not have a hole and eats a variety of animal food.

Marsupial mole (*Notoryctes typhlops*)

# Diprotodontia

Families: *Phascolarctidae, Vombatidae, Phalangeridae, Potoroidae, Macropodidae, Burramyidae, Pseudocheiridae, Petauridae, Tarsepedidae and Acrobatidae*

## Red kangaroo
## (*Macropus rufus*)

The kangaroo and wallaby family (*Macropodidae*) is large and contains animals which range in size from 10 inches to more than 5 feet. The three largest kangaroos, of which the red kangaroo is one, are called kangaroos, while all other members of the family are called wallabies. The red kangaroo, like all marsupials, is found in Australia, where it lives on large grass plains. It is herbivorous and

Red kangaroo (*Macropus rufus*)

Great grey kangaroo (*Macropus giganteus*)

Red-necked wallaby (*Macropus rufogriseus*)

eats grass and leaves. Adult males and females can be distinguished easily by their size; the male is much larger than the female. It can grow to a length of 5.5 feet, excluding the tail, and can weigh approximately 150 pounds. Its tail can be

Red kangaroo (*Macropus rufus*)

about 3 feet in length. Its hind feet are formidable thrusting weapons, which it uses when it feels threatened or when fighting with a member of the same species for the favor of a female. The red kangaroo can move very quickly. Over a short distance, it can reach a speed of approximately 50 miles per hour and it can leap more than 25 feet. It usually gives birth to one underdeveloped and blind young, which weighs only ⅓ of an ounce. After birth, the young animal crawls into the mother's pouch where it remains for approximately 8 months. After it has left the pouch, the young animal remains with its mother for an additional several months. The red kangaroo has another particular characteristic; there is a second (reserve) fetus in the womb besides the young animal that the mother carries in the pouch.

Sugar glider (*Petaurus breviceps*)

This fetus develops only if the first fetus dies or when it becomes independent. The great grey kangaroo (*Macropus giganteus*) is slightly smaller than the red kangaroo, but its way of living is very much like that of the red kangaroo.

## Red-necked wallaby
## (*Macropus rufogriseus*)

This small species of wallaby is found in South Australia and Tasmania and is active mainly at dusk and during the night. It is herbivorous and eats grasses and leaves. The female reaches sexual maturity between the ages of 1 and 1.5 years, while the male takes up to six months longer. She usually gives birth to one joey, which weighs less than $1/30$ of an ounce, after an average gestation period of one month. The young remains in the pouch for approximately 6 months and can fend for itself another 6 months later. An adult red-necked wallaby is approximately 35.5 inches long and weighs between 48 and 55 pounds. It can live for more than 10 years.

## Sugar glider
## (*Petaurus breviceps*)

The skin membranes between the front and rear limbs are the most striking characteristic of this common forest dweller. These skin membranes can be stretched by extending the limbs, so that the animal can glide relatively easily from tree to tree. It can travel relatively long distances in this way. The sugar glider is gregarious and lives in family groups, but it can be very aggressive toward animals from other groups. Its body is approximately 6 inches long and its tail measures approximately 7 inches. It usually remains hidden during the day in a hole in a tree trunk and appears at dusk to search for food. Its diet consists mainly of insects and other small animals, but it may also eat soft fruit and honey. Its natural habitat is Australia (particularly Eastern Australia) and Tasmania. It is sometimes kept as a pet and can become reasonably tame. A sugar glider raises an average of 2 young per year.

## Koala
## (*Phascolarctos cinereus*)

The koala is found only in Australia and is a member of the koala family (*Phascolarctidae*). It is nocturnal and lives a solitary life. It is arboreal and eats the leaves of certain types of eucalyptus trees, which are poisonous to other animals. An adult koala needs to eat about 2 pounds of eucalyptus leaves each day. It does not

Koala (*Phascolarctos cinereus*)

Common wombat (*vombatus ursinus*)

## Common wombat
(***Vombatus ursinus***)

The common wombat is a member of the wombat family (*Vombatidae*) and is found in the wooded regions of Australia. It lives a solitary life and eats mainly a variety of hard grasses. Like those of rodents, the teeth of a wombat continue to grow throughout its entire life. The wombat is a very large and extremely strong animal; it can grow to a length of more than 3 feet and weigh more than 90 pounds, although most animals are somewhat smaller. The wombat is a cumbersome animal, but can still reach a speed of more than 20 miles an hour. It is predominantly nocturnal and remains hidden during the day in an underground hole or network of tunnels. On average, a female wombat gives birth to one joey per year. The young spends its first 6 months in the mother's pouch and often remains with the mother for several more months to a year. A wombat reaches sexual maturity when approximately 2 years old and can live for approximately 20 years.

drink and gets liquid from the leaves that it eats. The female gives birth to only one joey per year, which weighs less than $\frac{1}{50}$ of an ounce. The young remains in the pouch for 6 to 7 months and is then carried on the mother's back for several months. A young koala is breastfed and cared for by the mother for almost one year. The species was once very common but its numbers have fallen drastically because its coat became popular in the fur trade and, since the koala is peaceful and not shy, it was an easy target for fur hunters. Luckily, this trade has been stopped and the species is now protected. Nowadays, the koala is the victim of forest fires, traffic and dingoes, but various contagious diseases also affect the koala. The current koala population is reasonably high in some regions, while in others, the koala is vulnerable and protection remains necessary. An adult male can weigh 22 to 24 pounds, while the female is a couple of pounds lighter. It grows to a length of between 27 and 31 inches.

## Pygmy glider
(***Acrobates pygmaeus***)

The pygmy glider is a member of the family *Acrobatidae* and is a common animal in eastern Australia. Its body grows to a length of approximately 3 inches and its hairy tail is about the same length. It weights between .25 and 0.5 of an ounce. It is nocturnal and eats mainly nectar, but may sometimes also eat insects. It has skin membranes between its front and rear limbs, which it can stretch by extending its limbs and which allow the animal to glide from tree to tree. The female builds a nest in the thick foliage of a treetop, usually high off the ground. On average, the female gives birth to 1 to 3 young, which she carries in her pouch. After a while, she no longer carries them in her pouch and lays them in the nest or carries them on her back when she goes in search of food. The young can fend for themselves when they are 3 months old. The pygmy glider reaches sexual maturity between the age of 8 and 10 months.

Pygmy glider (*Acrobates pygmaeus*)

# Xenarthra

Families: *Bradypodidae, Megalonychidae (subfamily; Choloepinae), Dasypodidae (subfamilies; Chlamyphorinae, Dasypodinae) and Myrmecophagidae*

## Nine-banded armadillo (*Dasypus novemcinctus*)

The nine-banded armadillo is found in South and Central America, as well as in the southern part of North America. It is nocturnal and spends the day in an underground hole which it digs itself. Its diet consists of worms, insects and insect larvae. It gets its common name from the typical bony shields that cover the top of its body, head, tail and a portion of its limbs and provide the animal with effective protection from attack by predators. The underside of the animal is usually hairy. All armadillos have claws which they use to dig holes when they feel threatened or to search for food. Armadillos have poor eyesight, but have an excellent sense of smell. This animal has a special peculiarity: the female always gives birth to identical quadruplets. The young are born fully developed, but still require milk from the mother for the first few weeks. The young animals develop quickly and a nine-banded armadillo reaches sexual maturity when only six months old.

Nine-banded armadillo (*Dasypus novemcinctus*)

Larger hairy armadillo (*Chaetophractus villosus*)

An adult has a body length of up to 20 inches, while the tail is usually somewhat shorter than the body. In Brazil, the animal is called *tatoe* and its meat is considered a delicacy.

## Larger hairy armadillo (*Chaetophractus villosus*)

The larger hairy armadillo is found in the northern part of South America, particularly in Argentina, Bolivia and Paraguay. It remains hidden during the day and is active at dusk and during the night when it searches for food. It is an excellent walker and can move relatively quickly. It eats small, live food. Like the nine-banded armadillo, it is a member of the family *Dasypodidae* and subfamily *Chlamyphorinae*.

## Giant anteater (*Myrmecophaga tridactyla*)

The giant anteater is a member of the anteater family (*Myrmecophagidae*). It has a total length of more than 3 feet and is the largest living anteater. It is found in the northern part of South America, where it lives both in wooded regions and on large open plains. The giant anteater lives alone and searches for other animals only during the mating season. After a gestation period of 6.5 months, the female usually gives birth to 1 pup, which rides on its mother's back while it is still small. The giant anteater has several special adaptations on its body which make it easier to catch its main food source, termites; it has very strong claws which it uses to unearth termite nests and its snout is very long and thin, like its sticky tongue, which it can extend up to 24 inches and which enables it to search the narrow network of tunnels in a termite hill. It does not use its front legs and large claws

Giant anteater (*Myrmecophaga tridactyla*)

Linne's two-toed sloth (*Choloepus didactylus*)

exclusively to search for food. They are also its sole, but formidable, weapon against predators because, the giant anteater has no teethlike all the members of this family.

## Linne's two-toed sloth (*Choloepus didactylus*)

The Linne's two-toed sloth is a member of the ground sloth family (*Megalonychidae*). A solitary, nocturnal mammal, it is found in the dense forests in the northern part of South America. The sloth moves very slowly and spends its entire life hanging upside down in trees and even its fur has been adapted to this. It cannot walk because its claws are far too long and are specially suited to hanging from branches, but it is an excellent swimmer. The sloth is herbivorous and its diet ranges from leaves to flower buds and fruit. The two-toed sloth gives birth to one young sloth after a gestation period of approximately 270 days. An adult two-toed sloth is approximately 24 inches long.

# Shrews, moles, hedgehogs, tenrecs and solenodons (*Insectivora*)

Families: *Solenodontidae, Nesophontidae, Tenrecidae (subfamilies; Geogalinae, Oryzoryctinae, Potamogalinae, Tenrecinae), Chrysochloridae, Erinaceidae (subfamilies; Erinaceinae, Hylomyinae), Soricidae, (subfamilies; Crodidurinae, Soricinae) and Talpidae (subfamilies; Desmaninae, Talpinae, Uropsilinae)*

## Tailless tenrec (*Tenrec ecaudatus*)

Of all mammals, the tailless tenrec can produce the most young per litter. It has 24 nipples and can give birth to more than 30 young. The tailless tenrec is nocturnal and is found only in Madagascar and the Comoros. It can grow to a length of between 10.5 and 15.5 inches. The tailless tenrec is not fussy about its diet and eats insects and worms, fruit and other plant material. The tailless tenrec hibernates for about 6 months.

## Western European hedgehog (*Erinaceus europaeus*)

The Western European hedgehog is a member of the hedgehog family and the subfamily of prickled hedgehogs. It is found throughout Europe and the in bordering regions of Russia along with several of its subspecies. The Western European hedgehog is a solitary animal which is active

Tailless tenrec (*Tenrec ecaudatus*)

Western European hedgehog (*Erinaceus europaeus*)

only at dusk and during the night. It remains hidden during the daytime and spends most of the day sleeping. The Western European hedgehog eats invertebrates, such as earthworms, as well as a variety of insects and snails. Less well known is that it also eats young mice, small reptiles and amphibians. It even eats poisonous animals; many poisonous animals are harmless to the Western European hedgehog. It also eats small quantities of vegetable material, such as berries and nuts. If a Western European hedgehog feels threatened and cannot escape quickly enough, it rolls itself up into a ball, causing its prickles to become erect. This offers excellent protection for the animal against an attack from cats and dogs but this does not put off large birds of prey and owls. The largest threat to the Western European hedgehog, however, is traffic. It usually produces two nests per year. To mate, the female makes her hind prickles go flat against her body so that the male is not obstructed. After a gestation period of more than 5 weeks, the female gives birth to an average of 6 young, which already have prickles when they are born. They remain in the hole for approximately 3 weeks and are reasonably independent after a additional 3 weeks when they leave the nest to lead a solitary life. The Western European hedgehog hibernates rolled-up for anywhere between 2 to 6 months. It can live for as long as 10 years. Hedgehogs are common throughout Europe and are often observed in urban areas. They are sometimes fed by humans or even kept as pets. Humans usually feed them bread with a saucer of milk, but it is better to feed them their natural food or, if that is not available, canned dog or cat food. Not all hedgehogs have prickles; some have normal, hairy fur and these animals are classified under the hairy hedgehog family (*Echinosoricinae*).

## House shrew (*Crocidura russula*)

There are about 265 different species of shrews, which can be recognised by their

House shrew (*Crocidura russula*)

European mole (*Talpa europaea*)

very thin, long snout and very small eyes. This animal is predominantly active at dusk and during the night. It is found throughout the world, except in South America, the Polar Regions, New Zealand, Australia and Tasmania and is particularly widespread throughout Europe. There are very small shrews, which measure no more than 2 inches and large species, which can grow to a length of almost 12 inches. Small shrews eat mainly insects, while the larger species also eat small mammals, amphibians and reptiles. The shrew does not hibernate and most species live a solitary life. Various species of small shrews are very common in Europe, such as the house shrew, garden shrew, field shrew and the smallest species, the Savi's pigmy shrew, which grows to a length of less than 2 inches. Small shrews are often mistaken for mice but they are actually not rodents. The house shrew prefers to live close to humans and is the only species of shrew that lives near or in urban areas.

## European mole (*Talpa europaea*)

The European mole is found throughout Europe, a large part of Russia and certain northern parts of Asia. It lives alone and an adult can grow to a length of approximately 6 inches, but can also be around an inch larger or smaller. The European mole has very small eyes, does not have any auricles and has a good sense of hearing. It prefers to use its sense of touch, however, and can detect vibrations very well. When a mole digs tunnels with its strong, large front claws, it pushes some of the soil against the walls of the tunnel to make them stronger. It pushes the excess soil behind itself, creating commonly sighted molehills. A mole does not dig very deep beneath the surface; a tunnel is usually only 8 inches below the surface. A network of tunnels consists of one or more holes and part of the network is used to store food. A mole eats anything it comes across, such as insects, larvae, invertebrates, snails, small rodents and small amphibians. It requires approximately 3.5 ounces of food per day, which equals the average body weight of a European mole. A mole rarely comes to the surface because it has many predators there, such as birds of prey, cats and foxes. It does so only if it cannot find enough food in its network of tunnels.

Common tree shrew (*Tupaia glis*)

# Scandentia

Family: *Tupaiidae (subfamilies; Tupaiinae, Ptilocercinae)*

## Common tree shrew
(*Tupaia glis*)

The common tree shrew is diurnal and is found in certain parts of Asia, particularly in wooded regions. Its behavior and way of moving is very much like that of a squirrel. It lives alone or with a partner in its own territory, which it does not share with any other common tree shrews. It is omnivorous, but eats mainly animal food, such as insects or even nestlings. The common tree shrew can produce more than one nest per year. After a gestation period of approximately 47 days, the female gives birth to 1 to 3 young, which

Philippine flying lemur (*Cynocephalus volans*)

are raised in a nesting hole in a tree. The young can fend for themselves after approximately 6 weeks.

# Colugo (*Dermoptera*)

Family: *Cynocephalida*

## Philippine flying lemur
(*Cynocephalus volans*)

There are only two species of flying lemurs, the flying lemur (*Cynocephalus temminckii*) and the Philippine flying lemur (*Cynocephalus volans*). The first species is found in Indonesia, Malaysia, Vietnam, Cambodia and Thailand, while the Philippine flying lemur is found in the Philippines. It shares several characteristics with prosimians and bats, as well as with marsupials and insectivores. The most striking characteristic of this arboreal animal is its large skin membranes. The skin membranes are somewhat comparable to those of some marsupials, such as the sugar glider but besides the skin membranes between the front and rear legs, it also has skin membranes between the front legs and neck and between the rear legs and tail. These skin membranes can be unfolded by extending its legs, so that the animal can glide from tree to tree. The flying lemur does not really fly. It is herbivorous and eats leaves and flower buds. It lives a solitary life and is active only at dusk and during the night. Its method of reproduction is similar to marsupials, although a flying lemur does not have a pouch. The underdeveloped infant, which is born after a gestation period of approximately 60 days, attaches itself to one of the mother's nipples. The Philippine flying lemur can grow to a length of approximately 16.5 inches and its tail is usually a little less than two thirds of its body length.

# Bats (*Chiroptera*)

Families: *Pteropodidae (subfamilies; Pteropodinae, Macroglossinae), Rhinopomatidae, Craseonycteridae, Emballonuridae, Nycteridae, Megadermatidae, Rhinolophidae (subfamilies; Rhinolophinae, Hipposiderinae), Noctilionidae, Mormoopidae, Phyllostomidae, (subfamilies; Phyllostominae, Lonchophyllinae, Brachyphyllinae, Phyllonycterinae, Glossophaginae, Caroliinae, Stenodermatinae, Desmodontinae), Natalidae, Furipteridae, Thyropteridae, Myzopodidae, Vespertilionidae, (subfamilies; KerivoulinaeVespertilioninae, Murininae, Miniopterinae, Tomopeatinae), Mystacinidae and Molossidae*

Egyptian fruit bat (*Rousettus aegyptiacus*)

## Egyptian fruit bat (*Rousettus aegyptiacus*)

The Egyptian fruit bat is found in Africa and a part of Asia. Its body can grow to a length of approximately 5 inches and its wingspan can reach 18 inches. It is gregarious and lives in extremely large colonies. It orients itself using echo sounding and emits a vibration with a very high frequency which cannot be heard by humans. Using the returned echo of its surroundings, it can orient itself to within a fraction of an inch, which makes it possible for the Egyptian fruit bat to fly in complete darkness. The Egyptian fruit bat is an exception because it is the only fruit-eating bat (*Pteropodidae*) which does not rely upon keen eyesight. The female gives birth to a single pup after a gestation period of 4 months.

Great mouse-tailed bat (*Rhinopoma microphyllum*)

## Great mouse-tailed bat (*Rhinopoma microphyllum*)

This very unusual species of bat has a body length of approximately 3 inches and has a thin tail which is just as long as its body. The great mouse-tailed bat is a member of the family *Rhinopomatidae* and can hibernate for a short period, during which time it can live off its own body fat. The female gives birth to a single pup after a gestation period of approximately 16 weeks. The great mouse-tailed bat is found in West and North Africa, as well as in several Asian countries. It is a gregarious, nocturnal animal and sleeps in a sheltered location during the day with its head pointed downward and its wings folded around its body (and sometimes also around its head) while hanging from a protrusion with one or two of its rear

Greater horseshoe bat (*Rhinolophus ferrumequinum*)

Common vampire bat (*Desmodus rotundus*)

legs. It appears at dusk and during the night to search for its food, which consists of a variety of insects.

## Greater horseshoe bat (*Rhinolophus ferrumequinum*)

The greater horseshoe bat has a very unusual, horseshoe-like nose which plays an important role in the echo-sounding by which the animal orients itself in the dark. The species is found in Europe and certain regions of Asia and Africa. It can grow to a length of approximately 5 inches and has a wingspan of approximately 13 inches. It eats a variety of insects which it finds mostly on the ground. The greater horseshoe bat hibernates for a long time in large colonies in caves and other sheltered, dark places. It can hibernate for as long as 6 months in some regions of its natural habitat.

## Common vampire bat (*Desmodus rotundus*)

This nocturnal bat is found in Central America and in several northern countries of South America. It can grow to a length of approximately 3.5 inches and has a wingspan of 7 inches. It is one of the most extraordinary bats because it feeds exclusively on animal blood. It approaches the animal from which it obtains the blood, usually a large mammal, not by flying but by creeping up on it across the ground. It makes a cut in the skin using its sharp teeth and licks up the blood.

Greater horseshoe bat (*Rhinolophus ferrumequinum*)

Barbastelle (*Barbastella barbastellus*)

## Barbastelle
## (*Barbastella barbastellus*)

This small species of bat is one of the best known and most common in Europe and is found in several North African countries as well. It is a small animal and grows to a length of just 2 inches and has a wingspan of approximately 10 inches. Its diet consists of a variety of flying insects which it catches in flight. Like almost all other species of bats, it is active during the night and at dusk. The bar-

bastelle hibernates in a dry, dark location, usually in a cave. The female gives birth to a single pup, which remains sheltered when the mother goes searching for food. On her return, she recognises her pup from as many as several hundred trough the unique noise that the young animal emits. When it is a bit older, the pup goes searching for food with its mother and after 6 to 8 weeks it can fend for itself. Although the animal develops very quickly, it takes a relatively long time before it reaches sexual maturity and most reach sexual maturity only during their second year.

Barbastelle (*Barbastellu barbastellus*)

Fish-eating bat (*Pizonyx vivesi*)

## Fish-eating bat (*Pizonyx vivesi*)

The fish-eating bat has, as its common name suggests, a very special diet. It eats nothing but fish, which it plucks from the water using its very sharp claws. It is found along the coasts of California and Mexico. An adult fish-eating bat is approximately 3 inches long and is a member of the family *Vespertilionidae*.

## Tent-building bat (*Uroderma bilobatum*)

The tent-building bat is one of the few species of bats which are diurnal instead of nocturnal. Its diet consists of fruit and it is found in southern Central America and the northern part of South America. It has a body length of approximately 3 inches and a wingspan of about 8 inches. The tent-building bat is a member of the family *Phyllostomatidae*.

Tent-building bat (*Uroderma bilobatum*)

## Primates (*Primates*)

Families: *Cheirogaleidae* (subfamilies; *Cheirogaleinae, Phanerinae*), *Lemuridae, Megaladapidae, Indridae, Daubentoniidae, Loridae, Galagonidae, Tarsiidae, Callitrichidae, Cebidae* (subfamilies; *Alouattinae, Aotinae, Atelinae, Callicebinae, Cebinae, Pitheciinae*), *Cercopithecidae* (subfamilies; *Cercopithecinae, Colobinae*), *Hylobatidae* and *Hominidae*

## Slender loris (*Loris tardigradus*)

The slender loris is a member of the loris family (*Loridae*). It is a tailless, slow-moving animal that is found only in Sri Lanka and certain regions of India. Most of the slender loris's life is spent in trees, where it leads a solitary existence rummaging for food. The slender loris is omnivorous and eats the leaves of trees, fruit, large insects, lizards, eggs and young nestlings. It is predominantly nocturnal and spends most of the day curled up on a branch sleeping. An adult has a body length of 7 to 10 inches.

Slender loris (*Loris tardigradus*)

Ring-tailed lemur (*Lemur catta*)

# Ring-tailed lemur (*Lemur catta*)

The ring-tailed lemur is a member of the lemur family (*Lemuridae*) and is found in Madagascar. The most striking characteristic of this prosimian is its very long, black-and-white ringed tail, which is generally longer than its body. The ring-tailed lemur is diurnal and prefers to bask in the sun in a very unusual sitting position. Its diet consists mainly of a variety of fruit, such as fig thistles, but it may also eat leaves. The ring-tailed lemur is gregarious. It lives in groups averaging between 15 and 22 animals in a territory in which no ring-tailed lemurs from other groups are tolerated, except maybe very young animals. The males are the inferior animals in the group. A female gives birth to an average of 1 to 2 infants with full hair per year. When born, the young have their blue eyes fully open and look exactly like adults. The mother breastfeeds the young for several months but, after time, the

Ring-tailed lemur (*Lemur catta*)

young start to venture out more often in search of food. The young animal can fend for itself when it is 6 months old and reaches sexual maturity a year later. A ring-tailed lemur can grow to a length of 3 feet, including its tail.

Aye-aye (*Daubentonia madagascariensis*)

## Aye-aye
## (*Daubentonia madagascariensis*)

The aye-aye is the only member of the aye-aye family (*Daubentoniidae*) and is one of the most striking prosimians. The aye-aye is found only in certain, densely wooded regions of Madagascar and is truly arboreal. It remains hidden during the day and appears only at dusk and during the night to search for food. One of the most important characteristics of this species is the thin, very long fingers on its front paws, of which the middle finger is the longest. This finger is used by the omnivorous animal to gather some of its food. For example, it uses this finger to pick larvae out of cracks and to hollow out plant stems. The aye-aye has large incisors in the upper and lower jaws which look much like those of rodents and which continue to grow throughout its entire life. Although it usually lives a solitary life in the wild, it easily forms pairs when kept in captivity. The aye-aye does not reproduce very quickly and usually produces only one infant every 2 or 3 years. The young aye-aye depends on the care of its mother for approximately 6 to 8 months. An adult aye-aye weighs approximately 6.5 pounds and has a body length of 16 to 18 inches. The tail is just as long, if not longer, than the body. The early indigenous people of Madagascar attributed supernatural powers to the aye-aye and have, therefore, never hunted the animal. Unfortunately, this has not stopped it from currently being endangered because later generations of indigenous people wanted to kill the it, as it was believed to cause bad luck. The increasing human population, which is reducing the natural habitat of the animal, has not increased the animal's chances for survival. Several aye-ayes are now held in reserves and these have already given birth to young.

## Tarsier
## (*Tarsius bancanus*)

This small prosimian is a member of the tarsier family (*Tarsiidae*). This family contains only 4 species with various subspecies, which all live alone or in pairs and look alike. The tarsier is found in wooded regions and places with an abundance of water on several Indonesian islands. An adult has a body length of 4 to 6 inches. It has a strikingly thin and long tail, which has hair only at the tip and which can be 1.5 times the length of the body, or even longer. Like all tarsiers, this animal can rotate its head fully without moving its body. The tarsier is an excellent jumper and climber. It remains hidden during the day and appears only at

Tarsier (*Tarsius bancanus*)

dusk to search for food. Its diet consists mainly of insects, which it catches with a quick movement of its hands. The female usually gives birth to 1 infant per year. At birth, the young has all its hair, its eyes are open and it is already able to walk and jump.

## Squirrel monkey
## (genus *Saimiri*)

The various species of squirrel monkey are all found in South and Central America. It is a gregarious animal and lives in groups of at least 10 to sometimes more than 100 animals. Large groups may actually be several groups which temporarily come together, as these animals are not particularly territorial. It is predominantly arboreal and rarely walks on the ground. Squirrel monkeys are omnivorous and eat insects and eggs. The female reaches sexual maturity at an age of approximately 2.5 to 3 years, while the male takes a year longer. After a gestation period of more than 5 months, the female usually gives birth to a single infant, which weighs 3.5 ounces and which the female raises. During its first 3 weeks of life, the young animal only drinks milk from the mother. After this period, it starts to eat more solid food until it can almost entirely fend for itself after 6 months. This species of ape usually grows to a length of approximately 27.5 inches, including the

Squirrel monkey

tail. On average, a male weighs almost 2 pounds and the female between 1 and 1.5 pounds. Many squirrel monkeys are kept in captivity, where they can live for more than 20 years. The life expectancy in the wild is approximately 10 years.

## Lar gibbon
## (*Hylobates lar*)

The lar gibbon's fur can be many different colors, ranging from dark grey or black to yellowish, although the top of its hands are always white. Like all other species of gibbons, the lar gibbon is very agile in the treetops in which it lives. Its strong arms allow it to swing easily from branch to branch and from tree to tree and its feet have a gripping toe, which it uses to maintain its balance when walking on a branch

Squirrel monkey

Withandgibbon (*Hylobatus lar*)

Lar gibbon (*Hylobates lar*)

Golden lion tamarin (*Leontopithecus rosalia*)

gregarious animal and is found in groups of 5 to 30 animals which are often led by a dominant male. The sexes can be distinguished easily by the size; the male is usually larger than the female. The white-throated capuchin reaches sexual maturity at an age of approximately 5 years. The female usually gives birth to a single infant every two years, which she breastfeeds up to the age of 1 year until it can search for its own food. The white-throated capuchin is found in the wooded regions of Central and North America and it is possible for the animal to live for as long as 40 years.

on its hind legs. The lar gibbon is a social animal and lives in small family groups. The female gives birth to a single infant once every 2 to 4 years after a gestation period of more than 7 months. The young animal remains with the mother for at least 2 years, during which time it is breastfed. It can take a lar gibbon 6 to 7 years to reach sexual maturity. A lar gibbon eats mainly fruit and leaves and it can grow to a length of approximately 22.5 inches. It is found in countries such as Thailand, Indonesia (Sumatra) and Malaysia.

White-throated capuchin (*Cebus capucinus*)

## White-throated capuchin (*Cebus capucinus*)

Like the squirrel monkey, the white-throated capuchin is a member of the subfamily *Cebinae*. It is a highly intelligent,

## Golden lion tamarin
### (*Leontopithecus rosalia*)

The golden lion tamarin is one of various species of tamarins, but it is the only species with a reddish orange coloring all over its body; other species of tamarins have dark hair on certain parts of the body. The golden lion tamarin is small; it has a body length of approximately 8 inches and its tail is usually an inch to 6 inches longer than the body. It is found in dense forests in the south-east of Brazil, where it lives in small groups. It spends most of its day in the shady treetops and eats leaves, fruit, insects, nestlings and lizards, as well as eggs. A female usually gives birth to 2 young after a gestation period of 4.5 months and both parents help raise the young.

## Emperor tamarin
### (*Saguinus imperator*)

Its bright white whiskers make the emperor tamarin one of the most striking species of tamarins. It is found in Bolivia, Peru and Brazil, where it lives is groups, usually in dense forests. The emperor tamarin is a small ape. Its body measures approximately 8 inches but the tail is much longer than the body. It eats fruit as well as small animal food, such as birds' eggs and insects. The female usually gives birth to 2 young after a gestation period of approximately 5 months. The emperor tamarin is a member of the family *Callitrichidae*.

## Brown-headed spider monkey
### (*Ateles fusciceps*)

The brown-headed spider monkey can cross large distances by swinging from branch to branch and from tree to tree. It is arboreal and rarely sets foot on the ground. Its diet consists mainly of fruit,

Emperor tamarin (*Saguinus imperator*)

but it may also eat leaves, bark, young twigs and honey, as well as animal food, such as (birds') eggs and insects. It is a diurnal, gregarious animal and lives in large groups, which are assumed to be family groups. Reproduction of the brown-headed spider monkey is not restricted to

Brown-headed spider monkey (*Ateles fusciceps*)

a certain season. A female usually gives birth to 1 infant once every 2 to 3 years after a gestation period of 7.5 months. The young animal is carried on the mother's belly for approximately 4 months. The young animal holds on tightly to its mother's fur and winds its tail around the base of the mother's tail. As the young animal becomes older and heavier, the mother carries it on her back. The spider monkey is found in the forests of Central America and in the northern part of South America.

## Eastern black-and-white colobus (*Colobus guereza*)

The eastern black-and-white colobus is noticeable because of the long, fringe-like hair on its back and tail. This ape and other apes which belong to the same genus are members of the subfamily *Colobinae*. A typical characteristic of this animal is its degenerate thumb. The eastern black-and-white colobus is a diurnal, gregarious animal and eats mainly leaves. The female gives birth to only 1 infant whose color is very different from that of an adult. The young animal is raised by both parents. The eastern black-and-white colobus is found in the eastern part of Central Africa and has a body length of approximately 24 inches.

Eastern black-and-white colobus (*Colobus guereza*)

Barbary ape (*Macaca sylvanus*)

Barbary ape (*Macaca sylvanus*)

## Barbary ape (*Macaca sylvanus*)

The Barbary ape is a tailless ape and is found in North Africa, particularly Morocco and Algeria, as well as in Gibraltar. It has a body length of 21.5 to 27.5 inches and the male is usually larger than the female. It lives on the rocks in groups which are made up of several dozen apes. It rests during the day and becomes active only at sunrise and sunset. The female gives birth to one infant after an average gestation period of 7 months and the young animal can fend for itself when it is approximately 6 months old. A Barbary ape is predominantly herbivorous and eats grasses, leaves and fruit, although a part of its diet consists of small animal food, such as insects.

## Japanese macaque (*Macaca fuscata*)

Not only is the Japanese macaque is the sole species of monkey found in Japan but it is also the only species which can withstand winter cold. The Japanese macaque is a territorial, gregarious animal and the size of the groups can vary greatly from only a couple to several hundred animals. The female gives birth to 1 infant after a gestation period of approximately 5 to 6 months. The young animal remains dependent on the mother for a very long time and often remains close to the mother even when it is an adult. The Japanese macaque is predominantly herbivorous and eats leaves and fruit. The species lives both in trees and on the ground and can live for 25 to 35 years.

Japanese macaque (*Macaca fuscata*)

Japanese macaque (*Macaca fuscata*)

## Crab-eating macaque (*Macaca fascicularis*)

The crab-eating macaque is a member of the family *Cercopithecidae*. Together with various subspecies, it is found on several Indonesian islands and the bordering areas of South-East Asia, where it prefers to live close to water. It is an excellent swimmer and collects a part of its diet from the water. Al one time, this monkey was worshiped on the island of Bali and large groups lived in the holy temples. The crab-eating macaque reaches sexual maturity between the ages of 4 and 5 years. After a gestation period of 5.5 to 6 months, the female gives birth to 1 infant, which is breastfed and cared for by the mother for over a year.

Crab-eating macaque (*Macaca fascicularis*)

## Owl-faced monkey
### (*Cercopithecus hamlyni*)

The owl-faced monkey is a member of the subfamily *Cercopithecinae*. One of its most striking characteristics is the male's bald, almost fluorescent blue scrotum. The vertical white stripe on the face is also a striking characteristic. The species is found in

Owl-faced monkey (*Cercopithecus hamlyni*)

Owl-faced monkey (*Cercopithecus hamlyni*)

Zaire and Rwanda, where it lives in large groups in the forests. Its body is approximately 22 inches long and the tail is several inches longer. It weighs 9 to 18 pounds.

## Marmoset
### (genus *Callithrix*)

There are various species of marmosets and they are all members of the family *Callithricidae*. The marmoset is found in eastern Brazil, where it lives in large groups in trees. It rarely sets foot on the ground. A group can contain as many as 30 animals. When an animal is born, it may be carried by the mother, although the father or one of the other members of the group often takes over this task and the young animal is only handed over to the mother to be breastfed. In the wild,

Marmoset (genus *Callithrix*)

A male hamadryas (*Papio hamadryas*).

Hamadryas (*Papio hamadryas*)

A hamadryas with its young (*Papio hamadryas*).

a marmoset does not generally live for more than 7 years, but it can live much longer in captivity, sometimes for as long as 20 years. It grows to a length of 8 to 12 inches, excluding the tail, and weighs between 10 and 18 ounces. The tail is just as long, or longer, than the body.

# Hamadryas
# (*Papio hamadryas*)

The hamadryas is found in Somalia, Ethiopia and southern Saudi Arabia and, in contrast to most monkeys, this animal is perfectly at home in rocky, semi-arid surroundings. The adult male has a long, silver-grey mane on its neck and shoulders. It is a diurnal, social animal. It retreats to the rocks or trees at night and spends the day searching for food. It is omnivorous and eats both plant and animal matter, particularly insects. The

hamadryas usually gives birth to a single infant, sometimes two, which remain with the mother for some time. A male hamadryas can grow to a length of approximately 35.5 inches. The female is usually 16 inches shorter.

# Mandrill
# (*Papio sphinx*)

The mandrill was once known by the scientific name *Mandrillus sphinx*, but the genus name has now been changed to *Papio*. The mandrill is a member of the catarrhine family (*Cercopithecidae*). The mandrill is noticeable not only because of its colorful facial skin, but also because of its large teeth. Its canine teeth can be up to 3 inches long and are extremely large in relation to the size of the skull. The mandrill is a diurnal, gregarious animal and is found in West African forests, such as in the Congo and Cameroon. A group usually consists of a dominant male with several females and their young. A mandrill eats fruit, plant leaves, nuts and a variety of animal food. It prefers to remain on the ground. It grows to a length of approximately 29.5 inches and its tail measures a maximum of 3 inches. The female is smaller and approximately half the weight of the male. The sexes can be distinguished by the intensity of the adults' facial colors; the coloring is less clear on the female and young male.

Mandrill (*Papio sphinx*)

A mother gorilla with her young (*Gorilla gorilla*)

Gorilla (*Gorilla gorilla*)

A female gives birth to only 1 infant. A mandrill can live for more than 25 years, but it does not usually live for so long in the wild.

# Gorilla
# (*Gorilla gorilla*)

The gorilla is the largest species of ape and is also believed to be the most intelligent, gentlest and most social. Adult male gorillas can weigh up to 750 pounds, although they do not usually weigh more than 375 pounds in the wild. They can be taller than 6.5 feet when standing fully erect. The female is smaller and half as heavy as the male. The gorilla is a terrestrial ape and rarely climbs high up into trees because its body is not suited to this purpose. It lives in close groups which vary in size. A male often lives alone and may sometimes join a group temporarily, even if there are already one or more males in that group, although every group has only one leader. This is a male and he can be easily recognised by the silver-grey hair on his back. The other, younger, males have black backs. It is herbivorous and eats leaves, berries and the cores of plant stalks. Gorillas lead a nomadic life, move through the forest in search of food and rarely sleep in the same place. Before going to sleep, they build a soft nest in a tree or on the ground. Like all anthropoid apes, the reproduction of gorillas is not seasonal. A female gorilla gives birth to 1 infant approximately every 4 years after a gestation period of more than 8 months. A newborn gorilla weighs more than 4 pounds and is completely helpless. After about three months, it can eat solid

Gorilla (*Gorilla gorilla*)

## Orang-utan
## (*Pongo pygmaeus*)

The orang-utan (Malaysian for "forest person") is found in the tropical forests on the Indonesian islands of Sumatra and Borneo. It is arboreal and is seldom seen on the ground. In the wild, it can live alone, in pairs or in small groups. It is a diurnal animal and spends the night sleeping and resting in a nest made out of tree branches. It spends the day searching for food, which consists mainly of fruit, but it may also eat a variety of plants, the leaves of trees, nestlings and eggs. An adult male and female can be distinguished easily; the male is larger (up to 5 feet, including the legs) than the female (up to 4 feet) and the male has a hairless jowl. An older male may also have a hairless throat sack. After a gestation period of approximately 8 months, the female

An orang-utan mother with her young (*Pongo pygmaeus*).

food and after six months, it no longer requires milk from the mother. A gorilla reaches sexual maturity at an age of approximately 6 years. As this age, or earlier, the young females withdraw from the group and join a different group to avoid inbreeding. The gorilla is found in certain areas of tropical West and Central Africa. There are three subspecies of gorilla; *G. gorilla gorilla* (Western lowland gorilla), *G. gorilla beringei* (Mountain gorilla) and *G. gorilla graueri* (Eastern lowland gorilla).

A male orang-utan (*Pongo pygmaeus*).

orang-utan gives birth to 1 infant, which is very dependent on breast milk. The young animal remains with the mother until it is around 4 years old, at whit point it can fend for itself. An orang-utan often does not reach sexual maturity for an additional 5 or 6 years.

## Chimpanzee
## (*Pan troglodytes*)

The chimpanzee is found in several African countries, including the Congo, Tanzania and Uganda and lives both in tropical forests and on open savannahs. Although its physique and muscular strength allow it to swing from tree to tree, it prefers to remain on the ground. It does, however, climb trees to catch food or to build a nest. A chimpanzee's diet depends largely on the area in which it lives,

Chimpanzee (*Pan troglodytes*)

although it does consist largely of plant material, which the chimpanzee supplements with animal food, such as insects and eggs. Some chimpanzees also hunt mammals, such as other, smaller species of monkey and small ungulates. Chimpanzees live in loose groups, the composition of which can change daily, as chimpanzees from other groups join, or vice versa. Fully-grown adults can be distinguished by their size. When a male walks on his hind legs, he can reach up to 5.5 feet and can weigh up to 110 pounds. The female, in the same position, is approximately 4 feet tall and weighs 90 pounds. After a gestation period of 8 months, a female gives birth to 1 infant, which weighs an average of 4.5 pounds. A young chimpanzee is totally dependent on breast milk for the first few months of its life. A bit later, it begins to eat solid food occasionally but usually continues to drink its mother's milk until it is 4 years old. The mother starts to ovulate again only once the young animal has been fully weaned. A chimpanzee reaches adulthood at the age of 5 years but it can take an additional 5 years, before it reaches sexual maturity.

Chimpanzee (*Pan troglodytes*)

# Carnivores
## (*Carnivora*)

Families: *Canidae, Felidae (subfamilies; Acinonychinae, Felinae, Pantherinae), Herpestidae (subfamilies; Herpestinae, Galidiinae), Hyaenidae (subfamilies; Hyaeninae, Protelinae), Mustelidae (subfamilies; Mustelinae, Taxidiinae, Lutrinae, Melinae, Mellivorinae, Mephitinae), Odobenidae, Otariidae, Phocidae, Procyonidae (subfamilies; Potosinae, Procyoninae), Ursidae (subfamilies; Ursinae, Ailurinae) and Viverridae (subfamilies; Viverinae, Paradoxurinae, Cryptoproctinae, Euplerinae, Hemigalinae, Nandiniinae)*

## Black-backed jackal
## (*Canis mesomelas*)

The black-backed jackal has a body length of approximately 31.5 inches and weighs about 22 pounds. This small, dog-like animal lives in small groups on African savannahs close to human settlements. It eats mainly small animals, varying from insects and reptiles to rodents

Czech and Saarloos wolf dog

Black-backed jackal (*Canis mesomelas*)

and birds, but a group of black-backed jackals may also catch a (newborn) lamb or calf. It may also eat carrion if food is scarce. A female black-backed jackal gives birth to between 4 and 9 young after a gestation period of approximately 2 months.

# Grey wolf
# (*Canis lupus*)

The grey wolf is a member of the family *Canidae* and is regarded as the most important ancestor of many domesticated breeds of dog in existence today. Wolves live in small groups called packs, where a strict hierarchy is constantly reconfirmed using body language. A male is usually the leader, the *alpha wolf,* but sometimes a female may take his place. Wolves hunt in groups, so that they can catch prey much larger than themselves. Usually, however, a wolf eats smaller prey, such as rabbits and small rodents. The color of the fur can vary greatly, from almost white to almost black, but grey is the most common colour. The female gives birth to between 2 and 7 pups in a hole that she digs after a gestation period of 63 days. The pups are breastfed by the mother for 2 months, but about halfway through the breastfeeding period, the mother starts to regurgitate food for the young animals, so that they become accustomed to solid food. The pups are defended by the entire pack from enemies. The wolf was once a common animal in Europe, as well as in many areas of Asia and North America, but its numbers have dwindled due to excessive hunting. Nowadays, it is found in certain regions of North America, certain regions of Europe and Asia, certain regions in the Middle East and in Japan. The body length of a wolf can vary from 3 to 5 feet.

Wolf (*Canis lupus*)

Black-backed jackal (*Canis mesomelas*)

Tibetan mastiff

Dachshund

Papillon

English cocker spaniel

Staffordshire bull terrier

Shar Pei

Bernese mountain dog

West Highland white terrier

## African hunting dog or hyena dog (*Lycaon pictus*)

The African hunting dog is one of the most colorful canine carnivores. It is not related to the hyena, but is instead a member of the family *Canidae*. In contrast to the hyena, the African hunting dog does not eat carrion. It lives in groups with a highly developed social system and a clear hierarchy. It is found in parts of Africa, particularly on savannahs. It does not have a territory, but leads a nomadic life, although when a certain location offers enough food, it may remain longer. Its prey consists of various large ungulates, such as zebras and gazelles, which it hunts in groups. Its tactic for catching its prey is to fasten its teeth onto the animal, usually the rear, until it is felled. After a gestation period of approximately 70 days, the mother retreats into a hole in

African hunting dog or hyena dog (*Lycaon pictus*)

Fennec (*Vulpes/Fennecus zerda*)

the ground to give birth. An average litter contains 7 young, but the nest can sometimes contain twice as many. The young animals start exploring the area around the hole when they are about 3 weeks old. The young are cared for, and protected by, the entire pack. They are big enough to take part in the hunt only when they are 6 or 7 months old. The body length of and adult African hunting dog is approximately 3 feet.

# Fennec
## (*Vulpes/Fennecus zerda*)

The fennec is found in the semi-arid regions of North Africa. It is a small fox with a body length seldom exceeding 16 inches and it does not weigh much more than 3 pounds. It is active mainly at dusk and during the night, when it hunts for insects, small rodents, birds and reptiles. The fennec lives either in pairs, which usually remain together for life, or in small family groups. The female gives birth to an average of 3 young after a gestation period of approximately 50 days. The fennec can live for about 10 years and is a member of the family *Canidae*.

# Kit fox
## (*Vulpes macrotis*)

The kit fox is a member of the family *Canidae*. Various subspecies are found in regions of North Africa and the north of Mexico. It has a body length of no more than 18 inches, a shoulder height of approximately 12 inches and weighs up to 6.5 pounds. It is nocturnal and lives on prairies and in wooded regions, where it spends the day in an underground hole. It lives alone in its own territory, where it hunts. It appears to prefer mice, however, it also eats a variety of small rodents, birds and even insects, as well as plant material. The kit fox usually gives birth to 4 or 5 young which are breastfed for 2.5 months. Although it is a solitary animal, the father also helps to take care of the young.

Kit fox (*Vulpes macrotis*)

## Red fox (*Vulpes vulpes*)

The red fox is found in wooded regions throughout Europe, parts of Asia (including Japan) and North America. The red fox is a solitary, territorial animal and lives in one or more holes with several exits. It uses the nest to sleep, for shelter when in danger and to give birth to, and raise, its young. The red fox gives birth to 3 to 6 young after a gestation period of 53 to 63 days. The young animals do not have adult coloring at birth, but are a brown to grey color with white markings at the tip of the tail and head and a white speck on the breast; they receive their adult fur coloring when they are 3 to 4 weeks old. Around that time, the young also start to explore the area around the hole. The red fox is not particularly fussy about what it eats. Its diet consists mainly of mice and voles, but it generally eats any prey it can catch, including insects, snails and carrion and sometimes plant material, such as berries. The red fox can transmit rabies, an illness which is dangerous to several species of animals, including humans. The red fox does not have many natural enemies apart from humans, although young animals often fall victim to large birds of prey and feline carnivores. The red fox is a member of the family *Canidae* and is, therefore, a canine carnivore.

Red fox (*Vulpes vulpes*)

## Northern lynx (*Lynx lynx*)

The northern lynx is a member of the subfamily *Felinae*. Various subspecies are found in the dense woodlands of Scandinavia, Central Europe (the Balkans, the Pyrenees and the Alps), Siberia and China. This solitary carnivore can grow to a length of approximately 3 feet, excluding its short tail, which is about 6 inches long. Its diet consists of a variety of small, live prey, such as rodents, lagomorphs, amphibians and birds, but it also hunts for deer and other large animals. A lynx hunts during the morning and in the evening and is rarely active during the day or night. It usually gives birth to between 1 and 3 young after an average gestation period of 70 days and the young often remain with their mother for a year before assuming their own territory. It reaches sexual maturity at an age of approximately 2 years. A northern lynx usually remains

Northern lynx (*Lynx lynx*)

loyal to the area in which it was born and its own territory is never far away. As with other felines, the lynx marks out its territory with its urine, feces and by scratching objects in strategic locations.

## Leopard cat
## (*Prionailurus bengalensis*)

The leopard cat is a small feline and is a member of the subfamily *Felinae*. Several subspecies are found in large parts of Asia. The color of its fur can vary according to the subspecies from a light yellow-brown or a deep yellow-brown to light grey or any color in between, but always with a black marking, which varies from a speck to a rosette-like marking. The end of the tail is always black. The leopard cat prefers wooded areas with abundant water, of which it is not afraid. Its diet consists mainly of rodents and birds. It

Leopard cat originated from the intermixing of wild leopard cat and domestic house cat

usually sleeps during the day and appears only at dusk to hunt. The leopard cat is approximately the same size as a domesticated cat. The leopard cat breed was created by cross-breeding leopard cats with domesticated cats.

## Fishing cat
## (*Felis viverrinus*)

The fishing cat inhabits the dense woodlands of southeast Asia, which have abundant water. It is active during the day and at dusk and usually sleeps or rests at night. In contrast to most small felines, this animal does not like climbing and prefers to remain on the ground. It is not afraid of water and is an excellent swimmer. Its diet consists mainly of fish, crustaceans and amphibians, which it catches in the water, however it may also eat birds. The fishing cat is a solitary animal and the male only seeks out female cats that are in heat to mate with before going off alone again. The female gives birth to an average of 3 young after a gestation period of 60 days.

Leopard cat (*Prionailurus bengalensis*)

Fishing cat (*Felis viverrinus*)

Ocelot (*Leopardus pardalis*)

## Large-spotted genet (*Genetta tigrina*)

The genet cat is found primarily in the grassland areas of South Africa. It is active at dusk and during the night and eats a variety of small, live animals, such as birds and mammals. The female gives birth to an average of 2 to 3 young after a gestation period of 57 to 72 days. Before giving birth, the mother makes a nest in

Large-spotted genet (*Genetta tigrina*)

a tree hollow or in a sheltered location in thick bushes. An adult large-spotted genet is 20 to 24 inches long, excluding the tail, which is usually slightly shorter than the body. The adult weighs between 2 and 7 pounds.

## Ocelot (*Leopardus pardalis*)

The ocelot is a member of the subfamily *Felinae* and is found in several South American countries. The ocelot can grow to a length of approximately 3 feet, excluding the tail, which can measure up to half of the body length. The color of its fur varies according to its habitat and can range from a grey-beige to a reddish yellow. It eats a variety of small animals, such as rodents and birds, but may also eat small species of monkeys and certain reptiles. In contrast to most felines, the ocelot is not a solitary animal, but lives in close pairs. However, like other felines, it marks out its territory with urine. The ocelot gives birth to an average of 3 young after a gestation period of about 10 weeks.

## Puma (*Puma concolor*)

The puma comes in a veriety of colors, ranging from grey to deep red. There are also a small number of black pumas. All young pumas have an unusual black mark on their body which fades as they get older. Its diet consists mainly of rodents and lagomorphs, but it also hunts larger prey. A puma lives a solitary life in its own territory which it marks out in a way characteristic of felines. After a gestation period of 3 months, the female gives birth to an average of 3 young, which often remain with the mother for a year or more before seeking out their own territory. A puma can grow to a length of 5 feet, excluding the tail, which usually measures 27.5 to 31.5 inches. The species is found in North America, in regions such as the Rocky Mountains, as well as many South American countries. It lives in both wooded and rocky, mountainous regions. The puma is a member of the subfamily *Felinae*.

## Serval (*Leptailurus serval*)

The serval is a diurnal animal that eats a variety of small animals and fruit. It has

Puma (*Puma concolor*)

a body length of 30 to 40 inches and a relatively short tail. Like most felines, it is a solitary animal, although females are tolerated in a male's territory. The fur color and markings of this species can vary greatly. Its diet consists mainly of rodents, lagomorphs and birds. It usually gives birth to 2 or 3 young after a gestation period of 10 to 11 weeks. The young are concealed in a sheltered location, usually a hole abandoned by another animal. The serval is a member of the subfamily *Felinae* and the various subspecies are found in several African countries, where it lives both in open grassland and wooded regions.

Serval (*Leptailurus serval*)

Serval (*Leptailurus serval*)

## Caracal (*Caracal caracal*)

The caracal is a solitary animal and is a member of the cat family (*Felidae*) and subfamily *Felinae*. It is also called a desert lynx and looks very similar to the larger lynx. The caracal is found in certain parts of Africa, the Middle East and Asia, where it lives mainly in prairies and semi-arid regions. Its diet consists of rodents, lagomorphs, birds and small ungulates. The caracal has a body length of up to 33.5 inches and the color of its fur can vary from a pale grey-beige to a deep red. Young animals can be recognised by the darker spots on their stomachs. These spots fade as the animal becomes older. The stomach of an adult is white. The female usually gives birth to 2 or 3 young after a gestation period of 10 to 11 weeks. The young animals can fend for themselves after approximately a year and reach sexual maturity a year later.

## Wildcat (*Felis silvestris*)

The wildcat is a member of the cat family (*Felidae*) and belongs to the subfamily *Felinae*. It has a very widespread natural habitat and is found in certain parts of Europe, Africa, the Middle East and China. Wildcats have also been introduced in South America, Australia and Canada, where several populations have survived. It lives in both wooded areas and fields with sufficient growth. The wildcat hunts mainly during the day for mice, birds and young rabbits. It is a solitary animal and lives in a territory which it marks out with urine and scratch marks. The female gives birth to an average of 3 young after a gestation period of 63 to 68 days. The young animals reach sexual maturity when they are 9 to 11 months old. The wildcat is fairly shy and is seldom seen in urban areas.

Caracal (*Caracal caracal*)

Wildcat (*Felis silvestris*)

Lion (*Panthera leo*)

Leopard (*Panthera pardus*)

Lioness (*Panthera leo*)

## Lion (*Panthera leo*)

The lion is a member of the subfamily *Pantherinae*. A lion can grow to a length of 5 to 6 feet and weigh between 330 and 530 pounds. The sexes can be distinguished easily because only the male has a mane. Most feline carnivores lead a solitary life of but the lion lives in groups, called prides. A pride usually consists of 2 or 3 males with 10 or more females. There are also prides which contain only young males and these males roam until they are strong enough to win a fight against an older male and so join an existing pride. Lions usually hunt in groups for large prey, such as gazelles and zebras. Interestingly, most hunting is carried out by the lionesses. A lioness gives birth to an average of 3 young after a gestation period of 15 to 16 weeks. The young animals have darker markings which fade as they become older. Before giving birth, the lioness separates from the rest of the pride and returns only when the young can walk. The young are immediately accepted by the group, cared for and even breastfed by the other lionesses. The young reach adulthood when they are approximately 1.5 years old. The young lionesses remain with the pride, while, to avoid inbreeding, the young males are usually chased away and have to look for another pride. The lion is found in several parts of Africa, except in densely forested regions.

## Leopard (*Panthera pardus*)

The leopard, or panther, is a member of the subfamily *Pantherinae* and various subspecies are found in several regions of Africa, as well as in certain parts of Asia (Vietnam, India and China). It is a solitary

Leopard (*Panthera pardus*)

Tiger (*Panthera tigris*)

Tiger (*Panthera tigris*)

animal and hunts within its own territory. It is not particularly fussy about where it lives and inhabits both densely wooded regions and vast open areas. Its body length varies from 3 to 5 feet. It has yellowish fur with black markings but, as in all other animal species, color mutations are possible. The best-known and most common color mutation is black; a black leopard is called a panther. The leopard eats large, able-bodied prey which it overcomes with a surprise attack and kills with a bite to the neck. After a gestation period of 3 to 3.5 months, the female gives birth to an average of 3 young, which are cared for by both parents. A leopard reaches sexual maturity at an age of 2 to 3 years.

# Tiger
## (*Panthera tigris*)

The tiger is a member of the subfamily *Pantherinae* and is the largest feline carnivore. The Siberian tiger grows to a length of up to 9 feet and is the largest subspecies. The tiger is a solitary animal and lives in a territory which it marks out in a way characteristic of felines. The size of the territory is largely determined by the amount of prey available. Females are usually permitted into a male's territory, but the male does not tolerate any other males. The female gives birth to an average of 3 young after a gestation period of 14 to 16 weeks. The young are born in a nest situated in a sheltered location which is covered with soft material beforehand. The young animals go hunting with their mother when they are 6 months old, but it may take 2 to 4 years before they can fend for themselves. A female tiger will normally not allow a male to mate with her again before her young become independent. The tiger hunts mainly for large, able-bodied prey, such as large deer and swine, but will also hunt other feline carnivores, such as lynxes, if they live in its territory. A tiger also eats smaller prey, such as fowl and even fish. It is not afraid of water and even prefers to live near water. The various subspecies are found in large parts of Asia, such as Nepal, China, India and Indonesia and certain parts of the former USSR, but most tigers are found in India. All tigers are threatened with extinction. The main reason for this is agriculture, which causes their natural habitat to decrease, as well as illegal hunting. There are only 50 South Chinese tigers left in the wild. The Bengal tiger has the largest numbers and estimates put this to be around several thousand.

Cheetahs (*Acinonyx jubatus*)

## Cheetah (*Acinonyx jubatus*)

The cheetah is a member of the cat family (*Felidae*) and the subfamily *Acinonychinae*. The species is found in large parts of Africa, where it lives on the savannahs. The cheetah, also called the hunting leopard, has a striking characteristic that distinguishes it from all other feline carnivores; its claws cannot be fully retracted. The cheetah can grow to a length of 5 feet, excluding the tail, which is usually half the length of the body. It does not usually weigh more than 130 pounds. A cheetah may live alone, as a pair or in a group. It often hunts alone or with several other cheetahs. It is the fastest land animal; over a short distance it can sprint at a speed of more than 60 miles per hour. Its prey consists mainly of medium-sized ungulates, as well as rabbits and hares. This animal relies not only on its great speed when hunting, but on its excellent vision as well, which is much better developed than its sense of smell or hearing. The female gives birth to 2 or 3 young after a gestation period of approximately 3 months. The young animals can be recognised by the long and lightly colored fur on their necks and backs. The young animals often remain with the mother for a year or two before they become fully independent. A cheetah is rather vulnerable in comparison to the other large feline carnivores, and hyenas or lions often steal its prey. If

Cheetahs (*Acinonyx jubatus*)

a solitary animal and usually lives with another animal only during the mating season. The female gives birth to an average of 2 to 3 young after a gestation period which may vary from 3 to more than 4 months. The young usually remain with the mother for a year before becoming independent. A cub grows to a length of 20 to 24 inches, excluding the tail, which is half the length of the body. The red panda is a member of the bear family (*Ursidae*) and the subfamily *Ailurinae*.

## Polar bear
## (*Ursus maritimus*)

The polar bear is found in the North Pole and the neighboring regions, particularly along the coasts. Its diet consists mainly of live prey, such as lagomorphs, fish, birds and, particularly, seals. It is not afraid to attack larger prey either, such as reindeer, and if possible, it supplements its diet with a small amount of plant material. It can travel large distances in search of food and is a very good swimmer. The

polar bear generally lives alone. After a gestation period of approximately 9 months, a female usually gives birth to 1 to 3 cubs once every two years, which sometimes remain with the mother for 12 months. A polar bear can grow to a length of 6.5 to 8 feet and weigh up to 2,000 pounds. It is a member of the subfamily *Ursinae*.

## Brown bear
## (*Ursus arctos*)

The brown bear is a member of the *Ursinae* subfamily of bears. It is found in certain parts of Europe, including Russia, as well as Asia and North America, along with several of its subspecies. Well-known brown bears are the grizzly bear and the Alaskan brown bear. The largest brown bear is the Alaskan brown bear, which can grow to a total length of 10 feet and weigh more than 1,600 pounds. It has a rather varied diet. Most brown bears eat vegetable material, supplemented by insects, snails and other small animals.

Polar bear (*Ursus maritimus*)

European brown bear (*Ursus arctos*)

Asiatic black bear (*Ursus thibetanus*)

Some bears prefer larger prey, such as ungulates, and others, such as the Alaskan bear, also eat salmon when it is the right season. The brown bear hibernates, during which time its body functions slow down, but its body temperature does not fall. It searches for a sheltered location, usually a crevice in the rocks, or digs a hole in the ground in which to spend the winter. A female usually gives birth to between 2 and 3 young

once every two or three years after a gestation period of 6 to 8 months. The young bears are very small in relation to the size of an adult. When born, they are blind and weigh approximately 20 ounces. The young animals often remain with the mother for more than a year and share her winter shelter. A female reaches sexual maturity at an age of approximately 3 years and a male reaches sexual maturity a year later.

Alaskan brown bear

## Asiatic black bear (*Ursus thibetanus*)

The Asiatic black bear is found in Asia, from Siberia to southeast Asia. It usually lives relatively high up in the mountains and has a long mane around its neck. Its diet consists mainly of vegetable material, such as fruit, nuts and leaves, but it may also eat insects and their larvae. It is very agile and a very good climber. A female usually gives birth to a single nest once a year containing 2 young. An adult Asiatic black bear has a shoulder height of approximately 31.5 inches and is 5 feet long.

## Malayan sun bear (*Helarctos malayanus*)

The Malayan sun bear is also known as the honey bear, although it rarely eats honey. It eats mainly soft fruit and may also eat small animals, ranging from

Malayan sun bear (*Helarctos malayanus*)

Spotted or laughing hyena (*Crocuta crocuta*)

insects to nestlings, although it is particularly fond of termites. It is not particularly harmful to humans. An adult Malayan sun bear can grow to a length of 5 feet and has a shoulder height of approximately 28 inches. The male is more solidly built than the female and weighs approximately 145 pounds. The female gives birth to 1 cub after a gestation period of more than 3 months. The Malayan

Malayan sun bear (*Helarctos malayanus*)

sun bear is found on several Indonesian islands and the southeast Asian mainland. It can live for approximately 18 years.

## Spotted or laughing hyena (*Crocuta crocuta*)

The spotted hyena is not related to the hyena dog. This species is a member of the hyena family (*Hyaenidae*), while the hyena dog is a member of the canine family (*Canidae*). The spotted hyena is found in several African countries south of the Sahara Desert. With a length of up to 5.5 feet, it is the largest species of hyena. The spotted hyena not only eats dead animals, but also hunts in groups for live prey.

# Whales, dolphins and porpoises (*Cetacea*)

Families: *Balaenidae, Balaenopteridae, Eschrichtiidae, Neobalaenidae, Delphinidae, Monodontidae, Phocoenidae, Physeteridae, Platanistidae and Ziphiidae*

Humpback whale (*Megaptera novaeangliae*)

## Blue whale (*Balaenoptera musculus*)

The blue whale is a member of the whale family (*Balaenopteridae*). It is found in large oceans throughout the world and is rarely found in coastal waters. The blue whale is the largest animal in the world; an adult female can be more than 100 feet long and weigh more than 275,000 pounds, while the male is several feet shorter. The heaviest blue whale found weighed 420,000 pounds. It eats enormous quantities of krill, crustaceans which are only an inch or so long; a large blue whale eats approximately 6.500 pounds of krill per day. The blue whale does not usually remain in the same location, but migrates each spring toward the North or South Pole and returns to warmer water in the autumn. A female blue whale gives birth once every 2 or 3 years after a gestation period of 11 to 12 months. They mate in the spring and the female usually gives birth to 1 calf, which

is 23 to 26 feet long and weighs 4.500 pounds. The young calf is breastfed by the mother for approximately 6 to 7 months and reaches sexual maturity between the ages of 5 and 8 years. It is sometimes found in large groups, but usually lives in groups of between 2 and 3 animals.

## Humpback whale (*Megaptera novaeangliae*)

The humpback whale gets its common name from the way it hunches its back when breaching. It is found throughout the world. It prefers coastal water and is rarely found in the open sea. It is usually a gregarious animal but solitary animals are also often found. It can grow to a length of approximately 50 feet and weighs more than 65,000 pounds. The female is usually larger than the male. The female gives birth to 1 calf after a gestation period of approximately 11 months. The newborn animal is relatively large and is usu-

Blue whale (*Balaenoptera musculus*)

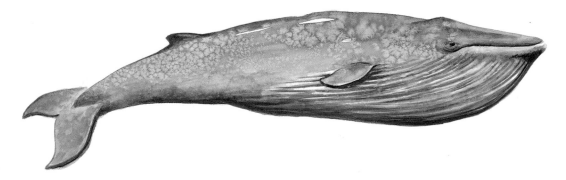

ally 13 to 16.5 feet long. The young animal is breastfed by the mother for approximately 5 months. The humpback whale usually reaches sexual maturity when 5 years old, but some animals are sexually mature when only 1.5 to 2 years old. Like the blue whale, the humpback whale is a member of the whale family (*Balaenopteridae*) and migrates to colder waters in the summer and warmer waters in the winter and may travel thousands of miles in doing so.

## Grey whale
## (*Eschrichtius robustus*)

The grey whale is a member of the grey whale family (*Eschrichtiidae*). It can grow to a length of up to 50 feet and eats a variety of small crustaceans, which it more or less scrapes off the bottom of the ocean. The way it collects its food means that the animal is rarely found in deep, open water, but mostly in relatively shallow coastal regions. The grey whale is usually found in the northern Pacific Ocean. In the spring, it migrates to more northern regions, even as far north as the Arctic Ocean and returns southward again in the autumn. The female always

gives birth in southern regions and mating also takes place in the south. After a gestation period of 11 to 13 months, the female usually gives birth to 1 calf every 2 years, although she may sometimes give birth to twins. Newborn young are more than 13 feet long.

## Killer whale
## (*Orcinus orca*)

The killer whale is a member of the dolphin and killer whale family (*Delphinidae*). It is a true raider and its diet consists of fish, birds, seals and other

Killer whale (*Orcinus orca*)

whales. Larger prey is often overpowered by a group of killer whales. The killer whale lives in groups which sometimes contain as many as 20 animals. The sexes can be distinguished easily by the animals' size. The male can grow to a length of 33 feet and weigh 9,000 pounds, while the female is no longer than 20 feet. The male also has a much larger fin. After a gestation period of about 12 months, the female gives birth to 1 calf, which is approximately 6.5 feet long. The killer whale is found in several areas, including the Atlantic, Pacific and Indian Oceans. Most are found in cold waters, particularly in the polar regions.

## Bottlenose dolphin (*Tursiops truncatus*)

The bottlenose dolphin is a well-liked member of the dolphin family (*Delphinidae*). It is found throughout the world, but particularly in warmer waters and is very common along the coasts of Florida and Hawaii. It is the most popular species of dolphin in dolphinariums and zoos. A great deal of research has been carried out on how this animal communicates. The bottlenose dolphin is a very social animal and always lives in groups. It grows to a length of 6 to 13 feet and

Common dolphin (*Delphinus delphis*)

usually weighs 330 to 440 pounds, the male being larger than the female. Its diet consists of fish and other sea animals, such as shrimp and cephalopods, of which it needs 11 pounds per day. The bottlenose dolphin mates in the spring or summer and gives birth in the spring or summer of the following year. A newborn animal is approximately 3 feet long and, on average, weighs 22 pounds. The young animal remains with its mother for 4 or 5 years and is breastfed for 1 to 1.5 years, although it eats solid food from the age of 6 months. A female usually gives birth to 1 pup every 2 or 3 years.

## Common dolphin (*Delphinus delphis*)

The common dolphin measures 5 to 8 feet and weighs 175 to 220 pounds and the female is always smaller than the male.

Bottlenose dolphin (*Tursiops truncatus*)

Sperm whale (*Physeter catodon*)

The common dolphin is very colorful and the body markings on each animal can vary. The species is found throughout the world in the Atlantic, Pacific and the Indian Oceans and is often found in the Mediterranean Sea, the Red Sea and the Gulf of Mexico as well. It is a very intelligent and social animal and lives in groups containing from 20 to sometimes thousands of animals. During the mating season, the males live with the females, but outside the mating season, the males tend to keep a distance from the group. Its diet consists of fish and cephalopods. When chasing fish, a dolphin can reach a speed of more than 30 miles per hour. Dolphins are known for helping others of its kind, such as helping an injured or sick dolphin to the surface so that it can breathe. There are also stories of dolphins saving drowning people, but some researchers doubt whether these stories are true. The female gives birth in the summer after a gestation period of 10 to 12 months. She usually gives birth to 1 pup, but may also give birth to 2 or even 3 young. A newborn dolphin is 35 to 40 inches long and weighs 24 to 35 pounds. A young dolphin begins to eat solid food after 6 months, but continues to be breastfed until it is more than a year old. The common dolphin is a member of the dolphin family (*Delphinidae*).

## Sperm whale (*Physeter catodon*)

The sperm whale is known as the best deep-sea diver among the whales. In its search for food, usually large cephalopods, it can dive up to 3,000 feet without any difficulty. It also eats large species of fish. The sperm whale is found throughout the world but mainly in temperate and warm regions. It lives in groups which consist of 1 male with several females and their young. Solitary sperm whales are always male. The sexes can be distinguished easily by the size of the adult animals. The male can grow to a length of 60 feet, while the female is usually 23 feet shorter. The female gives birth to 1 calf after a gestation period of approximately 16 months. A newborn sperm whale is approximately 13 feet long and is breastfed by the mother for 6 months. The sperm whale is a member of the sperm whale family (*Physeteridae*).

## Narwhal (*Monodon monoceros*)

The narwhal is a member of the narwhal family (*Monodontidae*) and is found mainly in the oceans around the Arctic Circle. The narwhal eats shrimp and other small sea animals. The male can be recognised by its characteristic, bent tusks, which can be 8 feet long. The female may have one tusk but it is never as long and developed as that of the male. The body of a narwhal is 13 to 20 feet long and it lives in small groups conposed of several males and females together. The

Narwhal (*Monodon monoceros*)

Dugong (*Dugong dugong*)

female gives birth to 1 calf after a gestation period of 14 to 15 months. The mother cares for the young animal for a considerable time and breastfeeds it until it is
1.5 to 2 years old.

# Dugong and manatees (*Sirenia*)

Families: *Dugongidae* and *Trichechidae*

### Dugong (*Dugong dugong*)

The dugong is a member of the dugong
family (*Dugongidae*). It lives alone and
spends all of its life in the water. Its diet
consists of seaweed and sea grasses. The
dugong grows to a length of 8 to 10 feet
and can weigh up to 440 pounds. The
species is found in areas between the Red
Sea and the coastal waters of Australia.

### Caribbean manatee (*Trichecus manatus*)

The Caribbean manatee is a member of
the manatee and round-tailed sea cow
family (*Trichechidae*). It can grow to

Caribbean manatee (*Trichecus manatus*)

a length of approximately 10 feet and is
found along the coasts and estuaries bordering the Atlantic Ocean, from Florida to
Guyana. It is not found in the open sea.
The Caribbean manatee is nocturnal. It
eats mainly a large quantity of aquatic
plants and an adult can eat up to
65 pounds of these a day. The length of
the intestinal canal has been well developed for this diet of vegetable matter and
is approximately 65 feet long. The
Caribbean manatee lives in family groups.
The female gives birth to 1 calf after a gestation period believed to be around 1 year
and the mother takes very good care of
the young animal.

Shetland ponies

New Forest pony

upper lip. It also does not have a lump on its neck, as the white rhinoceros does. The black rhinoceros is predominantly a solitary animal and eats leaves, twigs and young shoots. After a gestation period of 15 months, the female gives birth to 1 calf, which is breastfed for approximately 1 year and it remains with the mother for a approximately two more years. The young animal usually leaves the mother to fend for itself only when the mother has given birth again.

Black rhinoceros (*Diceros bicornis*)

## Square-lipped or white rhinoceros (*Ceratotherium simum*)

The common name *white rhinoceros* has nothing to do with the color of the animal, but was a mistake. It was once called the *wide-lipped* rhinoceros, which later became the *white* rhinoceros. The white rhinoceros can grow to a length of up to 16.5 feet and lives on the African savannahs. Female white rhinoceroses, and their young, usually live in small groups, while the males are inclined to occupy their own territory. It eats grass exclusively. After a gestation period of approximately 16 months, the female usually gives birth to 1 calf, which is breastfed for 1 year and often remains with the mother for approximately two more years. The white rhinoceros is a member of the rhinoceros family (*Rhinocerotidae*).

## South American tapir (*Tapirus terrestris*)

The South American tapir can grow to a length of approximately 6.5 feet and is found in several South American countries, including Brazil, Venezuela and Paraguay. This peaceful animal always remains close to water. It is herbivorous and eats aquatic plants, tree leaves and fruit. The female gives birth to 1 calf, weighing approximately 22 pounds, after a gestation period of about 13 months.

South American tapir (*Tapirus terrestris*)

Square-lipped or white rhinoceros (*Ceratotherium simum*)

Because of their beige color and lengthwise brown stripes, young animals look very different from their parents, although this marking fades as they grow older.

## Malayan tapir (*Tapirus indicus*)

This species of tapir has striking markings and is found in the marshy forests of southeast Asia. It eats aquatic plants and other plant material, including fruit, which

Malayan tapir (*Tapirus indicus*)

it finds on land. The female usually gives birth to 1 calf after a gestation period of more than a year. It is a solitary animal. A young Malayan tapir looks very different from an adult. A young animal is striped and spotted, but these markings fade as the animal grows older.

Square-lipped or white rhinoceros (*Ceratotherium simum*)

251

Aardvark (*Orycteropus afer*)

teeth only at the back of its mouth. Its diet consists mainly of termites. It digs the termite hills open using its strong claws and can easily collect the termites using its long, sticky tongue. It also uses its claws to dig a hole to defend itself against enemies. Although it usually eats termites in

An aardvark's claws (*Orycteropus afer*).

the wild, animals kept in zoos also do well with other food. The aardvark usually sleeps during the day and becomes active only in the evening when it goes in search of food. It is a solitary animal and looks for other aardvarks only to mate. A female usually gives birth to 1 pup after a gestation period of approximately 7 months. The young animal can fend for itself when it is 6 to 8 months old. The aardvark is found both in large open and wooded areas. It is found throughout Africa, except in the northern countries. Besides the large carnivores, which are its natural enemies, it is also hunted by humans for its aromatic meat. Its claws are also sometimes used as charms. Including its kangaroo-like tail, an aardvark can grow to a length of more than 6.5 feet and weigh between 110 and 190 pounds.

# Artiodactyls
## (*Artiodactyla*)

Families: *Suidae (subfamilies; Babyrousinae, Suinae, Phacochoerinae), Tayassuidae, Hippopotamidae, Camelidae, Tragulidae, Girafidae, Moschidae, Cervidaei (subfamilies; Cervinae, Hydropotinae, Muntiacinae, Capreolinae), Antilocapridae and Bovidae (subfamilies; Aepycerotinae, Alcelaphinae, Antilopinae, Bovinae, Caprinae, Cephalophinae, Hippotraginae, Peleinae, Reduncinae)*

## Hippopotamus
## (*Hippopotamus amphibius*)

Hippopotamus (*Hippopotamus amphibius*)

The hippopotamus is a member of the family *Hippopotamidae* and is found in Africa in areas with both water and open grassland to the south of the Sahara Desert. In contrast to most animals of this

Hippopotamus (*Hippopotamus amphibius*)

A hippopotamus with its young

order, the hippopotamus is more an aquatic animal than a terrestrial animal. It prefers to remain in the shallows along the edge of the water where it can stand, since it does not like deep water. It spends most of the day dozing in the water with only its ears, eyes and nostrils above the surface and come back onto land in the evening and at night to graze. The hippopotamus is herbivorous and eats grasses, leaves and a variety of soft fruit and plants. It is gregarious and most groups consist of both males and females, with an older male as the leader. It usually remains in the same location and does not often leave its habitat. An old male occupies a territory which it defends fiercely. A female hippopotamus gives birth to 1 calf approximately once every 2 years after a gestation period of more than 8 months. The young animal weighs approximately 110 pounds and is more than 3 feet long. The young hippopotamus is breastfed by its mother for 6 months and reaches sexual maturity when it is 5 to 8 years old. A male can grow to a length of 13 to 14.5 feet and a female can grow to a length of more than 11.5 feet. An adult sometimes weighs more than 6.500 pounds. The hippopotamus lives for about 40 to 45 years, although some animals have been known to live for more than 50 years.

Pygmy hippopotamus (*Choeropsis liberiensis*)

Bactrian camel (*Camelus bactrianus*)

## Pygmy hippopotamus (*Choeropsis liberiensis*)

Unfortunately, the pygmy hippopotamus is now rare and is found only in a few countries on the west coast of Africa. An adult can grow to a length of approximately 5.5 feet and the male can weigh up to 550 pounds. The pygmy hippopotamus is herbivorous and eats various aquatic and marsh plants. The male lives alone in his own territory and joins the female, who is also solitary, only to mate. The female usually gives birth to 1 calf after a gestation period of 6.5 to 7 months. The young animal is very dependent on the mother and often remains close to her for 1.5 to 2 years. The pygmy hippopotamus can live for approximately 35 years.

## Bactrian camel (*Camelus bactrianus*)

The Bactrian camel has two humps and is a member of the family *Camelidae*. In the wild, this animal is found almost exclusively in Mongolia and certain parts of China, where it lives in groups on the dry prairies of semi-arid regions. The species is domesticated in the rest of the world and is used to carry goods and people. Its meat is also eaten, its milk drunk, its hair turned into wool and its excrement used by nomadic people for fires. Domesticat-

Bactrian camel (*Camelus bactrianus*)

ed camels can be recognised by their heavier body structure and larger humps, which are often so heavy that they tilt over. Wild camels live in groups consisting of several females, and their young, led by a male animal. The female gives birth to 1 calf after a gestation period of 13 to 14 months. The young animal is breastfed by the mother for a long time and reaches adulthood only when it is 4 to 5 years old. A camel can grow to a height of 7.5 feet when measured from the ground to the top of one of its humps and weighs more than 1,300 pounds. Its diet consists of grass, plant material and leaves.

## Dromedary (*Camelus dromedarius*)

The dromedary, recognisable by its single hump, is a member of the family *Cameli-*

Dromedary (*Camelus dromedarius*)

*dae*. Although there are some wild populations of dromedary, particularly in the Middle East and Australia, where it has been introduced, their numbers are very small. Almost all dromedaries are domesticated. The dromedary is the most widely used animal to carry goods and people in North Africa and the Middle East. It is perfectly adapted to living in the desert. It can store fat in its hump which it can draw on when necessary. Its urine is also very concentrated, so that it loses as little fluid as possible. The dromedary can go a long time without water and food. Its body weight can be reduced by a quarter during difficult times without any long-term consequences. It can also replenish itself very quickly; a thirsty dromedary can drink more than 22 gallons of water in 10 minutes. The female usually gives birth to 1 calf after a gestation period of 12 to 14 months. A young animal can walk and graze fairly soon after birth, but

still remains with its mother for a full year, during which time it continues to breast-feed.

## Guanaco
## (*Lama guanicoe*)

The guanaco lives in the semi-arid regions of South America from Peru to Patagonia, where it eats grass. The animal forms herds consisting of a single male and several females, or only males, which contain 6 to 9 animals. After a gestation period of approximately 10 months, the female gives birth to 1 cria, which remains with the mother for a long time. A fertile female usually gives birth once every 2 years.

## Llama
## (*Lama glama*)

The llama is a domesticated guanaco. Like the Bactrian camel and the dromedary, this animal is a member of the family *Camelidae*. A llama can have a shoulder height of up to 5 feet. Large numbers of llamas are kept in Peru and Argentina. It is used to carry goods, its wool is used and its meat is eaten. Its fleece can be different colors and can even be spotted. A known fact about the llama is that is can direct its spit. The male animals spit at each other when fighting, but an irritated

Guanaco (*Lama guanicoe*)

Llama (*Lama glama*)

Llama (*Lama glama*)

A llama's feet (*Lama glama*)

llama will also spit at other animals or humans to defend itself. This is not its only weapon; a llama can also give a nasty bite and can kick using its front legs.

## Chital
## (*Cervus axis*)

The chital is found in India and eats leaves, grasses and soft twigs. The female has a gestation period of approximately 7.5 months. After giving birth, the mother leaves the newborn calf in a sheltered location and returns a couple of times a day to feed it until it is big enough to join the herd. In contrast to most deer, the chital can mate throughout the year and does not have a particular mating season. The chital can live for approximately 20 years.

Chital (*Cervus axis*)

## Red deer
## (*Cervus elaphus*)

The red deer designates a group of very closely related deer, all brought together in one genus with has many subspecies. In America, the animal's common name is *wapiti*. Its size varies according to the subspecies and the habitat, but is 5 feet at the most. The red deer is widely distributed. It is found in Europe and many Asian countries, but has also been introduced in North and South America, Australia and New Zealand. Its habitat varies from wooded regions to open grassland plains. The red deer is active mainly at dawn and dusk and its diet consists mainly of grass, although it may also eat leaves and suitable plants. The males and females live in separate groups outside the mating season. The males look for the females only during the rutting season in

A female red deer (*Cervus elaphus*) moulting its winter coat for a summer coat.

American red deer *wapiti* (*Cervus elaphus*)

Brow-antlered deer (*Cervus eldii*)

## Brow-antlered deer (*Cervus eldii*)

The various subspecies of this species inhabit the high plains of Central Burma, North India, Thailand, Laos, Cambodia and Vietnam and several subspecies are now rare. The brow-antlered deer eats grasses, reeds and plant matter. The male has antlers only during the mating season, although outside this season, the male can be recognised by its mane. The female usually gives birth to 1, sometimes 2, young after a gestation period of approximately 7 months. An adult brow-antlered deer is approximately 3.5 feet high and weighs between 200 and 310 pounds.

## Pãre David's deer (*Elaphurus davidianus*)

The Pãre David's deer is named after the French missionary who was the first European to bring the skin of this deer to Europe in 1865 and was, therefore, regarded as the man who discovered this species. Despite this, the deer was already well known to the Chinese by the name *sze poehsiang*. The species had been kept for many years in a game park by the Chinese emperor, where it enjoyed the best possible protection. Despite this, the animal became extinct in China due to many circumstances. Since a large number of deer had been exported to Europe, the

the autumn and fights sometimes take place to win the favor of a harem and to obtain or protect a territory. During this period, the hart makes loud noises. After an average gestation period of 8 months, the female gives birth to 1 fawn, which spends its first few days of life in a sheltered location. It is breastfed by the mother for approximately 9 months and remains with the mother until she gives birth to a new fawn. The young male has a small, unimpressive set of antlers during its first 2 years of life. It sheds the antlers each year early in the spring to make way for a newer, larger set with more tines. This continues until the deer reaches a respectable age and the antlers are then less impressive. The red deer is a member of the subfamily of deer (*Cervinae*).

species was preserved in zoos and game parks and its descendants have now been reintroduced in China. The Pãre David's deer has a shoulder height of approximately 4 feet and weighs approximately 375 pounds. The most striking characteristic of this majestic animal is its antlers, the tines of which point backwards. The antlers of all other deer point forwards.

## Fallow deer
## (*Dama dama*)

The fallow deer originally comes from Asia Minor, but is nowadays found throughout the world because it has been kept by humans for centuries. According to reports, the Phoenicians were the first people to keep the fallow deer and, therefore, contributed to its distribution. The fallow deer is undoubtedly the most common deer in animal parks and the most famil-

Pãre David's deer (*Elaphurus davidianus*)

Fallow deer (*Dama dama*)

A female fallow deer (*Dama dama*).

iar to humans. It has a shoulder height of approximately 35.5 inches. In the wild, the males and females usually live in separate groups.

## Western roe deer
## (*Capreolus capreolus*)

The western roe deer has a body height of 25.5 to 35.5 inches. It is a member of the subfamily *Capreolinae* and is, together with several subspecies, common in wooded regions throughout Europe, the Caucasus Mountains and some areas of northern Asia. The male sheds its relatively small antlers with few tines in November or December and these grow back in the spring. The first rutting season takes place in July and August. The gesta-

Western roe deer (*Capreolus capreolus*)

## Moose (*Alces alces*)

The moose is the largest deer known to man. It can grow to a height of more than 6.5 feet and weigh up to 1,750 pounds. The moose is a member of the subfamily *Capreolinae*. Its diet consists of a variety of plant material. Its relatively short neck indicates that it is not a grazing animal and it prefers to pluck its food from trees and bushes. The female usually gives birth to 1 or 2 young after a gestation period of approximately 9 months. The young animals remain with the mother for approximately 1 year and reach sexual maturity a couple of months after they become independent. The moose and several subspecies are found in the wooded regions of northern Europe (Scandinavia and Poland) and, via the northern part of the former USSR, in Mongolia and China, as well as Alaska, Canada and the northern United States. It prefers to live alone. During the mating season, it searches for a mate, but each subsequently goes its own way. The moose does not have its own territory.

tion period of the roe varies because the embryo can fall into a rest period where it does not develop. The female roe usually becomes pregnant during the first rut but some become pregnant in November during the second rut, although the young are always born in May and June of the following year. A roe usually gives birth to 2 or 3 young, which spend the first few days of their lives in a sheltered location. The mother comes to the young animals only to breastfeed them. The young animals can walk within their first week and then follow their mother. The roe eats mainly grass and several different types of herblike plants, which it prefers to search for on open plains. It usually retreats into the woodlands during the day and appears only in the evening and in the early morning. It lives alone or in small groups, depending on the time of the year and the age of the animals.

Moose (*Alces alces*)

# Reindeer
## (*Rangifer tarandus*)

The reindeer is gregarious and is a member of the subfamily *Capreolinae*. The reindeer and several subspecies are found in northern Scandinavia, Russia, Siberia, Mongolia, China, Alaska, Canada, Greenland and several of the northern United States. Both domesticated reindeer and wild populations can be found in several parts of the world. Most reindeer prefer to live on the tundra. The reindeer does not remain in a certain territory and constantly searches for locations where there is sufficient food. Its diet consists mainly of lichen, which, at certain times of the year, it must extract from under a thick layer of snow. Its body length varies according to the subspecies from 3 to 5 feet. After a gestation period of 6.5 to 8 months, the female usually gives birth to 1 calf, which is breastfed for 6 months.

Reindeer (*Rangifer tarandus*)

Reindeer (*Rangifer tarandus*)

Okapi (*Okapia johnstoni*)

# Okapi (*Okapia johnstoni*)

The okapi is a member of the giraffe family (*Giraffidae*). It is a solitary animal and leads a withdrawn life in the dense forests of the Congo. Its diet consists mainly of leaves and fruit, which it plucks from bushes and trees. It has a shoulder height of 5 feet and weighs more than 440 pounds. The male can be recognised by its horns, which the female does not have. After a gestation period of approximately 14 months, the female gives birth to 1 calf, which can walk soon after it is born. It is breastfed for 6 to 9 months, but can eat solid food when it is 2 months old.

# Giraffe
## (*Giraffa camelopardalis*)

Several subspecies of the giraffe are found in various parts of Africa south of the desert regions, where it lives in open and semi-open areas. Its diet consists mainly of tree leaves. A giraffe can also graze but its neck is so long that it must spread its front legs in order to reach the ground.

Giraffe (*Giraffa camelopardalis*)

A young giraffe (*Giraffa camelopardalis*).

Although the length of the neck suggests that the animal must have extra vertebrae, it has only 7, in fact, but these are much longer than the vertebrae of animals with a neck of a normal length. A giraffe can be up to 20 feet tall when measured from the ground to the top of the skull and weighs an average of 1,300 pounds. Both the male and female have small, rounded horns, which are covered with skin. The

Giraffes and their young (*Giraffa camelopardalis*).

gestation period of the giraffe is 15 months and the young animal is breastfed for approximately 10 months, although it can eat solid food within the first month. A giraffe reaches sexual maturity when approximately 3 years old. The giraffe does not have many natural enemies because most carnivores are discouraged by the giraffe's size and the giraffe can defend itself very well against attack by kicking its enemy. Together with the okapi, the giraffe is a member of the giraffe family (*Giraffidae*).

Cape buffalo (*Syncerus caffer*)

The young of an African buffalo (*Syncerus caffer*).

## Cape buffalo
## (*Syncerus caffer*)

This strong species of buffalo is found in various areas of Africa to the southern part of the Sahara Desert, where it lives in herds on the savannahs, usually close to water and in the protection of bushes and trees. It spends the day hidden in the foliage and appears at dusk to drink and graze. It usually lives in groups that contain both males and females or solely males, but it may also live alone. This buffalo is notorious for its aggression, but it will not usually attack if left alone. It can have a shoulder height of up to 5.5 feet and weigh 1,750 to 2.500 pounds. The female tends to be slightly smaller and less heavily built than the male. The female gives birth to 1 or 2 young after an average gestation period of 10.5 months. The young animal is breastfed for approximately 6 months, but reaches adulthood only when 1 to 2 years old.

## African buffalo
## (*Syncerus caffer*)

The African buffalo is found in Africa, where it mainly lives in densely forested regions. Its horns are well developed to its habitat and point backwards so that there is little chance of the animal becoming entangled in the trees. It lives in small herds, which are led by a male. The

African buffalo reaches sexual maturity at an age of 2 to 2.5 years. After a gestation period of 10 to 11 months, the female gives birth to 1 calf, which is breastfed for approximately 6 months. The African buffalo has a shoulder height of between 3 and 4 feet.

## Asiatic water buffalo
## (*Bubalus arnee*)

The Asiatic water buffalo is a member of the bovid family (*Bovidae*) and is found, together with several subspecies, in Asia. Domesticated animals are used as pack animals. It is a large animal with a length of up to 10 feet, a height of up to 6 feet and a weight of approximately 2,200

Asiatic buffalo (*Bubalus arnee*)

African buffalo (*Syncerus caffer*)

pounds. Because of its size and strength, it has almost no natural enemies, except for tigers. The sexes can be distinguished by the genitals, since the horns and size of the animal are nearly identical for both sexes. It has a gestation period of 10 to 11 months and the calf is breastfed for at least 6 months. An Asiatic water buffalo reaches sexual maturity when 2 years old and can live for approximately 25 years.

are smaller, can be a different color and have smaller horns. Both sexes have horns but the female's are smaller. Female yaks live in large herds, while males live alone or in small groups outside the mating season. After a gestation period of approximately 9 months, the female gives birth to 1 calf, which remains with the mother for at least 1 year.

## Yak (*Bos grunniens*)

The yak is a member of the subfamily *Bovinae*. It is found mainly in the wild in Tibet but also in India, Nepal and China. The yak lives at inhospitable heights and in areas where food is scarce. It does not remain in a particular territory, but is continuously migrating in search of food. A male yak can have a shoulder height of up to 6.5 feet and weigh up to 2,200 pounds, while the female is much smaller and lighter. Besides wild populations, there are also domesticated yaks, which

Yak (*Bos grunniens*)

Yak (*Bos grunniens*)

American bison (*Bison bison*)

## American bison
## (*Bison bison*)

The bison is a member of the subfamily *Bovinae*. The species was originally found throughout North America but because of excessive hunting during the colonial period, the animal can now be found only in several national parks in North America, Canada and Alaska. A bull can grow to a height of almost 6.5 feet and weigh up to 2,200 pounds, while the female is considerably smaller and not as heavily built. The bison lives in herds in which the male and female animals form separate groups outside the mating season. A bison reaches sexual maturity when approximately 2 years old. After a gestation period of 9 months, the female gives birth to 1 calf, which can walk as soon as it is born. The calf is breastfed for approximately 12 months. Besides the well-known American bison, one subspecies prefers to live in wooded regions and has a slightly different eating pattern. The first species is called the plains bison and the other the wood-dwelling bison.

## Bongo
## (*Tragelaphus eurycerus*)

The spectacularly marked bongo lives a slightly withdrawn life in West Africa, where it prefers to live in the protection of jungles and forests. The bongo usually rests during the day and appears at dusk to eat. It eats a variety of plant material, such as grasses, leaves, fruit, turnips and root vegetables. Depending upon the season, the sex and the age of the animal, this animal may live alone, in pairs or in small groups. The male can weigh more than 550 pounds and grow to a length of up to 8 feet. Both sexes have horns. The female usually gives birth to 1 calf after

American bison (*Bison bison*)

Bongo (*Tragelaphus eurycerus*)

Bongo with young(*Tragelaphus eurycerus*).

a gestation period of 9 to 10 months. The bongo is a member of the subfamily *Bovinae*.

## Addax (*Addax nasomaculatus*)

The addax is found in the arid regions of

Addax (*Addax nasomaculatus*)

Africa and eats withered grasses and bushes. It drinks very little and there have been reports of animals which have not drunk for 2 to 3 months. It is assumed that the animal gets sufficient moisture from its vegetable diet. The addax lives in small groups of 5 to 20 animals and rarely in larger groups. The herd is always led by a dominant male. The female gives birth to 1 calf after a gestation period of 8.5 months. An adult addax is approximately 4 feet long.

## Bontebok (*Damaliscus pygargus*)

The bontebok is a member of the subfamily *Bovinae*. Large numbers used to inhabit the African savannahs, but, it became extinct in the wild because of excessive hunting. Animals were kept and bred in captivity, however and the descendants of these animals were later released in their natural habitat and put under protection. These efforts have finally resulted in the bontebok returning to the wild in countries such as South Africa. It lives in herds, which can vary greatly in size. Its diet consists mainly of grasses. Both sexes have horns but the male can be recognised by its deeper color.

Bontebok (*Damaliscus pygargus*)

Springbok (*Antidorcas marsupialis*)

Impala (*Aepyceros melampus*)

Springbok (*Antidorcas marsupialis*)

## Springbok (*Antidorcas marsupialis*)

The springbok is a member of the sub-family *Antilopinae* and inhabits the flat grass pastures in Botswana, Namibia, Angola and, to a lesser extent, South Africa. It eats a variety of plant material. The springbok does not require much water and can obtain most of the water it needs from its food. It grows to a height of 31.5 to 35.5 inches and both the male and female have horns. It normally lives in herds numbering from about a dozen to several hundred animals, but in dry periods, various herds come together and move en masse to locations where there is enough food. The springbok gets its common name from the unusual spring that it makes.

## Impala (*Aepyceros melampus*)

The impala is a member of the subfamily *Aepyceronitae* and is found in various open plains of southern Africa. It lives in large herds, which consist of different groups of males with their females and young combined. The different groups appear to merge, but in times of danger,

Gemsbok (*Oryx gazella*)

268

the separate groups remain together. The male can be easily recognised by its horns, which the female does not have. The female usually gives birth to 1 calf after a gestation period of 6.5 to 7 months. An impala can grow to a height of approximately 3 feet.

## Gemsbok (*Oryx gazella*)

The gemsbok is found in South Africa, where it lives in herds ranging from approximately 10 to 20 animals. Both sexes are the same color and both have horns. The female usually gives birth to 1 calf after a gestation period of approximately 9 months. The calf spends its first month in a sheltered location and its mother visits to feed it. The mother and her calf join the rest of the herd once the calf is strong enough to walk. Like all the

Sable antelope (*Hippotragus niger*)

prairie animals in this order, the gemsbok's diet also consists mainly of grasses, but it may also dig for roots and turnips.

## Sable antelope (*Hippotragus niger*)

An older male sable antelope is dark brown to black, while the female and young animals are lighter brown in color. Apart from the colour, the male can also be recognised by its longer horns. A sable antelope has a mane on the top of its neck, which is very much like a horse's mane. An adult sable antelope has a shoulder height of approximately 4.5 feet. It is found in various parts of Africa and its diet consists mainly of grass. The sable antelope is a member of the bovid family (*Bovidae*).

## Addra gazelle (*Gazella dama*)

The addra gazelle is the largest living species of gazelle and one of the rarest. It has a shoulder height of 35 inches. It lives in the Sahara Desert in herds ranging from 5 to 25 animals and eats grass and leaves. Since food is scarce, the addra gazelle lives a nomadic life and the herds are continuously on the move in search of food.

Addra gazelle (*Gazella dama*)

## Common waterbuck
## (*Kobus ellipsiprymnus*)

The common waterbuck has a striking ring of white hair around its crotch. It is found in Central Africa and, as its common name suggests, prefers to remain close to water. It is gregarious and eats a variety of grasses. Only the male has long, ringed horns. The female gives birth to 1 calf after a gestation period of 9 months. An adult waterbuck has a shoulder height of approximately 4 feet and has an average weight of 440 pounds.

A characteristic of the common waterbuck (*Kobus ellipsiprymnus*) is the white ring around the crotch.

Common waterbuck (*Kobus ellipsiprymnus*)

## Tufted deer
## (*Elaphodus cephalophus*)

The tufted deer has a shoulder height of approximately 24 inches and weighs around 45 pounds and is, therefore, one of the smallest species of deer. It lives in the forest of Northern China and eats leaves and grasses, as well as eggs and larvae. The tufted deer makes a barking noise when in danger. The male has antlers which do not branch off and which are only about an inch long and completely hidden in the long hair on the crown of its head. This hair, which is sometimes longer than 5 inches, has contributed to the species' common name.

Tufted deer (*Elaphodus cephalophus*)

Barbary sheep (*Ammotragus lervia*)

Mouflon (*Ovis aries*)

# Barbary sheep (*Ammotragus lervia*)

The Barbary sheep is found in various countries of North Africa, where it lives in rocky mountains in desert regions. It has also been successfully introduced in Spain, Mexico and the United States. The Barbary sheep is predominantly active at dusk and during the night. It rests during the day while the sun is high in the sky. It is herbivorous and its food is very scarce at certain times of the year. It has adapted to a meagre diet and does not require a great deal of water. The sexes can be distinguished easily. The male is approximately 37 inches high and weighs at least 220 pounds, while the female is on average 4 inches shorter and often does not weigh more than 120 pounds. The horns of the male are also longer and more impressive than the female's. Finally, the hair on the underside of the neck and chest of the male is much longer. The female Barbary sheep lives in small groups, while the male lives alone outside the mating season. The male searches for a female during the rutting season and this can result in intense fights between males. After a gestation period of more than 5 months, the female usually gives birth to 1 or 2 young, which can walk soon after being born. Although it can eat solid food 2 weeks after birth, the young animal is still breastfed for 6 months.

# Mouflon (*Ovis aries*)

The wild mouflon is found in Turkey and several Middle Eastern countries. Although it originates from Corsica and Sardinia, it is now found in many countries throughout the world but these are usually half-domesticated animals which have been released into the wild. The mouflon's diet consists mainly of a variety of grasses and herbs. The ram can grow to a height of approximately 35.5 inches, while the ewe is usually no taller than 27.5 inches. The imposing horns of the male continue to grow throughout the animal's life. After a gestation period of approximately 5 months, the female usually gives birth to 1 lamb, which remains with the mother until a new lamb is born the following year.

Mouflon (*Ovis aries*)

# Bighorn sheep
## (*Ovis canadensis*)

The bighorn sheep is a member of the sub-family *Caprinae* and is found mainly in the mountainous regions of the north-western part of North America and, to a lesser extent, further south, as far as Mexico. It gets its common name from the enormous horns found on the adult ani-mals. Dominant males have the biggest horns, while females have smaller horns. A dominant male leads a herd and toler-ates rams with smaller horns within the herd as long as they remain submissive. The female gives birth to 1, sometimes 2, young after a gestation period of six months. The lamb remains with the moth-er for a long time.

Bighorn sheep (*Ovis canadensis*)

A female Himalayan tahr (*Hemitragus jemlahicus*)

A male Himalayan tahr (*Hemitragus jemlahicus*)

# Himalayan tahr
## (*Hemitragus jemlahicus*)

The Himalayan tahr behaves very much like a goat and eats a variety of plant material. Its shoulder height varies from 24 to 40 inches and it weighs up to 220 pounds. It lives in herds consisting of sev-eral dozens of animals. As its common name suggests, the animal is found in the Himalayas, but it is also found in neigh-boring areas and has been introduced in New Zealand and South Africa. The species is a member of the subfamily *Caprinae*.

# Takin (*Budorcas taxicolor*)

The takin has a body height of approxi-mately 4 feet and weighs more than 660 pounds. The takin was discovered only in

The Szechuan takin (*B.t. tibetana*) is one of three subspecies of takins.

1875 and lives in remote areas of the Himalayan mountains. It lives at a high altitude and is agile on the rocks, since its special hooves provide a solid grip on the difficult surface. It has thick fur which protects it from the cold. Taxonomists do not yet agree on whether it is a cow, chamois or a completely different species and it is provisionally classified as a member of the family *Caprinae*. The takin's diet consists of grasses and leaves. A herd of takins usually consists of females with their young and several young males, while an adult male lives alone or close to a herd.

# Babirusa
# (*Babyrousa babyrussa*)

The babirusa is found in the swampy forests and cane jungles of Sulawesi and the Sula Islands. The babirusa eats almost everything, from leaves to insects and berries. It lives in small groups, usually

Takin (*Budorcas taxicolor*)

Babirusa (*Babyrousa babyrussa*)

with a single male as the leader, but solitary animals have also been observed. An adult male can be recognised by the longer canine teeth in its bottom jaw. In both sexes, the teeth in the top jaw grow straight through the jaw, toward the eyes. The teeth of older animals are sometimes so long that they have grown into the

Javan warty pig (*Sus verrucosus*)

skull. The female gives birth to 1 or 2 young after a gestation period of 4 to 5 months. In contrast to all other animals which belong to the pig family (*Suidae*), the piglet of this species is not striped.

## Javan warty pig (*Sus verrucosus*)

The Javan warty pig gets its common name from the wart-like bulges which it has along its head. These are made from thick skin and cartilage and are most prominent in older males. The Javan warty pig is found on several Asiatic islands, including the Philippines, where it lives both in dense woodland and open areas. It usually lives in groups, the composition of which can vary. Many females live separately from the males, but some groups may temporarily be joined by a male. Males live alone and in small groups consisting only of males. A female can weigh up to 150 pounds, while the weight of the male usually exceeds 65 pounds. The female gives birth to 2 to 5 young after a gestation period of 5.5 months. A Javan warty pig can live for approximately 18 years.

Javan warty pig (*Sus verrucosus*)

African bush pig (*Potamochoerus porcus*)

Collared peccary (*Pecari tajacu*)

## Collared peccary
(*Pecari tajacu*)

The collared peccary is a member of the family *Tayassuidae* and is 30 to 35 inches long. It is found in the northern countries of South America, as well as Central America and several of the southern United States. It is most common in semi-arid regions but is also found in wooded regions. Water is not always available in the areas in which it lives and the collared peccary usually gets most of the water it requires from its food. It eats a variety of plant material, such as roots, grass and leaves, but also eats small animal food. The collared peccary lives in small groups of up to 30 animals. There is no competition between animals in the group, not even between the males during the mating season. The female usually gives birth to 2, sometimes 3, young after a gestation period of approximately 4.5 to 5 months. The newborn animals are small copies of their parents and can walk almost immediately. The collared peccary reaches sexual maturity very quickly; on average at an age of 8 to 10 months. The collared peccary can live for more than 20 years, but rarely lives for so long in the wild because it is a favorite prey for many predatory animals.

## African bush pig
(*Potamochoerus porcus*)

The African bush pig has long tassels of hair on the tips of its ears. It is found in the forests of West Africa and Madagascar, near abundant water, where it lives in small family groups with a single male as the leader. It finds its food by burrowing in the ground and eats roots, nuts and fruit, as well as insects, larvae and even carrion. The African bush pig builds a nest to sleep in from plant material. It is usually active during the day, but populations which are often disturbed have a more nocturnal existence. The female gives birth to between 3 and 6 striped young after a gestation period of 4 to 4.5 months. An adult African bush pig is usually 3.5 to 5 feet long.

The young of a collared peccary can walk almost as soon as they are born.

## Wild boar
## (*Sus scrofa*)

The wild boar lives in small groups and males often live alone close to a group and only join the group to mate. After a gestation period of 16 to 17 weeks, the female gives birth to 3 to 8 striped young, which can walk soon after being born. The wild boar is predominantly active at dusk and during the night. It eats a variety of plant material, such as nuts, roots and

Wild boar (*Sus scrofa*)

leaves, but may also eat animal food. The wild boar is found in large parts of Europe, northwest Africa and large parts of Asia.

## Blue wildebeest
## (*Connochaetes taurinus*)

The blue wildebeest lives on the prairies in the southern half of Africa. It can grow to a height of 5 feet and weigh up to 575 pounds. It is gregarious and can form large herds containing tens of thousands of animals. Its diet consists mainly of a variety of grasses. After a gestation period of approximately 8.5 months, the female gives birth to 1 calf, which can walk almost immediately. The blue wildebeest is a member of the bovid family (*Bovidae*) and, more specifically, to the subfamily of antelopes (*Alcelaphinae*).

Blue wildebeest (*Connochaetes taurinus*)

# Edentates and pangolins (*Pholidota*)

Family: *Manidae*

## Pangolin (genus: *Manis*)

There are 7 different species of pangolins. A striking characteristic that all pangolins share is the large overlapping scales which cover the skin and protect the animal from predators. When in danger, a pangolin rolls itself up so that its soft, scaleless and, therefore, vulnerable underside cannot be reached by the predator. Another characteristic of this species is that it does not have any teeth. Although all species are classified as belonging to the same genus, a difference can be seen between the Asian and African species. The African species are terrestrial and dig holes using their strong claws where they spend the day. The hole also functions as a place to give birth; an African pangolin usually gives birth to 1 pup at a time. Its diet consists almost entirely of termites and ants. It uses its strong front claws to dig open termite hills and can search the network of tunnels using its long, thin and sticky tongue. The Asian species also eats termites and ants, but only the kinds which build their nests in trees. It uses its strong

tail for gripping to make it easier for it to move from branch to branch. In contrast to the African species, the Asian species usually gives birth to 2 or 3 young each time. The young of an Asian pangolin are not born in a hole, but usually in a tree. The young animals can *ride* with the mother on her tail almost immediately after birth. All pangolins, except for the long-tailed pangolin (*Manis tetradactyla*), are active at dusk and during the night. Arboreal pangolins spend the day sleeping in a quiet and protected location in a tree or bush and the African species spend the day in a hole. Depending upon the species, this solitary animal can grow to a length of 16 to 30 inches, not including its tail, which is usually just as long as its body. The pangolin shown in the picture is the Chinese pangolin (*M. pentadactyla*), which can grow to a length of 3 feet and is found in Sri Lanka.

Chinese pangolin (*Manis pentadactyla*)

# Rodents (*Rodentia*, suborder *Sciurognathi*)

Families: *Aplodontidae, Sciuridae (subfamilies; Sciurinae, Pteromyinae), Castoridae, Geomyidae, Heteromyidae (subfamilies; Dipodomyinae, Heteromyinae, Perognathinae), Dipodidae (subfamilies; Dipodinae, Allactaginae, Cardiocraniinae, Euchoreutinae, Paradipodinae,Sicistinae, Zapodinae), Muridae (subfamilies; Murinae, Arvicolinae, Calomyscinae, Cricetinae, Cricetomyinae, Dendromurinae, Gerbillinae, Lophiomyinae, Myospalacinae, Mystromyinae, Nesomyinae, Otomyinae, Petromyscinae, Platacanthomyinae, Rhizomyinae, Sigmodontinae, Spalacinae), Anomaluridae (subfamilies; Anomalurinae, Zenkerellinae), Pedetidae, Ctenodactylidae and Myoxidae (subfamilies; Graphiurinae, Myoxinae, Leithiinae)*

## House mouse (*Mus musculus*)

The house mouse is a member of the sub-family *Murinae* and several subspecies are found throughout the world, close to humans. It is omnivorous. It is predominantly nocturnal, but is also active during the day with small rest periods in between. It is an expert climber and uses its tail, which is usually as long or longer than its body, as a rudder and grip. It has a body length of 2.5 to 3.5 inches. The

One of the color mutations of the domesticated mouse; the champagne & tan rump white.

house mouse is usually gregarious and is very tolerant of the other animals in the group. The dominant males and females in the group are the only animals able to reproduce during times of stress or over-population and in such a situation, the hormones of less dominant animals become very unsettled. The house mouse produces a large number of young. A female reaches sexual maturity before she is 3 months old and can produce 9 nests in a single year. A female goes into heat every 4 to 6 days. She gives birth to 4 to 9 completely naked and blind young after an average gestation period of 18 to 21 days. Not only the mother takes care of the young animals, but all the breast-feeding mothers from the entire group as well. A house mouse can live for 1 to 2 years, but since it is the favorite prey of many omnivorous and carnivorous animals, it rarely lives this long. Although the wild house mouse has been considered a destructive animal for many hun-

House mouse (*Mus musculus*)

Bald mice are used in laboratories.

Two-day-old mice

The white mouse has been kept as a pet since ancient times

## Eurasian harvest mouse (*Micromys minutus*)

The Eurasian harvest mouse is one of the smallest species of mice. An adult weighs approximately 0.5 of an ounce and has an average body length of 2.5 inches. It is found throughout Europe, except in the extreme north and extreme south and in Russia. The Eurasian harvest mouse lives in small groups and is active both during the day and at night, with short breaks in between. It is a very good climber and spends little time on the ground. It eats mainly seeds, but also requires animal food, such as insects and insect larvae. It reaches sexual maturity between the ages of 6 and 8 weeks. Under favorable conditions, a female can produce 4 to 7 nests in a single year. A female gives birth to an average of 4 to 5 young after a gestation period of approximately 21 days. Pregnant Eurasian harvest mice build an ingenious

dreds of years, domesticated animals have been kept as a pet for many centuries by the Egyptians, Greeks, Chinese and Japanese. The mouse is also popular today as a pet and for use in laboratories. Nowadays, there are countless color and fur mutations.

Satin Siamese colored mice

Eurasian harvest mouse (*Micromys minutus*)

nest from small pieces of plant material high up in a strong culm in which they give birth and raise their young. The newborn animals are blind and naked, but can leave the nest and eat solid food when they are 2 weeks old. The Eurasian harvest mouse can live for 2 years, but seldom lives this long because it is popular prey.

## Spiny mouse
## (genus *Acomys*)

The spiny mouse is a member of the subfamily of true mice (*Murinae*). There are several species of spiny mice, the best-known being the Sinai spiny mouse (*A. dimidiatus*) and the Cairo spiny mouse (*A. cahirinus*). Most species are native to North Africa and the Middle East. It has a body length of 3 to 5 inches and a tail which is usually slightly shorter than the body. Most spiny mice are active at dusk and during the night. They are not often seen during the day, but some species are

Sinai spiny mouse (*Acomys dimidiatus*)

sometimes active during the day with short breaks in between. The spiny mouse inhabits desert regions and its style of living and digestive system have adapted to this. It gets enough moisture from the food that it eats and, therefore, requires very little water. The spiny mouse is omnivorous. It gets its common name from the spiny hair on the top of its back. The rest of its body has normal hair. The spiny mouse is gregarious and lives in small groups. Its way of living is very sim-

Cairo spiny mouse (*Acomys cahirinus*)

Hairy-footed jerboa (*Dipus sagitta*)

of approximately 5 inches. Its tail, which has long hairs on the end, is longer than the body. Like most jumping mice, the hairy-footed jerboa lives up to 20 inches below the ground in a hole it builds for itself. It digs a separate hole in which to hibernate, which is sometimes a further 20 inches deeper. The female gives birth to an average of 3 young after a gestation period of 1 month. A female hairy-footed jerboa can produce more than 1 nest per year.

ilar to that of the house mouse; the females also raise their young together. Almost all spiny mice reproduce in the same way. The female is fertile when approximately 3 months old. She gives birth to 2 young after a gestation period of approximately 37 days. The young animals are already reasonably well developed when born; their eyes are open and they can move without help fairly soon after birth. They can eat a small amount of solid food when they are 1 week old. The average life expectancy of a spiny mouse is 2 to 3 years.

## Hairy-footed jerboa (*Dipus sagitta*)

The hairy-footed jerboa is a member of the jumping mouse family (*Dipodidae*). It is found from the Caucasian Mountains to northern China and has a body length

The tame rat is a descendant of the brown rat (*Rattus norvegicus*).

## Brown or Norway rat (*Rattus norvegicus*)

The brown rat originally comes from Asia, but the species has been found in Europe since 1728. It is very probable that the brown rat found its way to Europe via trade ships and it has also since made its way to the United States. Many brown rats prefer to live near humans and are found throughout the world in buildings, storage depots, harbors and similar loca-

One of the many colors which have been developed in tame rats

Black rat (*Rattus rattus*)

## Black rat
## (*Rattus rattus*)

The black rat has a body length of approximately 8 inches and its tail is usually approximately the same length as its body. The species originates from Western Europe, where it was a major cause of the spread of bubonic plague. The black rat has spread further throughout the world in the same way as the brown rat and can now be found all over the world wherever humans are. In contrast to the brown rat, the black rat is not particularly fond of damp environments. It is a very good climber and is often found in lofts and in the tree tops. The black rat is herbivorous and predominantly nocturnal. Its method of reproduction is very similar to that of the brown rat, although the gestation period is usually 1 to 2 days longer.

## Asian chipmunk
## (*Eutamias sibiricus*)

The Asian chipmunk is a member of the squirrel family (*Sciuridae*). The animal is also called a ground squirrel because it is predominantly terrestrial. It is found in northern Russia, the Kurile Islands, Japan, China and Mongolia. It is an active, diurnal animal and spends almost all day collecting food, which it stores in a hole. The hole is underground and can be several

Asian chipmunk (*Eutamias sibiricus*)

tions. It prefers to live in a damp environment, which is why the animal is also known by the less-flattering nickname of *sewer rat*. Some brown rats live in the wild and, in contrast to the animals which live near humans, these animals live underground in a network of tunnels they build for themselves. The brown rat can live in large colonies and is very tolerant of other animals in the group, although very little tolerance is shown to rats from other groups. Females often raise their young together. The brown rat is omnivorous and eats almost anything which is edible. It likes to eat insects, but will also eat larger, dead animals. The brown rat can produce more than 1 nest per year. The female is in heat every 4 or 5 days, but this may not occur if no males are available. After a gestation period of approximately 23 days, the female gives birth to 6 to 10 bald and blind young, which weigh about 0.5 of an ounce. Most young animals can fend for themselves when they are 4 or 5 weeks old. An adult brown rat can have a body length of 10 inches and weigh up to 14 ounces. Its tail is slightly shorter than its body. The tame rat, which is kept as a pet, is a descendant of the brown rat. Tame rats have been shown and bred since 1900 and are very popular as testing animals.

Solitary albino Asian chipmunk

feet deep. A typical characteristic of this animal is its cheek pouches, where it stores its food. It usually hibernates. It lives alone and seeks out other animals only to mate. Every animal has its own territory that it defends fiercely against intruders of the same species. The Asian chipmunk not only eats plant material but sometimes also eats animal food. It reaches sexual maturity at an age of approximately 9 months. The female is in heat for a couple of days almost every 2 weeks and lets the males know this by emitting an unusual whistle. After mating, the female does not allow the male near her anymore. She gives birth to 3 to 5 naked and blind young after a gestation period of approximately 30 days. The young animals leave the nest when they are about one month old to explore their surroundings and they can fend for themselves when they are 2 months old. The Asian chipmunk is 10.5 inches long, including the tail, and weighs an average of 3.5 ounces.

## Prevost's squirrel (*Callosciurus prevostii*)

The Prevost's squirrel and various sub-species, are found in Southeast Asia, particularly in Malaysia. It is one of the most strikingly marked squirrels and can grow to a length of approximately 11 inches. The Prevost's squirrel is diurnal. It is predominantly herbivorous and eats fruit and nuts, but it may also eat animal food. It usually lives in pairs and produces an average of 3 young per nest.

## Eurasian red squirrel (*Sciurus vulgaris*)

The Eurasian red squirrel can grow to a length of approximately 10 inches and its tail is usually 2 inches shorter than its

Prevost's squirrel (*Callosciurus prevostii*)

Eurasian red squirrel (*Sciurus vulgaris*)

body. It is a diurnal, herbivorous animal and eats nuts, pinecone seeds, mushrooms, fruit, berries, herbs and bark. An unusual characteristic of this animal is the way it stores its food; it hides any excess food in cracks in trees or in the ground. It then uses this storage of food when food is scarce. It does not hibernate. It may build its nest in a hole in a tree or may even build a round nest of twigs in a sheltered location in a tree. The female gives birth to 4 or 5 blind and naked young after a gestation period of approximately 5.5 weeks. When the young are approximately 6 weeks old, they leave the nest for the first time to explore their surroundings and most can fend for themselves 2 weeks later. The Eurasian squirrel and several subspecies are found throughout Europe, as well as in Asia — as far as China and Japan, where it prefers to live in coniferous forests.

Alpine marmot (*Marmota marmota*)

## Alpine marmot (*Marmota marmota*)

The Alpine marmot is a member of the squirrel family (*Sciuridae*) and is found in the Alps, the Tatra Mountains, the Carpathian Mountains and the Pyrenees. It is a gregarious animal and lives in groups which usually have a fixed territory in which no members of other colonies are tolerated. It digs a very ingenious network of holes as a base. Alpine marmots communicate with each other via typical whistles and body language. It is herbivorous and eats roots and grasses. The female gives birth to an average of 4 or 5 completely blind and naked young after a gestation period of approximately 5 weeks. The young animals can leave the nest for the first time when they are 1 month old. The Alpine marmot reaches sexual maturity at an age of 2 years and has then already grown to its adult length of 20 to 27.5 inches. The Alpine marmot hibernates in a hole which it lines with a large quantity of dried grass and stalks.

## Norway lemming (*Lemmus lemmus*)

The Norway lemming is a member of the subfamily *Arvicolinae*. It is the best-known species of lemming and is found in Scandinavia. It is well known because of a phenomenon that, for a long time, has been wrongly interpreted as mass suicide. The Norway lemming spends the summer on the tundra and migrates to the moun-

Norway lemming (*Lemmus lemmus*)

Muskrat (*Ondatra zibethicus*)

## Muskrat
## (*Ondatra zibethicus*)

The muskrat is a member of the subfamily *Arvicolinae*. It can grow to a length of 14 inches, excluding its flat tail, which is usually a fifth to a third shorter than its body. It weighs 1.5 to 2.5 pounds. The muskrat spends a large part of its life in water and is an excellent swimmer. The entrance to its hole is usually situated below the surface of the water, while the hole is situated above the water line so that the muskrat does not get wet. It is predominantly herbivorous and eats grasses and aquatic plants, but it may sometimes also eat aquatic animals. It is a gregarious animal and usually lives in small groups which share the same hole. The muskrat gets its common name from its typical musky smell which it excretes from its scent glands during the mating season. The female gives birth to an average of 3 to 5 young after a gestation period of approximately 1 month. A female muskrat can produce more than 1 nest per year. It is native to Canada and the United States. It was introduced in the former Czechoslovakia in 1905, from where it has spread throughout Europe and into the former USSR and, via Siberia, into Mongolia and China. In some countries, in particular in the Netherlands, the muskrat is considered a pest since its network of tunnels can weaken dykes.

tains before the winter sets in. Many lemmings die during the migration, particularly if their numbers have increased as a result of favorable conditions and sufficient food. Biologists, however, have been able to determine they do not commit mass suicide and that the large death rate is due to an unfortunate combination of circumstances. The population increases when there is sufficient food available. Since the animals require a large living space, they have to migrate further than normal and, consequently, several animals find themselves in unsuitable habitats. The Norway lemming is active both during the day and at night with breaks in between. It eats grasses and certain types of moss. The female gives birth to an average of 5 to 7 young after a gestation period of 2.5 to 3 weeks. She gives birth in an underground hole and the young are breastfed for more than 2 weeks. The young animals develop quickly and often reach sexual maturity when they are only 4 weeks old. A Norway lemming can produce more than 1 nest per year, but this depends on the amount of food available. An adult Norway lemming has a body length of approximately 5.5 inches and a short, stumpy tail.

The incisors of a muskrat (*Ondatra zibethicus*).

Golden hamster (*Mesocricetus auratus*)

# Golden hamster
## (*Mesocricetus auratus*)

The golden hamster is a member of the hamster subfamily (*Cricetinae*) and is found in the desert regions of Syria. The domesticated animal is extremely popular as a pet and now has many different types of fur and color mutations. The golden hamster is strictly a solitary animal. It has scent glands on its flanks which it uses to mark out its territory and the animals can identify each other from the odor. It is active only at dusk and during the night and spends the day sleeping in a sheltered hole which it digs itself. It searches for food at dusk, during the night and early in the morning. Anything edible, from insects to plant material, is stored in the pouches in its cheeks and taken to the hole. The golden hamster may hibernate if the temperature falls below 50°F for an extended time when the days get shorter. The hamster is a very clean animal and often defecates and urinates in the same location. The domesticated hamster reaches sexual maturity at an age of approximately 5 weeks and the female is in heat once every 4 days. After a gestation period of approximately 16 days, the female usually gives birth to 4 to 8 naked and blind young, which are approximately 1 inch long. The young animals leave the nest for the first time when they are 2 to 3 weeks old and can fend for themselves when they are 4 to 6 weeks old. The life expectancy of a golden hamster is 2 to 3 years, but wild animals seldom live for so long, since the animal is a favourite prey of many animals, from birds of prey to snakes.

# Dwarf Campbell's Russian hamster
## (*Phodopus campbelli*)

The dwarf Campbell's Russian hamster is a member of the hamster subfamily (*Cricetinae*) and is found in northern Mongolia, northern China, Manchuria, Altai and Tuva. The dwarf Campbell's Russian hamster is closely related to the dwarf winter white Russian hamster, which is very popular as a pet. It was once believed that they were the same species because the animals have the same number of chromosomes and hybridise among themselves. The habitats do not overlap in the wild, however. Although they have the same number of chromosomes, there are differences in the chromosomes of the two species. The dwarf Campbell's Russian hamster is kept as a pet, like the dwarf winter white Russian hamster. The dwarf Campbell's Russian hamster is predominantly active at dusk and usually sleeps during the day in a hole it builds for itself. It lives in small groups and can recognise

Dwarf Campbell's Russian hamster (*Phodopus campbelli*)

Chinese striped hamster (*Cricetulus barabensis*)

other animals by their smell. Its sight and sense of hearing are less well developed. It is one of the few hamsters which lives somewhat monogamously. A pair usually remains together for life and they raise the young together. The domesticated animal reaches sexual maturity at an age of approximately 6 weeks. After a gestation period of approximately 18 days, the female gives birth to an average of 5 completely naked and blind young, which weigh about $1/10$ of an ounce. When the young animals are approximately 2 weeks old, they have hair, their eyes are open and they can eat solid food. The dwarf Campbell's Russian hamster lives for 2 to 3 years.

## Chinese striped hamster (*Cricetulus barabensis*)

The Chinese striped hamster is found mainly in northern China. It has a varied natural habitat and lives both in open, barren areas and in dense forests. The Chinese striped hamster is predominantly active at dusk and during the night and spends the day sleeping in its hole. It is an excellent climber and it uses its relatively long tail to help it climb. It is a solitary animal. An adult Chinese striped hamster is very aggressive toward other Chinese striped hamsters and seeks out other animals only to mate during the short mating

A colored dwarf Campbell's Russian hamster (*Phodopus campbelli*)

Desert hamster (*Phodopus roborovskii*)

season. The female gives birth to approximately 6 blind and naked young after a gestation period of about 21 days. The young animals develop very quickly and sometimes become sexually mature at the early age of 5 weeks. The Chinese striped hamster measures approximately 4 inches, excluding the tail, which is approximately 1 inch long.

## Desert hamster
## (*Phodopus roborovskii*)

The desert hamster is found in the desert regions of Mongolia and several neighboring countries, where it lives in very small groups. It is active in the evening, during the night and early in the morning and spends the day in an underground hole. The desert hamster is less productive than other species of hamsters. The female usually gives birth for the first time only after the winter. Life expectancy for the desert hamster is not much more than 2 years. The young animals remain with their mother for approximately 6 weeks. It has a gestation period of approximately 21 days and the female can produce more than 1 nest per year. The desert hamster has a total length of 3 to 3.5 inches and the almost bald tail measures between 0.2 to 0.5 inch. The animal's fur becomes greyer in the winter than it is in the summer.

## American or Canadian beaver
## (*Castor canadensis*)

The American beaver is found in various parts of North America and there are also populations in Europe and Asia, but it is not native to these areas. The beaver always lives in forests with abundant water sources and spends most of its life in the water. It is an excellent swimmer and can remain under water for several minutes without having to breathe. It builds a strong nest, or lodge, from twigs and mud, usually several feet above the surface of the water. The lodge has several different entrances, which are always situated below the surface of the water. The lodge is so well built that it is almost impossible for a predator to break it open. To prevent the lodge from being exposed and the entrances from being accessible when the water level drops, the beaver builds dams at strategic locations in the water using trees which grow along the water. The beaver cuts the trees using its strong teeth so that they fall into the water. It sometimes also cuts down trees that are situated further from the water bank, which are then cut into manageable pieces and dragged to the desired location. These dams force the water to remain at an almost constant level. The lodge and dams are maintained with great diligence. Like the lodge, the dams are of a solid construction and can be quite large. Its diet consists mainly of bark and wood and, to a lesser extent, herbaceous plant matter. The female gives birth to an average of 3 young after a gestation period of 3.5 months. The Canadian beaver can be very large and an adult can grow to a length of 5 feet, including its tail, which is usually $1/5$ of the body length.

American or Canadian beaver (*Castor canadensis*)

Fat-tailed gerbil (*Pachyuromys duprasi*)

## Fat-tailed gerbil
## (*Pachyuromys duprasi*)

The fat-tailed gerbil originates from the northern Sahara Desert in North Africa. It spends most of the day sleeping and becomes active only at dusk when it goes in search of food. It is less active than other species of gerbils and it lives alone. The female gives birth to an average of 4 blind and naked young after a gestation period of approximately 19 days. The young animals can fend for themselves by the time they are 4 weeks old. The fat-tailed gerbil grows to a length of approximately 3.5 inches and weighs about 1.5 ounces. It gets its common name from its hairless, skin-colored, fat, short tail. The tail has an important function for the animal. This gerbil can store food (fat) and water in its tail, which it can draw upon when food is scarce.

# Mongolian gerbil
# (*Meriones unguiculatus*)

The Mongolian gerbil is found in the open, semi-arid regions of Mongolia and northern China. These are barren regions with little rainfall and little vegetation. The digestive system of this animal has adapted to a high-fiber, low-calorie, herbivorous diet. To protect itself from its many enemies, as well as the temperature fluctuations which occur in these semi-arid regions, the Mongolian gerbil lives most of its life underground in an ingenious network of tunnels which it builds for itself. The Mongolian gerbil is gregarious. It reaches sexual maturity at an age of approximately 4 months and remains sexually active until it is approximately 1.5 years old. The female goes in to heat once every 6 days and gives birth to 4 to 5 blind and naked young after an average gesta-

Mongolian gerbil (*Meriones unguiculatus*)

A black Mongolian gerbil

tion period of approximately 24 days in a nesting hole which is prepared beforehand. The newborn gerbils are approximately 1 inch long and weigh $1/10$ of an ounce. The young animals develop very quickly. They develop fur after the first week and open their eyes before they are 2 weeks old. Around this time, they leave the nest for the first time with their mother to explore their surroundings. They are almost completely weaned by the time they are 3 weeks old, but often still remain close to the mother. The father plays an important role in raising the young. The life expectancy of a Mongolian gerbil is between 3 and 5 years. It has a body length of approximately 5 inches, excluding the tail, which measures between 3 and 4 inches and it weighs between 2.5 and 4 ounces. The species is very popular as a pet and there are many different color mutations.

## Black tailed prairie dog (*Cynomys ludovicianus*)

The black tailed prairie dog is found on the prairies of the central United States. This animal looks nothing like a dog but gets its common name from its distress call, which is somewhat similar to a dog's bark. The black tailed prairie dog is a social animal which is very tolerant of other animals of the same species and lives in large groups.

Black tailed prairie dog (*Cynomys ludovicianus*)

It has several different nests which are connected by tunnels. It retreats into its network of tunnels when in danger or when it wishes to rest. The female gives birth to 2 to 10 young after a gestation period of 27 to 33 days. A black tailed prairie dog grows to a length of approximately 12 inches and weighs about 2 pounds. It has a life expectancy of 8 years, but animals in the wild rarely live for so long because they is prey to many carnivorous animals.

Black tailed prairie dog (*Cynomys ludovicianus*)

Black tailed prairie dog (*Cynomys ludovicianus*)

# Rodents (*Rodentia*, suborder *Hystricognathi*)

Families: *Hystricidae, Bathyergidae, Petromuridae, Thryonomyidae, Erethizonontidae, Chinchillidae, Dinomyidae, Caviidae (subfamilies; Caviinae, Dolichotinae), Hydrochaeridae, Dasyproctidae, Agoutdae, Ctenomyidae, Octodontidae, Abrocomidae, Echimyidae (subfamilies; Echimyinae, Chaetomyinae, Dactylomyinae, Eumysopinae, Heteropsomyinae), Capromyidae (subfamilies; Capromyinae, Hexolobodontinae, Isolobodontinae, Plagiodontinae), Heptaxodontidae (subfamilies; Clidomyinae, Heptaxodontinae) and Myocastoridae*

## Coypu (*Myocastor coypus*)

The coypu is a member of the family *Myocastoridae* and is native to certain areas of South America. It is also found on other continents, but these animals have been introduced or are descendants of escaped coypus. The coypu is seden-

Coypu (*Myocastor coypus*)

tary and a hole acts as a home base in its natural habitat. The hole can be underground, but some coypus build their nests above ground. It spends most of the time in the water, where it searches for its food: aquatic plants and a variety of small aquatic animals. The female usually gives birth to 6 young after a gestation period of approximately 4.5 months, although the nest can be larger. Besides wild populations, the coypu is also bred in captivity for its fur, although these animals usually have a lighter fur color.

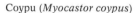
Coypu (*Myocastor coypus*)

Patagonian cavy (*Dolichotis patagonum*)

sometimes occupy a hole abandoned by another species of animal. It is herbivorous and requires very little water because it obtains most of its water requirements from its food. The female retreats into a hole before giving birth, usually to 2 or 3 young. A young Patagonian cavy looks like a smaller version of its parents. The young animals can walk soon after birth, they have hair and their eyes are open. The young remain close to their mother for more than six months before joining a group.

## Capybara
### (*Hydrochaeris hydrochaeris*)

The capybara is the largest living rodent and is a member of the family *Hydrochaeridae*. The capybara can grow to a length of more than 3 feet, weigh 110 pounds and have a shoulder height of approximately 20 inches. It does not have a tail. The species is found throughout South America, except in the extreme west and the south, where it lives in dense forests abundant in water. The capybara is also sometimes called the water hog because it spends a large part of its life in the water. It usually lives in small groups and the animals in the group are very tolerant of each other. It is herbivorous and eats aquatic plants and grasses. The female produces 1 nest per year and usually gives birth to 3 to 5 young after a ges-

## Patagonian cavy
### (*Dolichotis patagonum*)

The Patagonian cavy is a member of the family *Caviidae*. This gregarious animal can grow to a length of approximately 29.5 inches and weigh about 26 pounds. It spends its life in and around the holes which it digs itself, although it may also

Patagonian cavy (*Dolichotis patagonum*)

Capybara (*Hydrochaeris hydrochaeris*)

Capybara (*Hydrochaeris hydrochaeris*)

Chinchillas when only a couple of days old (*Chinchilla laniger*).

tation period of approximately 4 months. The young animals can see and walk immediately after being born and look like smaller versions of their parents.

## Chinchilla (*Chinchilla laniger*)

The chinchilla is a member of the chinchilla family (*Chinchillidae*) and is found in Chile. It is active only at dusk and spends the day in a hole. The chinchilla is a gregarious animal and lives in large groups. Its digestion system is adapted to a meagre, high-fiber diet of plant material. A chinchilla female reaches sexual maturity at an age of approximately 6 months. On average, the female is in heat for a couple of days once every 30 days and gives birth to 1 to 3 young after a gestation period of approximately 111 days. A newborn animal weighs approximately 1.5 ounces and looks exactly like its parents. After approximately 8 weeks, the young animals are independent enough to leave their mother. The average life expectancy of a chinchilla is about 15 years. A chinchilla measures about 12 inches from its nose to where its tail begins and its tail is approximately 5 inches long. It weighs between 1 and 1.5 pounds. The fur of this animal was once so popular in the fur industry that the animal was threatened with extinction, but chinchillas are now bred in captivity to meet the demand. The animal later also became popular as a pet and different color mutations have now been established. It is still found in the wild, but not in such large numbers as it once was.

Chinchilla (*Chinchilla laniger*)

Ebony is one of the types of chinchilla bred.

Crested porcupine with young (*Hystrix cristata*)

## Crested porcupine
## (*Hystrix cristata*)

The crested porcupine is a member of the porcupine family (*Hystricidae*) and is native to North and West Africa. It is also found in Italy and on the island of Sicily, where it was probably introduced. It spends the day in a hole and appears at dusk to search for food. It is quite adaptable, as is shown by animals kept in captivity, whose day and night patterns are opposite to those of wild animals. The crested porcupine is predominantly herbivorous and eats roots, nuts, bark and fruit. It also sometimes eats animal food, such as nestlings, small rodents, carrion or amphibians. It is a clean animal and defecates in the same place. The female gives birth to 1, or sometimes 2, young after a gestation period of approximately 112 days. A crested porcupine can grow to a length of approximately 29.5 inches and to a height of 10 inches. It weighs between 28 and 55 pounds and lives for approximately 16 years.

A crested porcupine when threatened.

## Degu
## (*Octodon degus*)

The degu is a member of the degu family (*Octodontidae*) and is found in Chile and Peru, where it lives on rocks with bushy growth. The degu is a gregarious, diurnal animal. It spends the evening and night in its network of holes and comes above ground in the morning to search for food. It usually rests in the middle of the day

Degu (*Octodon degus*)

# Naked mole rat
## (*Heterocephalus glaber*)

The naked mole rat has a very particular social structure which is very similar to certain insects, such as ants. In contrast to these insects, however, the naked mole rat spends all its life underground. The naked mole rat lives in colonies which can vary in size. Every colony has a *queen*, which is not only larger than the other members of the group but is also the only member able to reproduce. Almost all the other naked mole rats are *workers* and spend their time collecting food and digging tunnels. A small group, within the colony consists of non-working naked mole rats, one of which will take the place of the queen when she dies. A naked mole rat's diet consists of a variety of insects and roots. The naked mole grows to a length of only 3.5 inches and is found in Africa, particularly in Ethiopia and Somalia.

and becomes active again at the end of the afternoon. Its diet consists mainly of grain and grasses. The degu easily loses its tail if it gets stuck, after which it does not grow back. A female degu reaches sexual maturity at an age of approximately 4 months and comes into heat once every 2 to 3 weeks. She gives birth to an average of 5 young after a gestation period of approximately 90 days. At birth, the young animals have hair, their eyes are open and they are fairly agile. They can eat the same food as their parents when they are only a couple of weeks old, but they still require milk from their mother. The young animals can fend for themselves when they are 6 to 8 weeks old. The degu can live for 5 to 8 years. In the wild, a degu can grow to a length of approximately 16 inches, including the tail and weigh 7 to 10 ounces. The degu is very popular as a pet and the domesticated degu is much smaller than those found in the wild.

Naked mole rat (*Heterocephalus glaber*)

# Lagomorhps (*Lagomorpha*)

Families: *Ochotonidae and Leporidae*

## European hare (*Lepus europaeus*)

The European hare is a solitary animal and is found in large parts of Europe, Siberia and the Middle East. The species has also been introduced in North and South America, as well as in Australia and New Zealand. It gives off its scent using strong-smelling excrement, which it produces in addition to its usual excrement. It also has glands near its nose, which it brushes along objects to mark its territory. The animal is seldom active during the

European hare (*Lepus europaeus*)

day and ventures out of its lair only at dusk to eat. Its diet consists mainly of grasses and clover, but it also eats less moist plant material, such as tree bark. The European hare does not dig holes like the rabbit, but makes several nests (lairs) in sheltered locations in which it also gives birth to its young. After a gestation period of approximately 42 days, the female gives birth to an average of 1 to 5 young, which can walk as soon as they are born. Within a couple of days, they can gnaw some of the same food that their parents eat, but they are still breastfed until they are approximately 3 weeks old. What is striking is that a female hare can become pregnant again just before she gives birth. It is often the case that young are born from one uterus horn, while the next young are still in the embryonic stage

European rabbit (*Oryctolagus cuniculus*)

Rabbits when a couple of days old

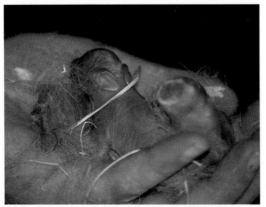

A rabbit marking out its territory

Flemish giant rabbit

German lop-ear rabbit

in another uterus horn; this is called superfetation. A female usually produces 2 to 5 nests per year. A hare grows to a length of 18 to 27.5 inches and has a short tail which is approximately 3 inches long.

## European rabbit (*Oryctolagus cuniculus*)

The European rabbit is a gregarious animal and lives in colonies with a strict social hierarchy. The colonies occupy a territory in which no other dominant male rabbit is permitted. The territory is marked by scent using scent glands on the underside of the head. The rabbit marks the objects by rubbing its chin along them. Since it is usually the buck which marks out the territory, this behaviour is often observed in bucks, particularly dominant bucks, and even the does in the group are marked in the same way. A rabbit may also mark its territory with urine and pellets. Like the hare, a rabbit can produce strong smelling pellets, which are then used to mark out the territory. The buck is also able to spray urine as a way of marking out its territory. The European rabbit grows to a length of approximately 16 inches and weighs an average of 5.5 to 6.5 pounds. The female gives birth to an average of 4 to 6 young after a gestation period of 28 to 31 days. Under favorable circumstances, a female can produce 4 to 5 nests per year. The species is found throughout Europe and North Africa. It has also been introduced in Australia, New Zealand and South America. In no

Angora rabbit

Rus rabbit

Snowshoe hare (*Lepus americanus*)

other country has the introduction of non-native fauna had such great consequences as in Australia. It is estimated that two to three million rabbits currently live in Australia and these cause a big problem for the native herbivores which rely upon the same food. The rabbit has been kept and bred in captivity as long as anybody knows. Through time, many color mutations have been produced which have served as the basis for a new breed. Rabbits were and are bred for wool (angora) or their fur, for their meat, or for both. The pigmy and small breeds are very popular as pets.

## Snowshoe hare (*Lepus americanus*)

This species is found in the northern part of North America, where it prefers to live in marshy areas. As with most lagomorphs, this species also has white fur during the winter and only the tips of its ears remain black. The normal fur color is greyish-brown, the same color as the European hare. After a gestation period of more than 1 month, the female gives birth to an average of 3 to 5 young with full hair, which can walk as soon as they are born. The female can bear approxi-

mately 3 nests per year and breastfeeds the young for about 4 weeks.

## Northern Pika (*Ochotona alpina*)

The northern pika is a member of the pika family (*Ochotonidae*), which consists of 20 different species. Pikas distinguish themselves from other lagomorphs for various reasons, the most noticeable of which is that they have relatively small and rather rounded ears and appear not to have a tail. The northern pika is widely distributed and is found in China, Russia, Mongolia, Japan and certain parts of North America. It is a social animal and lives in colonies. The northern pika communicates via a noise which resembles whistle. It can grow to a length of 8 to 10 inches. The female gives birth to an average of 2 to 5 young after a gestation period of approximately 1 month and she can bear 1 to 3 nests per year.

Northern pika (*Ochotona alpina*)

# Appendix

Condor

Barbastelle (*Barbastella barbastellus*)

Red-eared turtle or slider

European common toad (*Bufo bufo*)

# C

Lar gibbon

Red-necked wallaby (*Macropus rufogristeus*)

Grant's zebra (*Eguus burchelli granti*)

Common caracara (*Polyborus plancus*)

# E

Slender-tailed meerkat (*Suricata suricatta*)

bald eagle

Red kangaroo (*Macropus rufus*)

White-spotted laughing thrush (*garrulax ocellatus*)

Ocellated turkey (*Agriocharis ocellata*)

# H

Greater flamingo (*Phoenicopteridae ruber*)

European brown bear (*Ursus arctos*)

Lion (*Panthera leo*)

White spoonbill (*Platalea leucorodia*)

Male ostrich (*Struthio camelus*)

Herring gull (*Larus argentatus*)

African pigmy goose (*Nettapus auritus*)

Tiger (*Panthera tigris*)

A pack of wolves (*Canis lupus*)

## Q

## R

Eurasian eagle owl (*Bubo bubo*)

Black-winged stilt (*Himantopus himantopus*)

Northern lynx (*Lynx lynx*)

Asiatic black bear (*Ursus thibetanus*)

Przewalski's horse (*Equus przewalski*)

# T

European fire salamander (*Salamandra salamandra*)

European hedgehog (*Erinaceus europaeus*)